WITHDRAWN
No longer the property of the
Boston Public Library.
Sale of this material benefits the Library

A SHOT
IN THE
MOONLIGHT

ALSO BY BEN MONTGOMERY

The Man Who Walked Backward: An American Dreamer's
Search for Meaning in the Great Depression

The Leper Spy: The Story of an Unlikely Hero of World War II

Grandma Gatewood's Walk: The Inspiring Story of the Woman
Who Saved the Appalachian Trail

A SHOT
IN THE
MOONLIGHT

HOW A FREED SLAVE AND A
CONFEDERATE SOLDIER FOUGHT FOR
JUSTICE IN THE JIM CROW SOUTH

BEN MONTGOMERY

Little, Brown Spark
New York Boston London

Copyright © 2021 by Ben Montgomery

Hachette Book Group supports the right to free expression and the value of copyright. The purpose of copyright is to encourage writers and artists to produce the creative works that enrich our culture.

The scanning, uploading, and distribution of this book without permission is a theft of the author's intellectual property. If you would like permission to use material from the book (other than for review purposes), please contact permissions@hbgusa.com. Thank you for your support of the author's rights.

Little, Brown Spark
Hachette Book Group
1290 Avenue of the Americas, New York, NY 10104
littlebrownspark.com

First Edition: January 2021

Little Brown Spark is an imprint of Little, Brown and Company, a division of Hachette Book Group, Inc. The Little, Brown Spark name and logo are trademarks of Hachette Book Group, Inc.

The publisher is not responsible for websites (or their content) that are not owned by the publisher.

The Hachette Speakers Bureau provides a wide range of authors for speaking events. To find out more, go to hachettespeakersbureau.com or call (866) 376-6591.

Printing 1, 2020

ISBN 978-0-316-53554-0
Library of Congress Control Number: 2020947505

LSC-C

Printed in the United States of America

This book is for my children,
Asher, Morissey, and Bey

All being ready now, and the darkness opaque, the stillness impressive—for there should be no sound but the soft moaning of the night wind and the muffled sobbing of the sacrifices—let all the far stretch of kerosene pyres be touched off simultaneously and the glare and the shrieks and the agonies burst heavenward to the Throne.

—Mark Twain

A Winchester rifle should have a place of honor in every black home, and it should be used for that protection which the law refuses to give.

—Ida B. Wells

CONTENTS

Author's Note   *xi*

Chapter 1: The Whites Would Be Bent on Revenge   3

Chapter 2: "That Protection Which the Law Refuses to Give"   22

Chapter 3: "They Treated Him More Than Bad and Myself All So"   39

Chapter 4: "The People Say That Dinning Was a Worthless Negro"   45

Chapter 5: "We Turned and Shot Back at the House"   56

Chapter 6: To Defend Ourselves   72

Chapter 7: "There Was a Good Many Holes"   86

Chapter 8: "A Bullet Came Through My Hair"   *102*

Chapter 9: Son of the South   *115*

Chapter 10: A Bad Man   *129*

Chapter 11: "The Praiseworthy Act of Killing"   *157*

Chapter 12: "May the Lord Protect Us, Or the Devil Take Us"   *165*

CONTENTS

Chapter 13: "I Will Never Come Back to Kentucky"   183

Chapter 14: Indiana   199

Chapter 15: "Mass of Blood and Bones"   201

Chapter 16: The True Situation   210

Chapter 17: "A Negro's Life Is a Very Cheap Thing"   221

Chapter 18: Derby Day   227

Chapter 19: "There Was a Great Rejoicing in Hell This Morning"   236

Chapter 20: "The Outcome Is Regarded as Sensational"   241

Chapter 21: Squat and Fire   247

Chapter 22: "I Want to Die in the Old Blue Grass"   251

Chapter 23: "Some of This Falls Down to Us"   259

Acknowledgments   267

Bibliography   269

Index   273

Tampa, Florida
July 2020

Dear reader,

An old buddy called out of the blue a few years ago to say he was passing through Tampa and to ask if I had time to meet for drinks. I hadn't seen Ahmed in quite a while, so I cleared my schedule. He was road-tripping with some friends who were headed farther south for a hockey tournament. I suggested they drop him off a little east of Tampa, so they could easily jump back on the road.

When I greeted Ahmed at an off-ramp hotel, he was wide-eyed.

"Where the hell are we?" he asked.

I had completely forgotten about the flag.

In 2008, a local chapter of the Sons of Confederate Veterans had erected, on a quarter-acre plot of private property, the world's largest Confederate battle flag atop a 139-foot pole at the intersection of two main highways connecting Tampa to the rest of America. The controversial rebel flag—thirty feet tall and sixty feet long, about the size of a semitrailer—was unfurled over the gateway to Florida's third-largest city in time for the two hundredth birthday of Jefferson Davis, president of the Confederate States of America.

Welcome to Tampa.

And here stood Ahmed—whose last name, Cooper, was bestowed upon him by the white man who enslaved his ancestors, and whose father added an X to reject that heritage—shaking his head, totally miffed but not totally surprised.

"It's like the enemy telling me where they're at," he said. "This is probably what my ancestors felt when they went into sundown towns, like a reminder to stay in your place."

The problem with the Confederate flag and the granite statues of dead soldiers is that the Civil War never ended. It devolved into skirmishes and entanglements. As Nikole Hannah-Jones has written, it morphed into looser, legal forms of enslavement that are just as damaging as the whip. It rages on Facebook and in classrooms and in the streets of American cities, still. Its agents of trouble are Proud Boys and good ol' boys and police with no-knock warrants and whites who should know better but choose silence.

If you've been paying attention, George Floyd is just the latest name on the list of victims that extends back to April 12, 1861, and beyond.

"Contemporary police killings and the trauma that they create are reminiscent of the past racial terror lynching," reads a United Nations working report from a five-member group of experts who visited the United States. "In particular, the legacy of colonial history, enslavement, racial subordination and segregation, racial terrorism and racial inequality in the United States remains a serious challenge, as there has been no real commitment to reparations and to truth and reconciliation for people of African descent. Impunity for State

violence has resulted in the current human rights crisis and must be addressed as a matter of urgency."

That report? It was issued in 2016.

So we think about these symbols now, still, as statues fall. We think about the roots of hatred and racial supremacy manifest in flags and monuments and systems and songs as professional athletes kneel and bow their heads. We watch as armed Black protesters march through Louisville, Kentucky, to demand justice for Breonna Taylor, a twenty-six-year-old emergency medical technician who was shot to death by police who burst into her apartment with a battering ram around midnight on March 13, 2020, looking for evidence of drug dealing.

We see President Donald Trump on July 4, 2020, Independence Day, so named by and for white people, standing before Mount Rushmore, a sculpture memorializing two presidents who enslaved other human beings, carved by an artist aligned philosophically and politically with the Ku Klux Klan. We hear the president say, "We believe in equal opportunity, equal justice, and equal treatment for citizens of every race, background, religion, and creed," but we also hear him say, "Those who seek to erase our heritage want Americans to forget our pride and our great dignity, so that we can no longer understand ourselves or America's destiny. . . . Their goal is not a better America, their goal is the end of America."

But haven't we known for a long while that a day of reckoning would come, that men once considered heroes would be seen in a new light? Didn't the New York Times predict as much on November 5, 1864, as the Civil War raged? "But History executes a stern judgement," a prescient editorial reads. "She forgets the petty squabbles, the party fame of the day. She will judge the actors in our Revolution, especially in their relation to the great questions of morality

*which belong to all time. At that distant day, Slavery will
be as much a thing of the past as the inquisition is now
in Germany, or gladiatorial shows in Italy—a feature of
ancient barbarism and ignorance. But in their relation to
the great struggle for its destruction, all public men will
then be judged."*

*Isn't sculpting a better nation something akin to chiseling
a figure from stone?*

*So we look to past improvements of our shared experience
for comfort. To Rosa Parks refusing to give up her seat
on the Cleveland Avenue bus in Montgomery, Alabama, on
December 1, 1955. To the nine teenagers who enrolled at
Little Rock Central High School in 1957. To the four college
students refusing to vacate a lunch counter at Woolworth's
in Greensboro, North Carolina, on February 1, 1960. To
the march by six hundred activists across the Edmund Pettus
Bridge, through tear gas and billy clubs, near Selma, Alabama,
on March 7, 1965, known as Bloody Sunday. To Martin
Luther King, Jr., on April 3, 1968, the evening before he was
assassinated, telling striking Memphis sanitation workers that
he had been to the mountaintop.*

*These things we know and celebrate and memorialize.
But there are thousands of forgotten events and people upon
whose bones those brave activists stood. Their stories aren't as
accessible because they played out after the Civil War and
before the sustained civil rights movement, at a time when
there was little interest in preserving the stories and customs
of African Americans. The recorded history of that period is
white. When Black men and women were named in newspapers at the time, especially in the South, it was often either
for public ridicule, or because they had been marched to their
deaths the day before.*

In the winter of 2018, I was passing through Montgomery, Alabama, and I visited for the first time the new National Memorial for Peace and Justice, more commonly called the Lynching Memorial, which aims to ask white America to reckon with its bloodthirst for supremacy. It sits on six manicured acres overlooking the Alabama State Capitol. The memorial's main feature is a long walkway through and eventually under 800 coffin-sized steel boxes, each bearing the name of an American county and the names of those who were lynched there. There are 4,400 names. Thousands of names were new to me, but I was familiar with a few from my work as an investigative journalist for the Tampa Bay Times in Florida. I wrote about the lynching of Claude Neal by a mob of five thousand in Jackson County, Florida, for instance. I had the honor of interviewing Neal's daughter, Allie Mae. She was two years old in 1934, when her father was abducted and killed, and her family had been scared off to other towns in other states, her bloodline broken. I felt unworthy of her thanks after my story was published. The experience reminded me that our violent past is still with us, and that we face a reckoning, ready or not.

As I moved through the powerful memorial, I began to wonder about what was missing. Who was not listed here? It wasn't so much that I wondered about the lynching victims whose deaths had gone unrecorded, the extrajudicial killings that had not generated a single newspaper mention or public record. I suspect there are hundreds, if not thousands, of those. No, I wondered about the close calls, about the men and women who, against the odds, successfully defended themselves. I wondered about those who escaped the night riders. I wondered about those who survived and sought revenge or retribution or justice.

This is one of those stories. As you'll see, it is complicated by a helpful white man who did more than most to preserve the Lost Cause and the legacy of Confederacy, who had a huge hand in erecting those statues we deface and protect and destroy and argue over today.

This is a true story.

I've tried my best to be transparent, and to scrutinize the historical record with the aim of accuracy. In this book, I have taken no liberties, and I have made just a few of the very safest assumptions in service of the story. If something is in quotation marks, it came from a verified historic document. When I have used text from the historical record, I have left spelling and capitalization as they appeared at the time.

I have also tried to avoid muddying the text with inflation calculations, except where I felt it was absolutely necessary. So I'll note here that $1 in 1897 is equivalent in purchasing power to about $31 dollars in 2021; $10 in 1897 is equal to about $310 today; and $50,000 in 1897 is equal to about $1.55 million today.

I have spent no small amount of time in Simpson County, Kentucky, where much of this story is set, asking questions and searching in the archives and tromping through cemeteries. It's a rural community and now enjoys both a natural and a built beauty. The people I've met have been nothing but kind and gracious, and some have gone to great lengths to help me. While the record is incomplete, I'm appreciative of their help.

One last thing: in the spring of 2020, as protests against racism and police brutality again raged in hundreds of towns and cities across America, some threats on social media compelled the local chapter of the Sons of Confederate Veterans to take down their giant Confederate flag from the sky over

Tampa. I called Ahmed to see if he remembered his visit, and the flag. Of course he did.

"That system is alive and well, still," he said. "But I can't let that determine who I am and what I do. I never walk in fear."

That, right there, is the refrain of this book, and my hope is that it serves to inspire.

Thanks for reading.

Sincerely,
Ben

A SHOT
IN THE
MOONLIGHT

Chapter 1

THE WHITES WOULD
BE BENT ON REVENGE

January 21, 1897

When the guns fell silent and the white men took cover, George Dinning burst out the back of his little wooden house, wearing only his undergarments. He ran through the frigid January air, and when he reached the tall grass of a nearby field, he hurled himself down flat on his back, his lungs heaving, his breath visible and rising beneath a moon almost full and what seemed to be a million stars poking through a smoky blue-black midnight sky. He lay still and quiet and listened to the men's voices coming from the north, beyond the house. They sounded at first as though they were in a state of consternation, but the voices grew distant as time slid by, suggesting retreat. When he could no longer hear the voices over the heartbeat in his own ears, he sat up slowly, looked around, then darted across the field toward his house. His wife met him at the door with his boots, his heavy coat, and his hat, and he dressed quickly, without saying much, then turned away from the humble home he had built with his own hands, the only home his children had ever known, the home he had defended, and he disappeared into the darkness.

He ran, crashing through the near-freezing vegetation of southwestern Kentucky in close proximity to the Red River, which rolled silently west toward the Cumberland. He remembered the sight of his house surrounded by white men with guns and he tried to puzzle out in his mind the last few minutes, for what had just happened would determine which action he next chose. Who were those men? And whom among his neighbors could he trust?

He made his way first to the farm of Gib Hackney, a white man—a good man, he thought, a friend—who lived a half mile away, near the Tennessee state line. From the nighttime shadows Dinning bellowed, then waited, but he saw no light and heard no sound. He bellowed again and the same silence followed, so he turned and ran.

He cut through field and forest, and the sounds of his footfalls carried through the cold night. A mile away, at Price's Mill, he came upon the home of Zack Murray, another white man. Dinning called out to him, and Murray appeared in the doorway with a lantern. Murray held the lantern up to the heaving Black man standing before him and examined Dinning in the firelight. He first noticed the shotgun in Dinning's grip, one of two loads spent. He then saw blood oozing down Dinning's face, and then the wellspring: a gunshot wound in Dinning's forehead, as big around as the tip of his finger. He examined Dinning's arm and saw where his undershirt had torn, and saw a wound about a quarter inch deep and an inch and a half long.

Dinning followed Murray inside. When he'd caught his breath, he explained to his neighbor the evening's events, lantern light dancing on the walls around them:

He had eaten dinner at dusk. He had hauled some wood in. He had stoked the fire. His wife, Mollie, and children had climbed into bed. There was the baby, four months old; Emma, three years; Nannie, four years; Mertrude, six years; George Jr., eight years; Viola, ten years; and Eva, twelve years old.

He had drifted into a deep sleep, and woke when Mollie shook him. He had heard the dog barking outside, then voices. Then he heard someone call his name, "George!"

The men accused him of stealing from smokehouses, and he protested, said upstanding white folks would speak on his behalf. That was when the bombs came. He thought they were bombs, or dynamite, because they came from above and sounded like someone had cast handfuls of gravel on the floor. Murray tried to set him straight, said he and his whole family would be dead if somebody had thrown dynamite into his little house.

Whatever it was, Dinning told Murray that he grabbed his shotgun and started up the stairs, and just as he passed a window, he felt a sharp pain in his arm and looked down and saw his own blood. He rushed upstairs and threw open the window at the foot of his daughter's bed. He felt a great pain in the center of his forehead, and he pointed his gun at what seemed to be a yardful of men down below. He squeezed and the blast from his muzzle lit the night. The gunshot seemed to stop time for a split second, and a silence rushed over him, a silence that preceded a great deafening hail of explosions, of flying bullets, bullets flying over the heads of his children.

Murray asked if he'd recognized anybody. Dinning didn't know. Didn't think so.

The two men sat until 5 a.m., and Dinning told Murray he'd better head back to the house to check on his family, to face whatever might come. Dinning fetched his shotgun and headed toward the place he'd called home for fourteen years, but his friend Bob Lucas intercepted him a hundred yards away. Bob was a farmer, Black, younger than Dinning by eight years or so, and he lived nearby. In fact, the men who'd come the night before had asked Dinning if he knew where Bob Lucas was. He didn't, he said. The men told him they were looking for Bob

Lucas, too, and now here he was, coming down the road before sunup, carrying devastating news.

One of the men had been hit by George Dinning's birdshot, Bob Lucas told him, in the cheek and neck and shoulder. Had fallen from his horse in front of George Dinning's house. Had spilled blood in George Dinning's yard. Had passed in the night, George Dinning's name on his tongue.

You shot Jodie Conn, said Bob Lucas. Dinning knew Conn, had done work for him. Had no problem with the man. Hadn't known he was there that night. Conn was a wealthy farmer from the next county over, Logan. He was the thirty-two-year-old scion of the Conn family. And they would soon prepare his grave.

There was no time to go home, not under the circumstances. The whites would be bent on revenge. He had to trust that they wouldn't harm his babies.

He left the neighborhood on Friday for Franklin, the Simpson County seat, taking the Springfield road the whole way, careful, scared, walking nine miles. He left his shotgun with Dick Henry, a Black man who lived on the outskirts of Franklin, and promptly turned himself in to Sheriff Bud Clark at the county jail, a foreboding stone fortress. News of the shooting beat Dinning to the city, and the sheriff was already making plans to spirit him away. Clark loaded Dinning into a buggy and started across the brown and barren country for Bowling Green, in Warren County, some twenty miles away.

Even then, the agents of the fact-deprived press were preparing their dispatches, and those early reports, wrong as they were, would form the foundation of communal judgment, revulsion, and angst. They had never seen or talked to George Dinning.

"Prominent Farmer Assassinated" was the headline in the *Owensboro Inquirer*:

ADAIRVILLE, Ky., Jan 22—Mr. Jodie L. Conn, one of the best-known and most prosperous farmers of Simpson county, was shot to death from a window at Black Jack, Tenn., last night. He had gone with a party of friends from Price's Mill for the purpose of warning negro depredators to cease their work.

He was killed as he was riding along a street leading into the town. A posse is searching for his alleged slayer today, and will lynch him if found.

"WHITE CAPS STAMPEDED," said the headline in the *Fort Wayne News*. "A Gang of Whippers Fired on From Ambush":

ADAIRVILLE, Ky., Jan 22—A gang of white caps from Price's Mill were fired on from ambush last night while they were en route to Black Jack, Tenn., to punish some negroes suspected of theft. J.L. Conn, the son of a wealthy farmer, was instantly killed and the regulators retreated.

One of Kentucky's leading newspapers, the *Courier-Journal* in Louisville, spelled both men's names wrong and called Dinning "a worthless and dangerous negro." The shooting, the paper reported, "has caused great consternation and indignation here where Mr. Conn is well known and highly connected, being the son of Mr. Charles T. Conn, one of the largest and wealthiest farmers in Southern Kentucky." The paper pointed out that the Conn family was "one of the oldest and wealthiest in this part of the State, and stands high in the social scale," and that Jodie Conn, unmarried and in his thirties, "owned and managed one of the finest farms in Simpson County. He was a quiet, inoffensive man, whose friends were very close to him."

Citing "the most authentic reports," the paper explained that Conn and a group of a dozen neighbors had "been greatly annoyed by depredations and stealings" and were "determined to warn the negro who was suspected....After notifying the negro, who had responded to the call from an upper window of the house, they were preparing to leave when one of the party accidentally discharged his gun. The negro at once fired on Mr. Conn, who was standing in front of the window. The shot struck him in the neck and head, and he died in a few minutes." The paper reported that fifty or sixty of Conn's friends had been scouring the country for Dinning, and that they'd ridden toward Franklin "with the intention of lynching the negro if they had caught him." A headline in the Louisville *Evening Post* called Jodie Conn "One of Simpson County's Best Citizens."

In Nashville, about thirty miles due south of Price's Mill, the *Tennessean* reported that the killing had startled the country for miles around and ran an in-depth account of events, sure to stoke emotion. "Jodie Conn, one of the most highly respected and popular young men in Logan County was killed by George Dinning, a negro desperado," the front-page story read, then went on to exert some exaggeration and flawed logic.

> For some time the community for several miles around has been subjected to the depredations of a gang of thieves and incendiaries. When a theft was committed the loser was afraid to report the thief even if he was caught in the act. The whole country for a radius of five miles was in continual dread.
>
> About a week ago the smoke house of Newt Warren was robbed and burned. The people were at last determined that these depredations should cease. Last night a large

party of some of the best citizens visited several of the suspected thieves and notified them to leave the country within a certain number of days.

Two or three of these had been notified when the posse came to the house of George Dinning, one of the most desperate of the thieves and regarded as the fence for the gang. The house was quietly approached and they were preparing to call on Dinning to give him his orders when a gun in the hands of one of the men was accidentally discharged. This aroused Dinning, who was prepared for and evidently expected an attack. He discharged his gun from an upper window, the full charge taking effect in the left side of the face of Jodie Conn, a young man, who probably had more friends than any man for miles around and a member of the most prominent family in Logan County. Conn returned the fire but was soon seen to be badly wounded and died before he could be taken to the nearest house. As soon as Conn was taken away by his friends they returned, but Dinning had escaped. He remained in the neighborhood but this morning, discovering that Conn was dead, left armed. Large posses of men were formed and searched the whole country for miles around.

Such was the news that first day.

While George Dinning rode toward Bowling Green in the custody and protection of Sheriff Bud Clark, armed men showed up at his home and abducted his fourteen-year-old son, Hermann, who had returned home from his grandmother Mary's, where he had spent the night. The white men took charge of the house and held the boy all day, perhaps hoping George Dinning would return to rescue his son. When he did not, the men told Mollie that she must leave the county, and get at least fifty miles away before stopping, or she would hang.

Her husband had peacefully farmed these 125 acres for fourteen years, with no trouble to speak of. He'd grown up here, in fact, was born on this land in 1855, a son of slaves, a slave himself, one of about 1,850 men and women in bondage in Simpson County, Kentucky, each with a monetary value of about $380. The first Black settlers in Kentucky, many of them free men and women, came from the East—mainly Virginia, Maryland, and the Carolinas. But Irish, Scottish, and German planters brought enslaved Black people with them when they established the early settlements at Harrodsburg and Boonesborough in 1775. Planters migrated to the Bluegrass region, then slowly made their way west to claim federal land grants of several hundred acres, bringing slaves with them. The earliest Black people to settle in Simpson County lived in an area against the Red River known as Coffee Bottom, near Price's Mill and White Hill. They lived mostly in small board-and-batten cabins made of oak. Kitchen and living room downstairs, and a bedroom upstairs.

The U.S. slave roster of 1860, taken when George Dinning was five years old, did not record his name, or the names of his mother or father, but did list the name of his owner, David M. Dinning, descendant of a David Dinning who emigrated from northern Ireland to the American colonies with his parents in 1762 and migrated to Logan County, Kentucky, near the Red River, in 1817. In the 1860 slave roster, George Dinning was recorded as one of thirteen enslaved people who belonged to David M. Dinning. He is identified in the government record only by age, sex, and color: 5, M, and B.

He was a boy with no history. The recorded lineage and migration of his white owners could fill a book, but he could not say whether his own people came from Ogbomosho or Wushishi or Gombe, whether they crossed the vast Atlantic under a Portuguese or French or Dutch flag, whether they passed through Jamestown or St. Augustine or New Orleans, or whether they took some atypical journey. He could not say whether his ancestors were among the enslaved people who built the plantations of George Washington, Thomas Jefferson, or James Madison, or laid the foundations for the White House or the Capitol. His past had been eclipsed, or distorted, or wiped away. His father was given the name George, and he in turn gave the name George to his son.

He was barely a year old in late 1856, when fear of a slave insurrection spread through towns in western Kentucky. The whites imagined a coming revolt, an anxiety likely fueled by abolitionist activities across the country and the presidential run of antislavery politician John Frémont, the new Republican Party's first candidate for chief executive. He lost, but his bid scared white Southerners silly. That Christmas, intense panic spread along the nearby Cumberland River, in places like Hopkinsville, forty-five miles west of Price's Mill, and Clarksville, Tennessee, thirty-five miles southwest. A correspondent for a journal published in New York was traveling up the Cumberland for Nashville and stopped in one of the towns boiling with fear and vigilantism. "[T]hey imagine that Col. Frémont with a large army is waiting at the mouth of the River Cumberland until the night of the 23rd or 24th of December has arrived," the correspondent wrote in a dispatch printed in the *New York Times*. "Then all this army will help to deliver the slaves. They have been struck by the sudden swelling of the river, and attribute this circumstance to the great assemblage of men and ships at its mouth. Certain slaves are so greatly imbued with this fable that I have seen them smile while they are being whipped and have heard them say that 'Frémont and his men can bear the blows they receive.'"

Six suspected slave conspirators and a white man named Taylor were hanged in a single day in Dover, Tennessee, sixty miles west of Price's Mill. A Black preacher was hanged in Cadiz, Kentucky, and another was hanged in Pembroke, and one in Hopkinsville was jailed by a vigilance committee. Thirty slaves and six whites were arrested in Dover, Tennessee, under suspicion of planning an insurrection. A great panic passed from farm to farm through the region. The whites in the small town of Lafayette, expecting a rumored attack from six hundred Black men, asked neighboring Hopkinsville to send urgent help. A newspaper in Clarksville called for "swift and terrible examples" to be made and "if need be, the fagot and the flame should be brought into requisition to show these maniacs the fierceness and vigor . . . of the white man's vengeance" and, "if necessary let every tree in the country bend with negro meat." Six insurrection "ringleaders" were hanged just before Christmas, and credible reports of a man beheading the corpses and exhibiting the heads atop poles trickled out of Dover.

Such was the cultural tenor in the part of southern Kentucky where little George was learning how to walk and talk.

When he turned six, the South Carolina militia attacked Fort Sumter, near Charleston, and the Civil War was begun.

Then Kentucky's governor issued a proclamation of neutrality, saying the state would remain in the Union but wouldn't supply troops even though Confederate sentiment was strong in the Bluegrass region and the west.

Then, four months later, the Confederates invaded Columbus, Kentucky, 130 miles west of George Dinning's home.

Then the Confederates captured Bowling Green, twenty-five miles to the northwest.

The following summer, 1862, proslavery politicians met at a convention in Russellville, fourteen miles to the northwest, and formed the Confederate government of Kentucky, establishing Bowling Green as the seat of the provisional government. It was there, in late 1861 and early 1862, that an Alabamian named John Hunt Morgan organized the Second Kentucky Cavalry Regiment.

Dinning was seven years old on January 1, 1863, when Abraham Lincoln issued his Emancipation Proclamation, declaring that "all persons held as slaves . . . shall be then, thenceforeward, and forever free," but it didn't take in Kentucky because it only applied to "rebellious" states. Slavery would continue for another three years. Those who did break away and tried to join the Union in fighting, or tried to find freedom behind Union lines, which were often just north of where George Dinning was growing up, frequently faced a rugged reality. "They came at night, when the flickering campfires of the blue hosts shone like vast unsteady stars along the black horizon," W. E. B. Du Bois wrote about them in *Atlantic Monthly*. "Old men, and thin, with gray and tufted hair; women with frightened eyes, dragging whimpering, hungry children; men and girls, stalwart and gaunt,—a horde of starving vagabonds, homeless, helpless, and pitiable in their dark distress."

Nearly 180,000 Black men would serve the Union Army by war's end—more than one-fifth of the nation's Black male population. From the border states came the highest percentage. Enlistment was a path to freedom, and nearly 60 percent of eligible Black men in Kentucky served in the armed forces. In 1864, Isaac Dinning—who was either related by blood to George Dinning or had at least been enslaved by David Dinning of Simpson County—was among those who signed up.

Then in 1865, when Dinning was ten years old, on a day that would forever be known as the Eighth of August, emancipation finally reached the state in the form of the Thirteenth

Amendment. Despite a vote against the amendment by the Kentucky legislature, enslaved people in the Bluegrass State were free, if they could navigate that awkward exodus.

In December of the same year, six young Confederates met in a law office in Pulaski, Tennessee, just one hundred miles south of the Dinning home, and formed a secret society. Newspapers in the area began to report on the odd activities of the mysterious group, slowly at first. Its first public pronouncement came via letter, slipped under the door of the *Pulaski Citizen*:

TAKE NOTICE.—The Kuklux Klan will assemble at their usual place of rendezvous, 'The Den,' on Tuesday night next, exactly at the hour of midnight, in costume and bearing the arms of the Klan.

By order of the Grand Cyclops.

The editor ran the announcement but seemed confused. "The following mysterious 'Take Notice' was found under our door early yesterday morning, having doubtless been slipped there the night previous," he wrote. "Will any one venture to tell us what it means, if it means anything at all? What is a 'Kuklux Klan,' and who is this 'Grand Cyclops' that issues his mysterious and imperative orders? Can anyone give us a little light on this subject?"

The name was derived from the Greek word *kyklos*, meaning circle, and the Scottish-Gaelic word *clan,* and the original ambition was to frighten superstitious rural Black citizens into staying away from the polls, and staying put at home, under the pretense that they were preventing stealing. One early ruse: a masked Klansman in colorful robes would dismount before the home of a Black family and ask for a drink of water. He would pretend to drink and pour the water into a concealed hose and a bladder under his robes. After drinking an astonishing amount, the ghoulish rider would thank the family and say he hadn't had a drink since he died on the battlefield at Shiloh.

They began communicating locally using comically bad announcements in newspapers, which were willing to help spread the word. They claimed that their leader, the Grand Cyclops, was nine feet tall.

"But seek not to know the object and designs of the 'Mystic Klan,' or to impeach the authority of our Grand Cyclops to issue his mandates, for your efforts will be fruitless," read another letter published in the *Pulaski Citizen*. "If you see proper to publish our orders, and will do so, we thank you, but more of the 'Kuklux Klan' you cannot know."

The group's early intent might have seemed mysterious, but it set Black citizens on edge. The strange costumes and eerie communiqués struck fear in those leaning against the rail of newfound freedom. "The town and county are quiet as usual, unless it be some general and undefined dread among the negroes of a secret order that has recently made its appearance, known as the 'Kuklux Klan,'" read a letter from a resident of Maury County, Tennessee, to the Nashville *Union and Dispatch* in 1867. "No one, as yet, states publicly who compose the 'Klan,' or what are its purposes. One singular feature in it is the unbroken silence maintained by them while on parade. They dress in long red gowns, red pants and red caps, with black face-cloths covering their features. They have extended themselves all over Maury and Giles counties. Some of the negroes are wonderfully exercised over them, and some of the white Radicals have been heard to express the opinion that they were 'Rebel bushwhackers,' but as yet no one can say who or what they are."

By early February 1868, three new circles of Klan had organized in Nashville and Edgefield. On February 12, the weekly newspaper *Freedom's Watchman* pinned a murder on the Klan, the killing of a Black man named Hogg in Marshall County, south of Nashville. By March, the Klan had spread north into Montgomery County, Tennessee, just across the state line from Logan County, Kentucky, and it had grown militant—violent. The group's rapid rise was enough to spur a congressman from Tennessee to issue a resolution in the U.S. House of Representatives, asking the Committee on Freedmen's Affairs to investigate the "brutal outrages and murders on white and colored Unionists." In Rutherford County, Tennessee, Kukluxers, as they were called, posted placards in conspicuous places that carried ominous warnings:

BEWARE, OH YE UNGODLY,

FOR THE DAY IS CLOSE AT HAND.
KUKLUX

Twenty of them paraded through Murfreesboro one night that March. They wore tall white masks with lights burning in the peaks. They rode horses disguised with blankets. They lingered near the homes of teachers at the freedmen's schools for an hour or two. They slipped a note under the door of T. H. B. McCain, editor of the *Freedom's Watchman*. "Prepare thyself, your doom is sealed," it said. "We swear by our slumbering dust you will no longer oppose your downtrodden brothers."

By spring, the Kuklux Klan had organized in Georgia and Mobile, Alabama. On April 18, the Klan had infiltrated Kentucky. The Hickman *Courier,* in the southwest corner of the state, 135 miles west of the home of George Dinning, reported that the Klan, or someone purporting to be a Kukluxer, had posted placards around town telling "all the negroes to leave" and telling a certain enterprising citizen "not to employ any negroes," and threatening a penalty if he did. The paper's editor was resolute in repudiating the nonsense. "This is all wrong, and extremely foolish, and calculated to do the community serious injury," he wrote. "The persons issuing these orders...greatly misrepresent our people, and possibly might cause trouble. Our people have no desire to drive the negro from our midst, or to take any undue advantage of them. There is no such thing as a Kuklux Klan in Hickman or Fulton county."

But in the exact same paper, in the very next column, ran an account of a Klan "raid" into Hickman by "a squad numbering 30 or 40":

The Klan were dressed in loose gowns, with a horrid black cowl covering their faces. They made no halt at the Station, passing quietly and interrupting no one. The negroes of the neighborhood are terribly excited and alarmed, and gave various and some incredible stories of their operations during the night. It is said they went to the residence of Mr. John Shepherd, called for a certain negro at work on the farm, who hearing inquiry, we suppose in that terribly hollow voice peculiar to Kukluxers, which it is said sounds like an echo from an empty coffin, attempted to make his escape by running, and was fired upon by one of the Klan. The negro was permitted to make his escape, and their action indicated that they only intended to frighten him.

We have it, that at another place in the neighborhood, where there was a number of negroes congregated, the Klan made their appearance. Some of them dismounted and approached the cabin where the negro meeting was in progress. One of them opened the door, and stood before them in his sheeted robes. The negroes wilted; and a death-like silence prevailed. In a moment four stalwart Klansmen, masked and robed, stood by his side. The leader, raising his long bony finger meaningly, said:

"Boys! The Kuklux would befriend you! Go to work; be prudent; be industrious!"

At this the four assistants stepped out of the door, and the leader tapping himself three times mysteriously upon the breast, suddenly disappeared up the chimney.

We shall not vouch for the existence of the Klan, nor that the Klan did actually appear, but our informer is a truthful gentleman, and it is certain that the negroes and some others in the neighborhood give the above statements.

Several newspapers began to support the Klan, suggesting it was needed to protect whites from "secret leagues of Negro assassins," as reported by the Nashville *Banner*. By June 1868, the battles were raging.

In Chapel Hill, Tennessee, according to the newspapers, an elderly Black man said he was unafraid of the Klan and would shoot down any who trespassed. The Klan became "very much offended" by his "unbearable insolence" and decided to "whip him for using those expressions." On Monday, June 15, eight or nine Klansmen adorned in gowns visited the man's yard and told him to come out because they were going to give him ten lashes that would "teach him for the future to hold his tongue." They dragged him away from the house and had started whipping him when a shot rang out from the woods and a few of the Klansmen were hit. The old man scrambled away and the Klan retreated. The next afternoon, eighteen Black men armed with muskets and pistols marched down the road toward Chapel Hill, saying they were fed up and were going to kill all Klansmen in the vicinity. When word reached town, a group of fourteen whites armed themselves and marched out to meet the avengers. "Four or five of the white men were killed," the Nashville *Banner* reported. "The loss of the negroes is not known."

The next month, the *Banner* purportedly received the following edict from the Black K.K.K.:

more k k k Coming Soon. When the Black ones Come they Will bring fire With them you all thought the Black k k k Wood not Rise any more But th4 of July they Com to Life A Gain the Blacks that was kilt at Nashville an Richmon they is not A fraud of you no Way So Gmmean Look far your Self We have not Time to Look far you Time Brings all things home…the Time is at hand…the White k k k have com and now the Black k k k is A Coming

We have not yet Went to your houses your Wives and Children. We have Let you Go. But you have Went far A tough. We can't stand it

There's no indication whether George Dinning, in the midst of that chaos, ever left or made plans to leave Simpson County, Kentucky. He knew nearly everyone in the farming community. His mother and father, Mary and George, stayed put, too.

He grew and married and lived a life of toil. He claimed the land upon which he lived when David M. Dinning died in November 1884. He could not read or write, and he was unschooled, but he had managed to buy two horses, a plow, some farm implements, seven hogs, two dozen chickens, and four turkeys. He was industrious, and he'd built himself a two-story cabin, where he and Mollie were raising eleven children. His land was productive, rich soil above limestone bedrock. They lived in a region called the Pennyroyal, named after a prolific variety of wild mint, and the conditions there were perfect for growing the dark tobacco primarily used to make cigars, snuff, and chewing tobacco, which, at the time, were much more popular than cigarettes. Dinning's farm was profitable, and he owed no man. Would he steal? He was a well-regarded, hardworking longtime member of the community. He was self-sufficient, and lawful. There is no record of any preceding arrest or suspicion. George Dinning was, judging from all evidence available, a good, honest man.

Without her husband, and surrounded by the gun-hung whites of southern Kentucky, what choice did Mollie have? She did not protest that frigid January evening, though she was frightened and worried about her sick daughter. She quietly put Hermann on one horse and threw several featherbeds in front of him, over the horse's shoulders. She lifted Eva up to him. The girl was ill, and shaken. With her baby in her arms, Mollie mounted their second horse and helped the other children up behind her. At sundown, after one last look, the family started down the frozen road. They hadn't eaten that day, on account of the chaos. "I was so badly frightened when I left, that I did not take time to put wrappings on myself or children," Mollie would later say. Once they'd gotten a few miles away, charitable Black families carried food out to the road and handed it up to the outcasts. They rode until they reached the Tennessee line, and beyond that, the home of Mollie's brother.

Mollie and the children were long out of sight when the white men returned, sloshed out kerosene, and set fire to the main house, to the smokehouse, to the barn, and to the life-giving bottomland fields upon which she and her husband had toiled for fourteen years, from which they'd earned a hard and honest living as free people, to which they would never return. They wouldn't have smelled the first wafts on the night air of their own possessions catching fire—their threadbare clothes, their woodware, their feather beds, their schoolbooks. They wouldn't have heard the footfalls of the guffawing and lawless jackboots hustling across the spiny burdock, or the crackle and lurch of the cabin behind them as the fire came alive and consumed it and, hungry still, licked at the curling Kentucky sky.

Chapter 2

"THAT PROTECTION WHICH THE LAW REFUSES TO GIVE"

Sheriff Clark stepped out of the buggy at Bowling Green at seven o'clock on Saturday and walked his humble prisoner toward the jailhouse, bloodstains on the arm of his undershirt. Local reporters got their first chance to cast a few questions at George Dinning.

"Dunning does not deny the killing," reported the *Owensboro Messenger*, misspelling *Dinning*, "and says when the party came to his house Thursday night and called him out they told him that he had been stealing meat from them and must leave the country within ten days. He told them that he was not guilty of the theft, and was a citizen, owned his home and did not want to leave it. They told him that they did not want any of his d——d impudence and did not come to argue with him, but simply to tell him that he must leave."

"Dinning is apparently a hard-working negro and claims that he has a good character and that he owned the place at which he lived," the *Tennessean* reported.

Clark helped book him at the jail, apprehensive about what was happening outside.

"Conn's friends are greatly excited over the killing," the

Messenger reported, "and there is some uneasiness here over the report that a mob will try and get the prisoner out of the Warren county jail."

"The Simpson County officials report intense excitement and many think that a mob will come here tonight and attempt to take the prisoner from jail," reported the *Tennessean*. "If they come there will be trouble, as the officials will do their utmost to protect Dinning, as they would any of the other prisoners."

The deputy jailer, Matt Christian, noticed Dinning's wounds right away. He observed the fresh hole in Dinning's forehead and noticed quite a bit of swelling, and he said to himself that it had been made by a bullet. He examined the wound on Dinning's arm as well. Dinning was complaining about his head hurting, so Christian summoned a doctor.

The jailhouse doctor, W. R. Francis, inspected the wounds, which were beginning to produce the foul odor of infection. The doctor found a ragged hole in the middle of Dinning's forehead and a sort of swollen ridge that traveled up toward his hairline, then another wound about three inches away from the first. The area around the hole was bruised and rough. The doctor opened the crusty scab upon the wound and it expelled pus and bloody corruption. He cleaned it and probed the hole, which was granulated and inflamed. He ran the probe under the skin. In sixteen years of practice, the doctor had treated a number of gunshot wounds, and he knew what he was looking at. A small-caliber missile had entered George Dinning's forehead, traveled under the skin but over the skull, up about three inches, then exited Dinning's head near his hair. He was lucky to be alive.

The injury was terribly painful, but Dinning had other things to worry about as Saturday turned into Sunday. Even then, the sheriff was getting word that a new mob was forming and had plans to raid the jail at Bowling Green.

Two weeks before, in Sumter, South Carolina, a man named Simon Cooper had given himself up to authorities, but a mob of whites took him from the sheriff, strung him up in a sweet gum tree, pumped 150 bullets into him, then paraded him through town, his corpse sitting upright in a wagon. Two days before, two hundred whites raided the city jail in Amite City, Louisiana, and lynched John Johnson, Arch Joiner, and Gus Williams, then fired three hundred rounds into their corpses for good measure. And the very night George Dinning was attacked, January 21, 1897, a mob broke open the jail in Jeffersonville, Georgia, and hanged Charles Forsyth and Willis White from the same limb; the number of slugs discharged into their bodies was unknown. The newspapers reported that they wore hemp neckties and that their cries could be heard a mile distant.

Behind each of these barbaric events was an abject failure of the legal system, a lulling culture of apathy among government officials sworn to protect prisoners and uphold justice. When facing their bloodthirsty friends and neighbors, the lawmen simply feigned astonishment and, in a grand charade, gave up the keys to the jailhouses, no matter the shame that would shroud their towns long into the future.

Sheriff Clark, a strong Democrat, a Baptist, and a member of a secret fraternal order that promoted philanthropy and friendship, stood apart from his scarecrow peers in the rural South, and he and the Warren County officials did not want to be disgraced by a lynching. The other man standing between George Dinning and the lawless mob was the governor of Kentucky, W. O. "Bill" Bradley. Bradley fired off telegrams daily, monitoring the situation.

"Is there any danger of violence to Dinning in your county when he goes there for trial?" he wrote to Sheriff Clark on Monday. "Have you sufficient force to protect him that you can rely on? The honor of the state must be protected at all hazards and a fair trial had."

Clark wrote back, betraying his fears.

"The killing was just in the edge of my county, on the border of Logan Co. and the Tennessee line. There is no talk of a mob here but I hear considerable talk from Tenn + Logan Co.," he wrote. "The Father of the young man that was killed [says] that he intends for the law to have it and will not have a mob. But I believe [Dinning] will be in danger when brought back here. I intend to give him all the protection in my power and will keep you [informed] as to the matter as I can."

Bill Bradley—no one called him William or Will—was a stocky man, five feet eight and 235 pounds, and the political pundits liked to joke that he was the biggest man intellectually and the most roly-poly physically among the active Republicans of Kentucky. He wore a dark beard and a white Alpine hat and they sometimes called him Billy O. B. He had a sharp wit, a fantastic memory, and a fine speaking voice that carried as well across the Appalachian hills in the east as it did the Bluegrass. He liked to surprise political rivals by sending them bottles of fourteen-year-old Kentucky bourbon. As a Republican in a Democratic state, he knew the bitter flavor of defeat. He'd been trounced in two congressional races and in his 1887 campaign for governor. But he kept fighting, and his next opponent's main political tactic was an appeal to Democratic voters to stop "Negro domination" by Republicans. Bradley had always enjoyed strong support from Kentucky's Black citizens, in part because he promised to end lynchings. Finally, in 1895, he was elected governor by a margin of nearly ten thousand votes.

His term in office had been haunted by violence—feuds in eastern Kentucky, the tollgate wars over free roads in the central region, and the killing of Black men and women by lynch mobs all over. So had his life. Born in 1847, Bradley had lived through an intense period of racial violence in the Bluegrass State. The end of the Civil War sucked a tide of race-based killing into a border state that had officially remained loyal to the Union, and the decade after emancipation was marred by the forced exodus of Black workers from rural towns, ambushes on Black churches and schools, slayings, and attacks on returning Black soldiers who had fought for the North. Because Kentucky never joined the Confederacy, the federal government didn't open a Freedmen's Bureau immediately after the war, as it had in other Southern states. Formally called the Bureau of Refugees, Freedmen, and Abandoned Lands, the Freedmen's Bureau established outposts to help former enslaved people find shelter, education, protection, and access to the legal system. With no bureau in Kentucky, violence filled the void.

Black Kentuckians begged for a bureau for protection, and the government finally opened one in January 1866. A month later, agent S. F. Johnson wrote a supervisor expressing desperate fears of white supremacists in Logan County, saying "there is a reign of terror in this country, such as has never been before." He pointed out that Black people were robbed and shot each day, and that the outlaws were hateful, intimidating, and violent. When federal agents toured Kentucky in the following years, they found Black people still in bondage, as though the Thirteenth Amendment had never been ratified. One agent reported "sixty cases of outrage in a limited district and period, unparalleled in their atrocity and fiendishness; cruelties for which in no instance . . . is there the least shadow of excuse or palliation."

Before the Freedmen's Bureau was established, whites almost never faced justice for crimes against Black people. Black citizens couldn't even testify against whites in Kentucky state court until the early 1870s. So, starting in the late 1860s, the bureau began moving cases from state courts to the United States district court at Louisville, where Judge Bland Ballard doled out rulings in favor of Black litigants such as the state had never seen. The federal docket was soon crowded with cases that centered on Black testimony, and Ballard was exceptional in his fair-mindedness.

Even so, the Kuklux Klan held power—and if it wasn't the organized Klan, it was white vigilantes or Whitecappers or night riders—and the legislature refused to pass laws to quell mob violence. Some lawmakers openly supported the Klan's tactics. Some even swore allegiance to the group.

When Bradley entered politics as Garrard County attorney at age twenty-three, in 1870, the Klan was on the rise and nearing the apex of the postwar bloodshed. In his own county, the Klan was known to fill courtrooms when a trial involved a Black man, to make certain the jury ruled according to the Klan's wishes. In early 1871, in nearby Frankfort, seventy-five masked men raided the jail to free Thomas Scroggins, who was to be tried in federal court for murdering a Black man. The mob didn't seem to fear the law, and the violence spread far and fast until white rebels controlled fifteen Kentucky counties. In Bradley's hometown of Lancaster, a race war broke out after the election of 1874, forcing Black residents to hole up in the home of William Sellers, head of the local Republican committee. The white mob killed at least four Black men and burned Sellers's house to the ground before two hundred soldiers arrived and stopped the fighting.

The killing was close, ever-present, clockwork. Bradley lived alongside it, took it in with his supper, like every son of the South.

When bloodshed was averted, it was often only because Black men were armed. Black leaders tried to work within the system to achieve equity, but that was seldom enough. Sometimes Black writers and speakers urged their brothers and sisters to take up arms.

"The whites concoct all kinds of devilish schemes in the South, and lay them on the colored man or woman, so they can slyly exterminate us by mobs or imprisonment," wrote an anonymous writer in 1885 in the *New York Freeman,* which was widely read in several Kentucky cities. "We have seen our mothers, wives, sisters, and daughters beaten, shot, cut, seduced, deprived of the protection of the law." The writer had lost patience with the corrupt and spineless judicial system and jailers who "open his prison doors to the mob."

"We cannot stand it any longer," the column read. "We should kill as well as be killed."

As George Dinning was establishing himself as an independent farmer surrounded by white folks, the violence peaked. In 1892, a year in which 161 lynchings of Black people were recorded, journalist Ida B. Wells wrote, "Of the many inhuman outrages of this present year, the only case where the proposed lynching did not occur, was where the men armed themselves in Jacksonville, Florida, and Paducah, Kentucky, and prevented it. The only times an Afro-American who was assaulted got away has been when he had a gun and used it in self-defense."

In both Florida and Kentucky, Black men had armed themselves and surrounded the jails when they learned that whites planned to lynch a Black man arrested for a petty crime.

"The lesson this teaches and which every Afro-American should ponder well," Wells wrote, "is that a Winchester rifle should have a place of honor in every Black home, and it should be used for that protection which the law refuses to give. When the white man who is always the aggressor knows he runs a great risk of biting the dust every time his Afro-American victim does, he will have a greater respect for Afro-American life. The more the Afro-American yields and cringes and begs, the more he has to do so, the more he is insulted, outraged and lynched."

By late January 1897, when George Dinning turned himself in, Bradley was under intense scrutiny. In his thirteen months in office, nine men and one woman had been lynched in Kentucky. The very day Dinning surrendered to Sheriff Clark in Franklin, newspapermen were preparing stories about a posse in Fulton, Kentucky, that aimed to search the woods for a Black man accused of assaulting farmer John Carver's daughter in the barn, and one about Whitecappers in Albany, Kentucky, who stabbed to death a boy named John Porter, and one about a mob forming in Hodgenville, Kentucky, with plans to kill Joe Pierce and John Howell, recently indicted in the slaying of Henry Baird. Even though Bradley was publicly critical of judges and sheriffs who didn't protect prisoners from the mob, he was nearly powerless to stop lynchings.

"The commission of crime to punish crime can find no apologist in Christian civilization," he had told the Anti-Mob and Lynch Law Association. With each new extrajudicial killing, it seemed, the Democrats reminded the public anew how impotent Bradley was, delighting in his failure to stop lynchings. He was often condemned in the newspapers, even Republican organs. "It must have dawned upon him by this time that the Democratic Administrations were not, after all, wantonly remiss in the matter of crushing out the mob spirit in the State, and that it is a much bigger undertaking than he imagined," editorialized the Bowling Green *Times*.

But at least he was trying. And by and large, he made a good governor. He did things because they were in the best interests of all the people instead of for a particular faction.

"Bradley has never used the negro voter in the offensive

manner so characteristic of the carpet-bagger and the scalawag politician, but no Republican in the state has ever had such a hold as he has upon the Black man," wrote one magazine writer.

Bradley took steps to prevent a lynching in Paris, Kentucky, in late 1896. Without waiting for local police to ask for help, he had troops on alert in a town nearby. And he was constantly wiring officials to ask if they needed help preventing violence.

So when George Dinning turned himself in to the local sheriff, Bradley was determined to do everything in his power to make sure Dinning was safe.

"Please answer immediately when Dinning will be taken from Bowling Green to Franklin [and] whether you can give him safe conduct," Bradley wrote in a telegram to Warren County's head jailer.

"Goes to Franklin in March," came the reply from jailer C. J. Hagerman on Monday, January 25. "Will need protection then."

They told Dinning about the governor's assurances of protection and told him he was safe, that he would not have to die.

"God bless the governor," Dinning said.

Hagerman was still worried. As night came on, he stationed extra armed guards outside the jail, but he grew suspicious of some activity in the neighborhood. He received several credible-seeming reports that a mob was preparing to attack the jail. Hagerman began making plans to transport Dinning to Louisville, but he couldn't do so safely after dark on one of the coldest nights of the year. The threats grew so intense, and Hagerman so worried, that he decided to distribute weapons to some of the prisoners with instructions to start shooting if the mob broke down the strong outer doors and advanced into the corridors. He chose the most trustworthy and handed them rifles, and there they sat, waiting for the outraged friends of a dead man to kick open the doors and face their hell.

Bradley, meanwhile, took the first steps to call a special session of the legislature. He was sick of mob violence. The Dinning affair was at the front of his mind when he told the press the next morning that he would be bringing lawmakers back to Frankfort in March. He told them the recurrence of kukluxing in Kentucky was the cause. He wouldn't say what the answer was, but he swore to the reporters that he had a cure for the vigilantes.

George Dinning arrived in Louisville on the one o'clock train on January 27, 1897, under the careful custody of Warren County Sheriff Rodes and Deputy Sheriff Waddle.

"DINNING ESCAPES THE MOB," the next day's headline would read in the *New York Times*. "Kentucky's Governor Protects a Negro Who Shot a Regulator."

Dinning did not seem to the reporters to be unusually worried, but he struck them as reticent. He told reporters that he had simply been protecting his home, and that he felt he had only done his duty.

Then Deputy Waddle took the unusual position of defending his prisoner. He told the press that Dinning had many sympathizers at Bowling Green, that folks believed him. He said that a number of Bowling Green citizens had volunteered to defend Dinning from the mob. The deputy said he, too, believed Dinning, believed his version of the story to be true.

"The negro appears to be honest, and I for one believe his story," Deputy Waddle said. "He gave me no trouble on the train."

The sentiment about Dinning in the newspapers, racist as it was, seemed to be changing. The stories were still discriminatory and mean-spirited, but it helped that reporters saw him for themselves, sized him up.

"The prisoner is inoffensive looking and is a typical Southern negro," reported the correspondent for the *Courier-Journal* in Louisville.

"Dinning looks to be a peaceable and inoffensive negro, rather an old-fashioned Southern darkey," reported the Louisville *Times*.

Some writers assumed the worst and still found the killing justifiable.

"For 'a quiet, inoffensive, intelligent and wealthy young man,' the late Mr. Jodie Conn and a dozen of his neighbors were engaged in very disreputable business when they banded together and went about in the night warning other citizens, who had been convicted of no crime, to abandon their homes and leave the community," wrote the editor of the Louisville *Times*. "George Dinning may be a bad negro and an undesirable neighbor, but if he was a violator of the law he should have been proceeded against according to the law."

"This Negro, mean as he doubtless is, has done the state a service by killing one of the midnight raiders," wrote the editor of the *Interior Journal* in Stanford, Kentucky, "and he should be protected if the entire State Militia is necessary to do so. Gov. Bradley says he shall not be mobbed and we hope he will see to it that the law takes its course in this case especially. Conn and every member of his lawless band deserved what he got, and if all mobs could meet with such reception, few of such gangs would disgrace the State."

Dinning had waived his right to an examining trial, so he would not be traveling back to Simpson County and the nest of Conn's bellicose friends until the next circuit court session in March. And he would go only if the grand jury could deliver an indictment, which was an important aspect of the case and one the press noticed in the following days. No impartial person bore witness to the chaos that night. If Conn's friends wanted George Dinning to go to jail, they would have to tell a grand jury that they had armed themselves and ridden on horseback to his home around midnight, and that there had been an exchange of gunfire.

Two of the so-far-unnamed vigilantes took a train to Louisville to consult with lawyers about what they should do, and they were advised to hold their tongues. To step forward and publicly say that they had armed themselves and approached a Black man's house as vigilantes or regulators required confidence that a Simpson County jury would find Dinning guilty.

"The members of the mob have since sworn vengeance," the *New York Times* noted as the case began to gain national attention. "They know full well, however, that Dinning acted in self-defense, and that they cannot testify against him without incriminating themselves."

In a story on January 27, *The Tennessean* noted that fascinating fact as well. "Another important feature in the case, which did not come to light until to-day, is that a night or two after the killing the house of Dinning, just on the line between Simpson County and Robertson County, Tenn., was burned to the ground and his family is now scattered over the neighborhood," the paper reported. "If in the prosecution of Dinning the names of the so-called 'vigilance committee' are brought out, his attorneys will at once institute suits of big damages against all of the men who composed it."

Days slid by, and January turned into February, and Sheriff Clark wondered if that meant the night raiders were organizing to end the ordeal in bloodshed rather than risk outing themselves. He knew already that the vigilantes had gone after other Black folks living in Coffee Bottom, those they found "objectionable." They told several families to leave the county immediately and never come back, and those families packed their things and left.

A reporter for the Louisville *Times* who had been investigating the case reported on the mob's plan. "The general opinion is that the negro will be hanged," he wrote. "The grand jury will return an indictment and a change of venue will be prayed for and refused, as the killing took place in the extreme west corner of the county, and an unbiased jury can be impaneled in the east portion. When the negro is brought back here for trial a mob will take him from custody and wreak swift and terrible vengeance."

That had happened here at least twice before.

In 1882, a mob of one hundred men on horseback abducted eighteen-year-old Bob Sarver from a sheriff's deputy who was trying to spirit him safely away to Bowling Green by train. Sarver had been accused of trying to "outrage" Tennie Ruby (or Tina Ruley), sixteen, in broad daylight on one of the busiest roads in the county, eight miles north of Franklin. The coroner found him hanging from a small tree near the same spot the next day, his feet nearly touching the ground. The papers said the white girl was "beautiful and pure, with an untarnished name." Sarver was called a "black beast," a "burly brute," and a "negro ravisher." Just five years before the Dinning case, in 1892, John Redfern killed his employer after a dispute and turned himself over to the sheriff. That night, a mob of twenty-eight masked men woke the jailer, put a gun to his head, and demanded the large key to Redfern's cell. The helpless Redfern was found hanging the next morning at Sharp's Branch, near the junction of Franklin and Gallatin Road with the L&N Pike.

Though he'd not been indicted, Dinning's assigned lawyers had already begun preparing his defense, and they'd made several investigative trips from Bowling Green to Franklin, the Simpson County seat. What they found was outrageous enough to prompt a letter to the governor.

County Court day in FRANKLIN, Ky.

A postcard depicting a typical court day in Franklin, Kentucky, at the turn of the century. (*Courtesy of the Simpson County Historical Society*)

"We feel that it is our duty to our client to inform you of the peril of his condition," wrote lawyer Virgil Hagerman, of the firm of Grider & Moss. "If he goes to Franklin without a strong guard he will not live to be tried. Of this we feel morally certain."

The attorney told Governor Bradley that many folks they had interviewed in Simpson County couldn't see how Dinning could be blamed for the killing under the circumstances, but those same people would not dare to take sides with Dinning. Hagerman also said they had noticed that the crowd they feared the most were now offering the greatest assurances of tranquility, peace, and a fair and impartial trial.

"This we believe to be a shifting tactic," Hagerman wrote to the governor. "They saw their mistake, and they would now lull us into a sense of security. We do not believe, nor have we seen any man...who does not believe, even to a conviction which amounts to absolute knowledge, that Dinning will ever live to stand his trial unless protected."

The lawyers were itching for the case to go to trial, no matter the danger. They felt confident that they could prove beyond doubt that Dinning had fired only after he himself had been shot in the head, and his house shot into. They'd interviewed several men—neighbors—who had seen the house the following morning, before it was burned, and they would testify to seeing bullet holes in the doors and finding rifle balls on the floor inside the house.

"His life we are certain is in your hands, and you alone can save him," Hagerman wrote. "We believe he did no more than any other man would have done in defense of his home, and he should have a trial."

In late February, members of the Fifth Street Baptist Church in Louisville, the first Black congregation in the city, took up a collection and bought George Dinning, whom they had never met, a full suit of clothes to wear when he was taken back to Franklin for trial. The church's pastor, the Reverend John H. Frank, informed Governor Bradley that a traveling minister who had spent two weeks in Franklin said he'd overheard that the whites in town were planning to mob Dinning as soon as he arrived, before the judge even called court into session. "Governor, you must not allow it. It will be a shame from which we can never recover," Frank wrote. "Not only must he be protected to and during the trial but after his discharge (I do not see how it can be anything but a discharge) and if he can not come away with the soldiers owing to lack of means or owing to the state's failure to provide him transportation, I am prepared to furnish him [a] return ticket."

The circuit court term began on Monday, March 1. Governor Bradley immediately wrote to Sheriff Clark and Dinning's lawyers, asking for an update. More than a month after the shooting, the sheriff still couldn't come up with a single witness to testify against Dinning. None of the Whitecappers had the courage to step forward. Sheriff Clark sent a telegram to the governor on March 2. "Geo Dinning is not indicted. We fail to find a witness to testify before grand jury. Will wire desired information if Dinning is indicted." Dinning's lawyer, Virgil Hagerman, also wrote back on March 2, saying there was no indictment. "The general impression among those who have an opportunity to know is that he will be hung unless guarded by soldiers and we are exceedingly glad to know that you are going to protect him," the lawyer wrote.

Bradley was hard at work in Frankfort, and that month he called for a special session of the legislature, urging lawmakers to pass a bill that would make each county liable for damages from lynchings. His logic was that if citizens stood to suffer financially, they would stop lynchings. He also felt that law enforcement officials—sheriffs, jailers, peace officers—should be held accountable, and should resign from their elected offices if they failed to keep a suspect safe. Most radical was his proposal to arm prisoners if a mob was lurking nearby. "No mob would be able to stand before the prisoner fighting for his life and the jailer or sheriff fighting for his office," the governor reasoned. The bill wouldn't be ready for vote until May, but many praised Bradley's ambition.

On Thursday, March 4, President William McKinley was inaugurated in impressive fashion in Washington, D.C. Representing the former Confederates in the grand inaugural parade along Pennsylvania Avenue were 200 horsemen and 2,000 foot soldiers, each wearing a ribbon that said THERE SHALL BE NO NORTH, NO SOUTH, NO EAST, NO WEST, BUT A COMMON COUNTRY.

Meanwhile, back in Kentucky, they all waited: Sheriff Clark in Franklin, the lawyers in Bowling Green, the governor in Frankfort, and George Dinning alone in a jail cell in Louisville, wearing the same clothes he wore the night the white men tried to kill him.

Franklin was eerily quiet that week.

Charles T. Conn, the father of the dead man, showed up to speak to Sheriff Clark. He said he discouraged anything like violence, and swore that he would see to it that the honor of the state was upheld by a fair and impartial trial.

And on Saturday, March 6, the Simpson County grand jury— having heard testimony from several of the white men present at the killing of Jodie Conn on a cold and moonlit night, those who had decided that they would tell what happened and trust it would all end with Dinning's conviction and sentencing because they were white and he was Black—handed down an indictment signed by its foreman, J. C. Baird, in a case styled Commonwealth of Kentucky v. George Dinning: Willful murder, no bail.

Chapter 3

"THEY TREATED HIM MORE THAN BAD AND MYSELF ALL SO"

Mollie Dinning struggled to keep her family fed that spring. She was living with her mother-in-law in Black Jack, Tennessee, just across the state line, but she had no income, no husband, no meat or bread. No clothing for the children save what they wore when they were forced to leave.

Everything she and George had built together was gone.

She missed him. She missed their routine, their security, their little home near the Red River, set back a hundred yards from the nearest road. Their picket fence and hitching post. She went there sometimes in her mind, to the bottomlands, and she could hear the chickens squawking and the wind whipping around the corners of the house. Their house, free and clear.

George bought the place from John Dinning in 1877 on a promissory note for $350, at 8 percent interest. He began making payments almost immediately, $70 here, $48 there—all proceeds from his seasonal tobacco earnings. He had the land paid off in seven years, by 1884, or so he thought. After John Dinning's death, the man appointed administrator of his estate filed suit in circuit court claiming that George Dinning had not fully paid off the note. Dinning disputed that and called as a witness the sheriff, Joseph Plummer, who testified that he remembered collecting the final payment from Dinning. The case was settled in 1886, with George Dinning paying an additional $23.33, the only amount left in dispute. From that day forward, a tract bordered by the Red River on the south, and on the east, west, and north by white farm families, belonged to a man who had been born into bondage and set free by the Thirteenth Amendment in 1865. His white neighbors, some of them, would for years wrongly suspect he was not the true owner of the place.

The house wasn't much, but it was sturdy. It had a fireplace, tongue-and-groove flooring, plank shutters on the windows. A room upstairs. And it was theirs. Their things. Over the years, Dinning would wander off on Saturdays and Sundays to visit estate sales in far-flung corners of Simpson County, and he'd come home dragging a spotted cow, or a saddle and bridle, or some rusty hay hooks. They'd accumulated enough to live comfortably and to farm their fertile acreage.

Now Mollie faced the uncertainty of the future, and making a life on her own. She wasn't sure where to turn for help, so in May 1897, she—or someone close to her—wrote to the governor of Kentucky, William O. Bradley.

"I take in hand my pin to write you a few lines to let you know my present condishion is one left most awfuly bad," the letter said. "I am the wife of George Dinning whoes case is now before you being accuse of the death of Jody Conn. The mob that come to kill my husband that night they treated him more than bad and myself all so."

She told the governor her version of the entire saga, of what she had lost.

"And after they found that they could not get my husband they came and burnt our house and smoke house and gear house," the letter said, "and they wood not let me get nothing out at all for me and my children."

She told the governor that her neighbors were cold and gave her little relief. She speculated that the mob had threatened them, too.

"Governor Bradley if a change is not made for me and my family to live we shall all like wise pearish on account bad treatment from the mob threatening us because they could not get to kill my husband George Dinning who are now in Louisville Ky jail," the letter said. "How Governor Bradley please tell me can you take some steps to provide a way by which I may live and have something for my family to live on for we air suffering here. Every thing we have is burnted in to ashes."

She spoke, too, of the injustice her people would feel if the mob was left unpunished.

"Mr. Hon. Governor if in such cases there is not sumthing done for defence we as a collered people can not live here," the letter said. "We want too and will be lawbiding citerzens and in such cases we look for protection by law where as we air poor and helpless. Not able to defend our selves regarding the capital sutch as the money but a poor woman as I am and in my condition I believe the law will defend against all sutch treatments. I am in hope that your Honor Governor Bradley will make arrangment for us me and George my husband to get pay for damage done to us from this County."

She signed the letter:

"Yours truly, Mollie Dinning the wife of George Dinning, the present prisoner now in the Louisville Jail, George Dinning, Collored"

It is unknown what reaction the handwritten plea drew from the governor, but Mollie followed it on May 11 with a sworn affidavit, recounting for him the night her husband fired on the mob. She reported a short exchange of dialogue that started with the men outside telling George they were his friends and they wanted to see him.

"That is not much of a friend if he will not give him name," Dinning responded.

"George," one of the party said, "we will give you ten days to leave here."

"What for?" Dinning responded.

"You have been stealing," came the response.

"Stealing what, gentlemen?" Dinning said.

No response.

"I can prove by responsible men where I got everything I have," Dinning shouted.

"You keep quiet in there," one of the men hollered, "or we will tear this damned shack down, and take you out and hang you now."

That was when the first shot rang out, and a bullet exploded through their front door, struck something, and fell to the ground.

Dinning grabbed his gun and started up the stairs and two more bullets came through the front door.

"I heard George fire from the window upstairs, and almost simultaneously there was a regular volley fired from the outside at the window from which George fired his gun," Mollie swore.

George Dinning also sent the governor a sworn letter, recounting much of what Mollie had witnessed.

"I have never seen my wife or any of my children since the night I left home as stated," his statement said. "I feel confident that my life is in great peril if sent back to Franklin for trial. I do not feel that I have violated any law of my country; I had nothing against Mr. Cohn, and regret the unfortunate circumstance which lead to his death. I only acted in what I believe to be in defense of my home and my family, and I do not feel that I should suffer for it, which I know that I must do unless your Excellency interferes in my behalf, and I respectfully petition Your Excellency to pardon me and not require me to go back to Franklin for trial."

His trial was scheduled to start in ten days.

Before closing, he reminded Governor Bradley that he had a family, homeless now, and that he was obliged to protect them, and to do that he needed to stay alive.

"I earnestly beseech you to pardon me," he wrote, "for my sufferings have already been great and as I feel undeserved."

And so it came to pass that a Republican legislator and friend of the governor introduced an antilynching bill into the Kentucky Senate. The bill was called "An act to prevent lynching and injury to and destruction of real and personal property in this Commonwealth." It was broken into eleven sections. The first few defined what made up an unlawful mob and charted the penalties for Whitecappers who kidnapped suspects from law enforcement and harmed or killed them. The fourth section gave sheriffs the right to command able-bodied men in the community to help protect a prisoner, and to arm prisoners so they could defend themselves. Another section established that a county judge or sheriff who failed to protect a prisoner had to forfeit his office and face a fine of up to $500. Another gave the governor and county judges the option of offering financial rewards for the apprehension of members of lynch mobs. It also allowed the governor to dispatch detectives to help local officials investigate lynchings. Another section made it possible for any person injured by a mob to sue the mob for damages. Another established a penalty for anyone circulating threatening letters. And the last section put the law into effect immediately:

"As mobs and riotous assemblages of persons in certain counties of this Commonwealth have for several months past been engaged, and are now engaged, in injuring and destroying real and personal property, and the good name of this Commonwealth demands that such unlawful conduct should be stopped as soon as possible, it is hereby declared that an emergency exists, and this act shall take effect when approved by the Governor."

There was little, if any, debate. Perhaps the bill was being ignored, given the apathy about lynching in many quarters. Or perhaps the legislators would simply let it die so they could hustle to Louisville for the upcoming Kentucky Derby. But then came a surprise. On May 11, the bill passed the Senate with huge support and was sent to the House. Some expected it to die there.

"It is a decided improvement, but it is said that the House will not adopt it," wrote the editor of the *Interior Journal* in Stanford, Kentucky. "The members are afraid of their lawless constituency."

There was a little more debate on the House floor, but when called to a vote, the bill passed, 52–2.

When it landed on Bradley's desk, he immediately signed it.

Chapter 4

"THE PEOPLE SAY THAT DINNING WAS A WORTHLESS NEGRO"

Simpson County, Kentucky, 1897: honeysuckle and barbed wire, wheat threshers and smokehouses and kerosene lanterns. Woodware, glassware, tinware. Baptists, Catholics, and Methodists, thick as fiddlers in hell. Runabouts, surreys, and stanhopes, and briar tangled in the roadside fences across rolling country, around cornfields and orchards. Fatback, Sunday clothes, linen suits and alpaca coats, red clay, knee stains, handwritten receipts. Pullman sleeping cars, steam laundry, notions, Franklin Hardware Co., McCartney & Swan's, R. L. Booker & Short Grocery Store, and the Boisseau Hotel, the best stagecoach stop between Louisville and Nashville. Everything's a nickel. A dime is a double nickel. Pig in the Parlor, Shoot the Buffalo, *Southern Harmony*. Dr. Peffer's Royal-Tansy Pills. Bronze turkeys and Berkshire hogs and Ben-Hur Bicycles. Clod crushers, Dr. Price's Cream Baking Powder, twenty-five pounds of blackberry sugar for a buck, a bushel of meal for fifty cents. Blood remedies and carriage repair and Family Bibles and Kentucky Dew Whiskey, and $15 for a hogshead of tobacco makes the newspaper.

On Sunday, June 27, the Simpson County judge ordered the Jefferson County jailer to turn George Dinning over to the Simpson County sheriff, and he ordered the Simpson County sheriff to turn Dinning over to the Simpson County jailer. So a bevy of fresh-faced soldiers boarded trains at Winchester and Franklin and made their way to Louisville to retrieve George Dinning from jail and escort him back home.

The sun rose shortly after four o'clock on June 28 over the small city of Franklin, the county seat, named after Benjamin Franklin. Soft morning light fell on the stately new courthouse, topped by a metal roof and a handsome clock tower, which was squared in by chalky dirt roadways and low brick buildings, each with a hitching post. And soon those hitching posts were lousy with horses, and soon the streets filled with the curious, the reticent, and the hostile. They swarmed the dusty boulevards, a crowd such as few had ever seen.

An illustration of downtown Franklin, Kentucky, incorporated in 1820. The jailhouse sat on College Street, a block from the central courthouse. (*Courtesy of the Simpson County Historical Society*)

Reporters, too, came from neighboring towns and cities to bear witness to whatever might unfold. Even the *New York Times* hired a correspondent to cover the sensational trial.

"This case has attracted more attention than any case that has been tried in this county for years," wrote a reporter for the *Tennessean* in Nashville, "and the interest is growing now that the negro has come to trial or will doubtless in the next few days."

And already they were making predictions.

"It is the universal opinion that the jury will bring in a verdict placing Dinning's penalty at death," wrote a correspondent for the *St. Louis Daily Globe-Democrat*. "The people say that Dinning was a worthless negro."

George Dinning sat inside the jailhouse alone, the sun creeping in through the narrow vertical slats in the thick stone walls. Nearly three hundred soldiers in two companies had escorted Dinning to Franklin, a fraught journey. He could hear them outside now. Their presence was a remarkable show of force.

"From a reliable source we have information that it is the intention of the friends of the man Dinning killed to make an effort to take the negro away from the troops as soon as they arrive in Franklin," Adjutant Charles Coin had told a reporter for the *Cincinnati Enquirer* as the troops headed toward Simpson County.

"It has been said that a regiment of soldiers can't prevent his being hanged," Coin said. "We have good prospects for a lively time."

Even as the jury was impaneled, dangerous men stalked the streets.

While it might have seemed as though lynching was typically reserved for men accused (often falsely) of murder or rape, more Black men in Kentucky were lynched for other reasons: being "uppity," being "troublesome," having "bad character." A few were even hanged on "general principles." In Kentucky alone, at least 166 people were lynched without trial in the last twenty-five years of the nineteenth century. The numbers were much

A cell in the Simpson County Jail, where Dinning awaited trial. (*Courtesy of the author*)

higher in Deep South states like Mississippi, Alabama, and Louisiana, but Kentucky was far worse than other border states when it came to racist lynchings. The very day Dinning arrived back in Simpson County, a mob of masked men in Aberdeen,

Mississippi, 230 miles from Franklin, overpowered the city jailer and abducted Perry Gilliam, a Black man accused of robbing a white woman. They carried him five miles from the jail and hanged him from a tree in the middle of a big road, where passersby found his lifeless body twisting in the wind the next morning.

Dinning feared for his life. It's impossible to say what ran through his mind as he sat in the small, stone-walled cell. It's possible he recalled John Henry Grainger, who might even have been a friend. They didn't live far apart. Newspapers near and far said Grainger was "obnoxious," and that "he talked too much," and that his white neighbors were tired of his threats, but he was just a man who sometimes said what was on his mind. The story about his argument with Bell Witt was muddled. Nobody knew for a fact what words they exchanged that hot day six years before, in late July 1891. But everyone knew that a band of mounted men rode to Grainger's house at night and called him to the door. And he came out. That was what was hard to understand. Why comply, when he must have known what they were there for? Why would a man like Grainger, who could read and write, who wasn't afraid of speaking his mind, come outside when called? The newspapers don't mention it, but he had a wife and three children. Perhaps he was worried about their safety.

The mob bound him, tied him to the lead horse, and carried him to a spot where the woods skirted the road. The men, none of them wearing masks, told him to prepare for death. They put a rope around his neck and threw the other end over a protruding branch and drew him up into the air to strangle. Those who cut him down the next day found a note pinned to John Henry Grainger's breast, warning the other Negroes of Simpson County to keep out of trouble with white men and refrain from making threats of violence.

There was nothing Dinning could do to protect himself now. His safety was in the hands of others.

In court that morning, fearing mob violence at worst and a tainted verdict at best, Dinning's attorneys filed a motion for change of venue. They had a better shot at justice in another county. Dinning would have been safer a hundred miles away. But after reading their motion and supporting affidavits, and hearing witnesses for the Commonwealth, Judge W. L. Reeves overruled the motion. The trial would commence in Franklin, Simpson County, as soon as a jury was assembled.

Governor Bradley had departed the Commonwealth on June 12 for a three-week visit to Colorado Springs, leaving in charge of state affairs Lieutenant Governor William Jackson Worthington. Worthington was a farmer and ex–Union Army soldier from the red-brush section of eastern Kentucky whose political speeches were said to rustle the cobwebs from the rock-ribbed Democracy of the grand old Commonwealth. Worthington, like Bradley, swore to protect Dinning from the mob. Everyone expected him to send soldiers to guard Dinning in Simpson County, but reporters were stunned when they saw the soldiers loading two cannons onto flatcars in Frankfort. Cannons, Worthington had decided, would send the message.

When the troops arrived with their guns, the people of Simpson County were outraged and insulted. They grumbled about the outsiders who would think them so uncivil. They groused about the governor. "The people of Simpson county are insulted and highly indignant because Gov. Bradley ordered the troops there, as they did not ask for them and the officials of the county had informed the governor that they were able and willing to protect Dinning," wrote a reporter for the *Russellville Ledger* in neighboring Logan County. "But the governor...wanted to show the people that he was a big man with a little head and therefore ordered out the militia, and the abuse that the good people of this county have heaped upon Billy O'Bradley is an elegant sufficiency." To show their displeasure, the good people of Simpson County hanged in effigy William O. Bradley and Lieutenant Governor William Jackson Worthington on the courthouse lawn.

Something else happened that seemed to be a harbinger of bad things to come. Tom Bryant, the Black porter at the depot in Franklin, was killed on a train somewhere near Elizabethtown, ninety miles away. His death was a mystery, his killer or killers at large. His mangled corpse arrived at Franklin by the same locomotive Sunday, and the Black citizens of Simpson County took it to be an omen of summary vengeance.

The *Louisville Times* ran on its front page a drawing of Dinning under the headline: "HIS LIFE IS IN DIRE DANGER." In the drawing Dinning is wearing a handsome—if rumpled and short-in-the-sleeves—frock coat and waistcoat and an ascot, most likely the suit donated by Reverend John H. Frank and the Fifth Street Baptist Church. His left hand rests on a chair back, and in his right he holds a fedora. He's modestly built, slouched at the shoulders. His eyes seem tired, and his face is remarkably expressionless.

Late Monday night, a terrible explosion rocked the jailhouse and sent the jittery soldiers scrambling to their feet and grasping for their rifles. It seemed for a moment that the jailhouse was under attack, and in the commotion the soldiers began firing shots. Lieutenant F. L. Gordon of the Frankfort militia saw three men riding away on horseback and fired his revolver at them desperately. When the dust settled, the soldiers haltingly crossed the street to find a huge hole in the side yard of the house opposite the jailhouse, where the garden of a Ms. Norris had

Drawing of George Dinning in the Louisville *Times*.

once been. Someone had lobbed dynamite in their direction. A warning, perhaps.

Given the circumstances, Colonel E. H. Gaither, the slender, mustachioed man in command of the Second Regiment sent to protect Dinning, suspected someone might take a potshot at Dinning once his trial commenced. So the next morning he beseeched Judge Reeves to ban guns in the courtroom and allow his soldiers to search each person who entered. But Reeves refused, saying it would give the military authority in a time of peace and therefore be unconstitutional, as citizens are free from unreasonable search and stigma. Colonel Gaither argued that having armed citizens at the trial would place his soldiers at a great disadvantage. He told the judge he was nearly certain that someone would try to shoot Dinning during his trial, and he threatened to keep his soldiers out of the courtroom and to protect Dinning only while in custody of the jailer and going to and from court.

But Gaither wasn't known to quit. In fact, everyone in Kentucky knew the best story about the old Confederate soldier. He was near Brentwood during the war, and he had started over a hill to get some water from a spring when he came across six Yankees walking in his direction. Knowing he was outnumbered, he shouted, "Surrender!" The Yanks misunderstood. They threw up their hands and Gaither marched them back to his camp in triumph. He had courage, and good fortune.

Gaither called on Governor Bradley, who quickly wired his orders that all spectators be searched. Gaither also decided to place soldiers with Springfield rifles in positions surrounding Dinning for the entire trial.

Gaither's moves made the locals mad. "UNWELCOME GUESTS," read a headline in the *Louisville Times*. "Many People in Franklin Indignant Over the Presence of Bluecoats."

"Col. Gaither's reputation for daring courage is well-known throughout the state, and he is very outspoken in his denunciation of the persons who are trying to bring on trouble," wrote a reporter for the *Richmond Climax*. "It is probable that he himself will be made the object of wrath of Jody Conn's friends."

JUDGE WILLIS REEVES.

Judge Willis Reeves, depicted in the Louisville *Times*.

As jury selection began on Tuesday, Gaither searched and disarmed everyone who entered the courthouse, and everyone protested, even Judge Reeves. "There's a feeling of uneasiness and it is feared the negro will be lynched before the trial is over, regardless of soldiers," wrote a reporter for the *Knoxville Sentinel*.

A reporter for the *Lexington Morning Herald* asked a prominent citizen if there would have been trouble if the soldiers had not come. "Not a bit," the man replied. "They would just have taken him out and hung him up." The reporter opined that he had "no doubt that if opportunity offers, Dinning will be assassinated."

By two o'clock on Wednesday, June 30, a jury of twelve had been impaneled: John Gibson, Joe Gibson, Nute Temple, J. D. Uhls, J. M. Kirby, E. Jones, J. H. Gibson, J. M. Pistole, Burle Mayes, William Henson, Tom Snider, and John Snider. All were men. All were white. All lived on the east side of Drake's Creek, which divided the county, some sixteen miles away from the scene of the alleged crime. And by the time they had been sworn in, the crowd in the courtroom had grown beyond all expectations. Tensions ran high. And it was hot. The temperature had climbed to 96 degrees by the time the judge took the bench. The sun's burning breath enveloped the land in torrid air. The earth outside shriveled to cauterized cakes like crusts of bread on a hot stove. The grass fell down in a faint. The leaves hung listless on motionless boughs. Dogs plodded down dusty lanes, their tongues hanging out. Cows lay flat on the ground. Brooks babbled tepid eddies over stones that rose up out of the water with tops like hot coals. All of nature sizzled and sweated. In the still air inside the courthouse, even the gauziest shirtsleeves were saturated like dishrags freshly hung on a clothesline.

George Dinning sat alongside his lawyers at the defense table, his new three-piece suit a boiling catacomb. Eight soldiers guarded him: one on each side and six leaning against the railing that separated Dinning from the spectators. The lawyers were planning to call sixty-two witnesses to testify, and up first were the men who had come to visit Dinning on that moonlit January night.

Chapter 5

"WE TURNED AND SHOT BACK AT THE HOUSE"

First came Albert Green Freeman, a thirty-four-year-old white farmer who had known George Dinning his whole life, had grown up right down the road.

"Where do you live?" asked the prosecutor for the Commonwealth, G. T. Finn.

"Right down here in the lower edge of Simpson County," Freeman said.

"How long have you lived there?"

"I reckon for about ten or twelve years," Freeman said.

"Were you acquainted with Jodie Conn in his lifetime?"

"Yes, sir."

"Were you acquainted with the defendant, George Dinning?"

"Yes, sir."

"Were you at defendant Dinning's house the night Jodie Conn was killed?"

"Yes, sir."

"I will get you, Mr. Freeman, to go ahead and state all that occurred there and how came you there and for what purpose."

"Well," Freeman said, "we went down there because there had been some stealing going on in the neighborhood. We went down there and Doc Moore went up to the door and I don't know that I can tell all he said. I am not certain but I believe it was about this. He went up to the door and he says, 'George, George.' And he says, 'Huh.' And Doc says, 'Come out to the door.' And he says, 'Who's there?' And Doc says, 'Your friends.' And he says, 'I ain't coming.' And Doc says, 'We didn't come to hurt or harm you and if you will not come to the door just listen to what we have got to say.' And he told him that there had been some stealing going on in the neighborhood, and he told him he was suspected as being one of the parties, and, if he was, he must leave the neighborhood in ten days."

"Did George Dinning make any reply?" the lawyer asked.

"He asked what had been stolen," Freeman said, "and Doc told him meat had been stolen and some houses set on fire, and turkeys and chickens had been stolen, and he said he did not know anything about the stealing and that he had not stoled anything and could prove by his neighbors and friends that he made his living honest, and Doc told him if he could prove it that was alright."

"Did anything else occur there?"

"When he said that, we turned and started off and he said something about—maybe he would and maybe he wouldn't—and we started off and I heard a racket upstairs, and I reckon I was about fifteen or twenty feet from the house, and I looked back and saw someone fire from the upstairs window, and someone says, 'Anybody hurt?' And Jodie Conn said he was."

"What happened?" the prosecutor asked.

"We turned and shot back at the house," Freeman said.

"Whereabout towards the house?"

"At the window upstairs where we saw the blaze come from."

"About how many shots? Can you say?"

"I can't tell," Freeman said. "I do not know. There was a good many shots fired."

"How many was in the party that night with you?"

"Twenty five," Freeman said.

"With Conn?"

"Yes, sir."

"Up to the time Jodie Conn was shot or at any time before he was shot there at George Dinning's that night, state whether or not Jodie Conn or anyone in the crowd there offered any violence toward George Dinning or any of his property," the prosecutor said.

"No, sir," Freeman replied. "He was not harmed in any way at all."

"Any harsh words?"

"No, sir."

"Any abuse?"

"No, sir," Freeman said. "Nothing at all."

"Did you all hurt or harm him or any of his property there?"

"No, sir."

"Make any threats?"

"No, sir."

"He refused to come to the door?"

"Yes, sir."

"And, yet, you told him the purpose for which you all had come?"

"Yes, sir."

"I understood you to state that you were starting to leave and were leaving?" the lawyer asked.

"Yes, sir," Freeman said. "I was outside of the yard. Just outside of the yard."

"Where was Jodie Conn?"

"He was outside of the yard to the left of me, to the north of me."

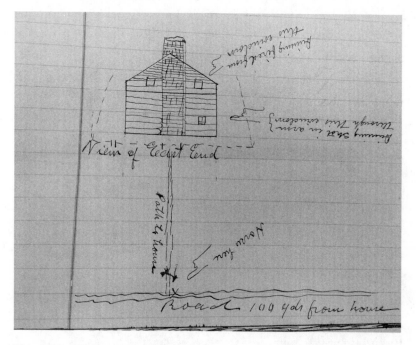

This drawing of the east end of Dinning's cabin was used in the case. Pointers indicate where the horses were tied up near the road, the lower window through which Dinning was shot in the arm, and the upper window from which he fired. (*Original held with the petitions for pardon in the papers of Governor William O. Bradley, Kentucky Department for Libraries and Archives, Frankfort, Ky.*)

"Had you all been in the yard?"

"Yes, sir."

"Had Conn been in the yard?"

"Yes, sir."

"What kind of night was it, Mr. Freeman?"

"A light, moonshiny night," Freeman said.

"What kind of man was Mr. Conn? Describe his personal appearance...how tall?"

"I do not know exactly, but about six feet high," Freeman said.

"Was he slender?"

"Yes, sir."

"Was he accustomed to wearing a peculiar dress," the lawyer asked, "and was he peculiarly dressed that night?"

"Yes, sir," Freeman said. "A little peculiar to anyone in the neighborhood."

"How was he dressed that night?"

"Dressed about like he was every day," Freeman said. "His overcoat struck him way down here." Freeman motioned below his knee. "Same clothes he wears every day in the winter."

"What sort of hat?" Finn asked.

"Black hat with broad brim," Freeman said. "Broader than this right sharply." He removed his own hat, which was felt and had a narrow brim.

"Broad-brim black hat and a long overcoat?" Finn asked.

"Yes, sir," Freeman said. "And I think he had the overcoat turned up at the collar."

"Anybody else in the crowd dressed in that manner?" Finn asked.

"No, sir."

"How far was Conn from the house at the time which the shooting took place . . . at the time he was shot?"

"I reckon he was about ten steps from the house."

"How far was the fence from the house?"

"I reckon it was about halfway between him and the house."

"Now," Finn said, "from that upstairs window to where Mr. Conn was, could he have been easily recognized?"

"Yes, sir," Freeman replied. "I think he could."

"Could anyone well acquainted with him recognize him at that distance?"

"Yes, sir," Freeman said.

Dinning's lawyers could see how this was shaping up.

"What took place and what became of Jodie Conn?"

"Me and some more boys carried him up to the road and some of them said he was shot right bad, and we took and set him on his horse and had to take him off and he died right there," Freeman said.

"How long after he was shot before he died?"

"We hadn't brought him but about fifty or sixty yards until he died."

"How long after he was shot by George Dinning until he died?"

"I can't tell you," Freeman said. "It was but a little while."

"How far did Conn live from where Dinning lived?" the lawyer asked.

"About two miles," Freeman said.

"Had Conn said anything to Dinning that night or do you know?"

"No sir," Freeman said. "He did not say a word until he was shot."

"Before or after shooting, did Mr. Conn fire his gun or not?"

"If he did," Freeman said, "I did not see him."

"Could you have seen him had he done it?"

"I was not right close to him; about ten feet from him, maybe," Freeman said. "Of course, when the shot was fired I looked back."

"You saw the fire flash from the gun from the upper window?"

"Yes sir. And one of the crowd said, "Look out from the upper window.""

"Up to that time had anyone fired a shot?" Finn asked.

"No, sir."

"Anybody fire or explode any bombs or dynamite?"

"No, sir."

"Anything of that kind in the crowd?"

"No, sir."

"Any bombs or dynamite thrown into the house that night?"

"No, sir."

"Any explosions or any discharge of any firearms or weapons or anything of the kind until *after* the flash come from the window and Mr. Conn was shot?"

"No, sir."

"Any harshness?"

"No, sir."

"I will ask you to state whether or not the conduct of these parties along with Mr. Conn upon that occasion, whether or not their conduct was boisterous?" Finn said.

"No, sir," Freeman said. "There was nothing of that kind by any of the party."

"Was there any purpose or determination or demonstration on the part of anybody present there that night to hurt or harm him or his property?" Finn asked.

"No, sir."

"Up to the time Jodie Conn was shot and you all were leaving the premises, did you or any member of your crowd there that night make any demonstration of purpose or determination to do Dinning any personal harm?"

"No, sir."

"All that occurred before the shooting and all that was intended on that occasion was simply to tell Dinning that there had been a good deal of thieving going on in the neighborhood and that he was suspected?"

"Yes, sir," Freeman said.

"When you told Dinning what you had come there for, was there anything then said as to whether or not you proposed to hurt or harm him or that you were there to harm or molest him?"

"No," Freeman said. "We told him that we didn't come there to hurt or harm him."

"Did you all tell him for what purpose and reason you came there?"

"Yes, sir."

"Then what was it that Dinning said?"

"He said something about he may leave and he might not, that we had better make him leave that night," Freeman said.

"About how long after that conversation with Dinning before the shot was fired?" Finn asked.

"A few seconds."

"Was there anything said to Dinning that night about having been to other places that night?"

"He was told he must leave and that some of his white neighbors had been notified to do the same thing."

"He was told that some of his white neighbors had been suspected, too?"

"Yes, sir," Freeman said, "and were visited for the same purpose he was."

"Up to the time that you all had started to leave was there any cursing upon the part of Dinning or not?"

"If he did, I did not hear it," Freeman said. "There was some loud talk in the house but I couldn't hear what it was from where I was."

"Do you remember what night in the week it was?" Finn asked.

"Thursday night."

"About what time?"

"Between 10 and 11 o'clock."

"I believe you said it was a light, moonshiny night?" Finn asked.

"Yes, sir. The moon was shining bright."

"Do you know whether it was a three-quarter moon, full moon, or what?" Finn asked.

"I do not know."

The courtroom was hot and stuffy as Finn took his seat and

John Grider, Dinning's attorney, stood to question the witness. The people in the overflow balconies, which ran the length of the courtroom, leaned forward to listen.

"How far do you live from where Dinning lived?" Grider asked.

"A mile and a half or so," Freeman replied.

"How far from Jodie Conn?"

"About one-half mile."

"Is Jodie Conn a married man?"

"No, sir."

"Did he live at his father's house?"

"No, sir."

"Was he house-keeping?"

"Yes, sir."

"He was keeping bachelors' hall?"

"Yes, sir."

"You say twenty five were down at Dinning's house in that party that night?"

"Twenty five was in the party," Freeman said. "Four of them didn't go any closer than the gate or fence."

"How far is the gate from the house?"

"One hundred yards."

"Twenty one went down to his house?"

"Yes, sir," Freeman said. "Four of them stayed up there."

"Did that party get together by accident or by some pre-arrangement?"

"I reckon it was made up...a man told me."

"Told you that a party was going to start out and make the rounds?"

"Yes, sir."

"Where did you meet that party at?"

"About a half-mile from George's house."

"Did you all meet there on regular occasions?"

"No, sir."

"Did they stop at the house of anybody before they got to Dinnings'?"

"Yes, sir," Freeman said. "At three places."

"Did the party have any guns or pistols?"

"Some of the party had some guns."

"Any of them pistols?"

"If they did, I didn't see them."

"How many guns in the party?"

"I can't tell you."

"Was the party all armed?"

"No, sir," Freeman said. "I was not."

"In your opinion how many of that party were armed?" Grider asked.

"About ten or twelve."

"What kind of guns did that ten or twelve have," Grider asked. "Shotguns or rifles?"

"Shotguns."

"Was anybody disguised with any apron or cloth over their face?"

"No, sir."

"Did you stop on the way down to George Dinning's, at Ben Conn's?"

"Yes, sir."

"Did you go to Ben Conn's house?"

"No, sir," Freeman said. "I was out in the road."

"You were looking towards the home—did you see some parties go to the house?"

"Yes, sir."

"Didn't you see a man standing on one side of his door with a gun at 'carry arms' and another by his side with an apron over his face?"

"No, sir," Freeman said.

"Did you see anybody down at Dinning's house that night with anything over their face?"

"No, sir."

"Now just repeat as near as you can what occurred at Dinning's house that night," Grider said.

"We went to the door and said, 'George, George!' And knocked on the door, I think—I ain't certain—and he says, 'Heh!' And he says, 'Come to the door.' And George remarked, 'Who is that?' And he remarked back, 'Your friends.' And George says, 'I ain't coming.' And he says, 'If you won't come to the door—we didn't come here to hurt or harm you—listen to see what we have to say.'"

"Was Dinning downstairs or upstairs when that conversation occurred?"

"Downstairs," Freeman said.

"Who was doing the talking to Dinning?"

"Doc Moore," Freeman said.

"Did you notice any light in the house?"

"No, sir."

"What time was it?"

"Ten or 11 o'clock."

"Were the Dinnings in bed when you got there?"

"I reckon they had," Freeman said. "I didn't see any light in the house."

"Were you doing any talking?"

"No, sir."

"Did you hear parties talking at the doors on both sides of the house?"

"No, sir."

"You say you told Dinning he must get away from there in ten days?"

"We told him there had been a great deal of stealing going on in the neighborhood and he was the cause of it and he must get away in ten days," Freeman said.

"Did you tell him at what distance he had better not stop?" Grider asked. "Did you tell him he had better not stop within forty miles of there?"

"No, sir."

"You say that these instructions was all said kindly to Dinning, in a kind manner?" Grider asked, as if he was rolling his eyes.

"Yes, sir," Freeman said. "And he said he didn't do any stealing and could prove by his neighbors that he didn't."

For the next few minutes, Grider asked Freeman to explain how the men were situated around Dinning's house, and how it came to be that they were all walking away when they heard a shot ring out from the upstairs window. He asked what Conn was doing when he was shot, and Freeman testified that he was walking away, just as all of them were. Grider interrupted.

"At the time Conn was shot, was he standing still or moving off?" Grider asked.

"He was standing still," Freeman said.

"He was not moving at the time he was shot?"

"No, sir," Freeman said. "He had turned back when he heard the racket upstairs."

"You all turned back to the house when you heard the noise and racket upstairs?"

"Yes, sir."

"And were standing still?"

Freeman must've realized his mistake. "I did not look to see," he said. "I could not see what Conn was doing when he was shot."

"You all turned around when you heard the racket upstairs and saw the fire come from the window?"

"Yes, sir," Freeman said. "Some of us did, I know."

"You all fired into the house after Dinning shot?" Grider asked.

"Yes, sir. Someone asked if anybody was hurt and Jodie Conn said he was and they ordered for us to shoot from where the blaze came from."

"You all were on the east side of the house?"

"No, sir," Freeman said. "Some were on one side and some another and some were on the southeast and some on the northwest."

"How many shots did you all fire?" Grider asked.

"I don't know," Freeman answered. "I can't tell you."

"How many shots did Dinning fire?"

"I do not know. When he shot they ordered for us to shoot where the blaze come from, and I couldn't tell how many he shot."

Hoping to catch Freeman off guard, Grider quickly switched subjects.

"Did you go back to that house the next day?"

"No, sir."

"Have you ever been back there?"

"No, sir."

"Do you remember Mr. Doc Moore calling the negro out when you got there?"

"No, sir," Freeman said. "He never called him out. He told him to come to the door."

"Do you remember Doc Moore talking to Dinning in a disguised voice?"

"No, sir."

"Didn't he have something over his face?"

"If he did, I didn't see it."

"Didn't he say he had put something over his mouth to disguise his voice?"

"He didn't tell me so."

"Now, Mr. Freeman, you say you didn't see any man with a white rag or apron over his face there that night?"

"No, sir. I never saw anything over their faces."

"You are certain that none of them had anything over their faces?"

"If they did, I didn't see it."

"You do not know whether or not they did anything down at Ben Conn's and if there was anything over their faces down at Ben's you didn't see it?"

"Yes, sir," Freeman said. "I didn't see it."

"Had three shots not been fired through that door before Dinning went upstairs?"

"No, sir."

"What side of the house were you on?"

"South side."

"You were not around at the door on the north side?"

"No, sir."

"You do not know what occurred at that door?"

"No, sir," Freeman said. "If there were any shots they didn't make any noise."

"You do not know what parties were around there?"

"No, sir."

"You do not know when Dinning went upstairs?"

"No, sir."

"You saw Mr. Conn after he had been shot at his house the next day, didn't you?"

"No, sir. I never saw him next day. I saw him on Saturday."

"Where was he shot?"

"In this side of the face," Freeman said, pointing to the left side of his own face. "Down along here."

"What appearance did the shot place or the wound seem to have?" Grider asked. "How did the shot range?"

"It ranged downward," Freeman said.

With that, Grider returned to his seat and Finn again rose to question the witness. The room was quiet.

"You say that you had started off and heard a noise and stopped and turned around?" the prosecutor asked.

"Yes, sir," Freeman said. "There was a noise like something had shot the shutter against the house, had thrown it back."

"That is what attracted your attention?"

"Yes, sir."

"How long after the noise of the shutter or whatever it was before the shot was fired which struck Conn?"

"A few seconds."

"How many could you count?"

"I couldn't count very many," Freeman said. "By the time I looked back, the blaze came from the upstairs."

"You say that before that racket had occurred Mr. Conn was leaving the house?"

"Yes, sir. Went out of the yard with me."

"You and Mr. Conn were both leaving when you heard the racket?"

"Yes, sir."

"That is what attracted your attention and caused you to look around?"

"Yes, sir. We left together and went out through the palings and he went out the palings a little lower down than me."

"Mr. Grider asked you where all those parties stood down at the house," Finn said. "I understood you to say that so far as you knew that they were out on the east or southeast and southwest, is that correct?"

"Most of them had stopped at the door, the south door," Freeman said, "and some of the others had come in the yard, sorta down at the corner of the house. The most of them was standing right around me."

"Was there any noise or any other violence offered?"

"No, sir," Freeman said.

"And Conn was about fifteen steps away?"

"Yes, sir. About fifteen steps from the house."

The lawyers wrapped up with A. G. Freeman, and the judge dismissed him. One remarkable fact never surfaced during his questioning. Freeman's wife was the sister of two other men there that night: the Flowers brothers. And two of his sisters were married to men there that night as well: Joseph Copeland and Thomas White. The mob was a family affair.

A reporter noticed that George Dinning's face was twitching occasionally and presumed it was due to fear.

Men gather at the Simpson County Courthouse in Franklin, Ky. (*Courtesy of the Simpson County Historical Society*)

Chapter 6

TO DEFEND OURSELVES

As the afternoon dragged on and the mercury continued to climb, the state next called William S. "Doc" Moore, fifty-two, the man who had done the talking that night. He was an ex-Confederate soldier who had served with the Kentucky Mounted Infantry during the Civil War. After the war he had patrolled Simpson County for some years as a constable. He was ten years older than George Dinning, and they'd lived in the same neighborhood all their lives, save the war years.

Moore put his hand on the Holy Bible and promised to tell the truth. He had met Jodie Conn only three or four times, but his testimony was key to the state's case against Dinning.

"Do you know George Dinning?" prosecutor G. T. Finn asked.

"Yes, sir," Doc Moore said.

"State what occurred there," Finn said.

"We got down at the gate about one hundred yards from the house—a gate of bars—and hitched our horses and walked down to the house and knocked on the door and said, 'George, George!' And he says, 'Who's that?' And I was doing the talking, and I said, 'George, some of your neighbors and friends want to talk with you. Get up and come to the door.' And he said he wouldn't do it and I told him to just stay there and listen to what we had to say, and I told him there had been some stealing going on in the neighborhood, meat houses had been broken into and meat taken and the houses set on fire and chickens and turkeys and such had been taken and that we had visited some of his white neighbors and the neighborhood thought he was concerned in the stealing and that we wanted him to leave the neighborhood in ten days," Doc said. "He remarked that he had done no stealing and I said that was alright. And I asked him if Bob Lucas was there, and he said he was not, and I told him that the neighborhood wanted him to leave also in the same way for he was concerned in the same business. And then he remarked that he could prove by his neighbors that he done no stealing. And I told him if he could do that, that was alright, and as I left the door and got about five or six steps away he said, 'You had better take me tonight.' And I told him that so far as that was concerned there was enough of us to do it, and I heard him say something that I didn't understand. I was leaving the house at the time and was some five or six steps away and I heard some of the boys say, 'Lookout!' And at the same time, a shot was fired. My back was turned to the house, and some of the boys fired back at the house, and somebody asked if anybody was hurt or shot and Jodie Conn said, 'Yes, I am shot.' I didn't shoot, and we started off to the bars and after we got a good piece from the house someone asked Conn if he was hurt much and he said he was shot badly.

"When we got to the horses, we put him on his horse and put his feet in the stirrups and had to hold him, and we took him down from his horse."

"What became of him then?" Finn asked.

"We carried him to Mr. Williams' house."

"Did he die there?"

"No, sir," Doc Moore said. "He died as soon as we took him off his horse."

"Doc," Finn asked, "was anything said to Dinning there on that occasion with reference to hurting or harming him?"

"No, sir," Moore said. "We told him we didn't come there to hurt him."

"Did he come to the door?"

"No, sir. He said he had no business there."

"Then it was you said, 'Listen to me from where you are?'"

"Yes, sir."

"Now, where was he when you were talking to him?" Finn asked.

"I suppose he was in bed in the house."

"Downstairs?"

"Yes, sir."

"Did you hear him leave downstairs and go upstairs?"

"I understood him to say, 'You had better take me out now.' And I said, 'George there is enough of us to do that,' but didn't want to do him any harm. And I heard him talking in the house and heard a racket and somebody hollered, 'Lookout!' And, in a second, a gun was fired."

"You were going away from the house?"

"Yes, sir."

"Did you hear anything at the upstairs window?" Finn asked.

"I heard a noise upstairs," Moore said, "and somebody said, 'Boys, lookout!'"

"Where did that voice come from? Somebody in the crowd say that?"

"Yes, sir."

"That was just before the gun fired?"

"Yes, sir, and my back was to the house at the time."

"Did the crowd disguise in any way?"

"I had a handkerchief over my mouth," Moore said. "I was the only one."

"Across your mouth?"

"Yes, sir."

Finn seemed satisfied with Moore's answers. He sat back down as Grider prepared his questions.

"Mr. Moore, when did you all make the arrangements to visit Dinning that night?" he asked.

"Mr. Conn sent me word the day before," Moore said.

"Then you all had pre-arranged to visit Dinning and the other parties that night?"

"Yes, sir."

"What time of the night did the party get together?"

"I suppose it was about 9 o'clock."

"At what place did they meet?"

"In the big-road."

"You say you all met there about nine o'clock?"

"Right about there somewhere."

"That was rather a late hour to go out visiting wasn't it?"

"I don't know," Moore said. "Sometimes that will do."

"You think sometimes it is better to visit late at night?"

"I do not know."

"How many houses did you stop at before you got to George Dinning's?" Grider asked.

"Three," Moore said.

"You came in an eastwardly direction to the house?"

"Yes, sir."

"Did you go to the South door?"

"Yes, sir."

"How many went there?"

"I think about the whole crowd."

"How many were in the crowd?"

"About twenty-five."

"The greater part of them went to the South door but you do not know where the balance of them were?"

"No sir," Moore said. "Some stayed up at the horses I think."

"How many?"

"I think about four. I do not know."

"You had a talk at the door?"

"Yes, sir."

"You told Dinning it was friends out there?"

"Neighbors and friends."

"You disguised your voice so he would not know it?"

"Yes, sir."

"You say you told George that parties had been stealing and if he had been doing it he must get away within ten days?"

"I told him that the neighbors had called on him to ask him to get away."

"Did you have a gun or pistol?"

"I did not have anything."

"How many guns or pistols were in the crowd?"

"Not more than eight, I think."

"Was there not twelve or thirteen guns along?"

"I do not know."

"Was one-half of the crowd armed with guns?"

"No, sir," Moore said. "I do not think there was."

"You don't know?"

"No, sir."

"Did you see several of the party with guns?"

"Yes, sir."

"You all started out on a friendly visit that night did you?" Grider asked, mockingly.

"Yes, sir," Moore said. "We did not mean to do anyone any harm."

"You were prepared?"

"Yes, sir. To defend ourselves."

"You were afraid of having a fight and you wanted to defend yourselves?"

"I was unarmed," Moore countered.

"You were not looking for someone to fight you were you?" Grider pressed.

"No, sir," Moore said. "But we thought we would be ready."

"Where twenty-five men get together and start out on a business expedition of any kind, is there any danger in being unarmed?"

"No, sir. I think not."

Grider let it slide, and again started trying to make the case that the mob had had the house surrounded. He had drawn a sort of rough floor plan of George Dinning's cabin and used it to show the jury where the Whitecappers were positioned.

"Do you know whether anybody was at the north door at the time you were at the south door?"

"No, sir."

"Was the party when this firing was done down near the window here?" Grider said, pointing to the easternmost window.

"I think they were all due east of the house," Moore said.

"Was your party due east of the house when they shot at him?"

"Yes, sir."

"How many shots were fired back?"

"I couldn't tell you."

"The party was all together when they shot?"

"Yes, sir."

"You cannot state how many were fired but you can state that they were all due east of the house?"

"Yes, sir."

"Where these parties were standing when they shot, they

could not shoot into the north door or the south door either could they?" Grider asked.

"I do not reckon they could," Moore answered.

"You said you were standing east of the house?"

"I was standing right along here," Moore said, pointing to the east side of the house on the drawing.

"That shot came from the window upstairs?"

"I do not know," Moore said. "I could not see it."

"How far were you standing from Conn when that shot was fired?"

"I do not know," Moore said. "He was in the crowd."

"Was the crowd bunched together?"

"They were scattered."

"Where was the crowd at?"

"Right along here," Moore said, pointing again at the east side of the house.

"All around near the east end of the south door?"

"Yes, sir."

"You say you saw no one at the north door?"

"No, sir."

"Were there shots at the south door?"

"I reckon so."

"They could not have shot in the North door?"

"I do not think that anybody was around there."

"Could they have done it?"

"No sir."

"You told George if he were stealing you would give him ten days to get away?" Grider asked.

"We asked him to get away," Moore replied.

"Did you ask him if he was stealing?"

"We told him if he was concerned in the business he must get away."

"And you told him he must get away in ten days?"

"We told him if he could prove [he wasn't stealing] it would be alright."

"He said he could prove it?"

"Yes, sir."

"Did you all tell him he needn't go away?"

"No, sir. Told him to do it."

"Did you all tell him how far he had better go before he stopped?"

"No, sir."

"I believe you stated that he said, 'You had better take me out now.' What did you say to that?" Grider pressed.

"I told him if he didn't believe we could, that there was enough of us to do it."

"I will ask you if some of the parties didn't make this remark," Grider said, checking his notes. "'You shut up in there or we will tear this damn shack down and hang you now'?"

"No, sir."

"You told him he had better get out, and he said, 'You had better put me out.' And you told him, 'There is enough of us to do it'?"

"Yes, sir."

"Was Conn between you and the house?"

"He was in here," Moore said, pointing to a spot between where he was standing and the house.

"Some of the party were at the south door here?"

"No, sir. They were following me. I was in front."

"How many shots did Dinning fire?"

"I do not know."

"How many fired from the window?"

"There was one that I heard and I didn't see where it came from."

"You say there was one shot from the house?"

"I didn't see anything of the shot from the house at all."

"Did you hear the report of several guns coming from the house."

"I heard the report of several guns it seemed coming from the house."

"They were from your party?"

"Several was," Moore said.

Grider finished and Finn stood to reexamine.

"When you were walking off or leaving and heard the report of a gun, not up to that time had there been any gun fired there?" Finn asked his witness.

"No, sir," Moore replied.

"Any bombs?"

"No, sir."

"Any dynamite?"

"No, sir."

"Any violence offered?"

"No, sir."

"Now, Doc, Mr. Grider asked about where you were when that shot was fired and then he asked you where the rest of them were. Do you undertake to remember where all that party was at the time the shot was fired?"

"No, sir."

"So far as you can state—and that is all you mean to state— is that a good bunch of them were in that direction?" Finn said, pointing to the east side of the house on the drawing.

"Yes, sir."

Finn was finished. Grider had a few more questions.

"You say when you were out here," he said, pointing to the east side of the house, "you do not know whether there were men at the north door?"

"No, sir."

"You could not tell?"

"No, sir."

"I believe you said you could not see Conn when he was shot and you did not see what he was doing when shot?"

"No, sir," Moore said. "He came out here"—he pointed to the front of the house—"and says, 'I am shot.'"

"He was out here at this fence?" Grider asked.

"No, sir," Moore said. "He was about ten steps from the fence."

"What part of the body was he shot in?"

"He was shot in the head here," Moore said, touching his own head and neck. "I did not look at him at the time."

"What side?"

"Left side. He was going in an easterly direction, I reckon."

"His back would have been to the house then would it not?" Grider asked, pointing out the obvious conflict in Moore's story.

"He was making a turn," Moore said.

"If he was going from the house in that direction," Grider said, pointing to his drawing, "his left side would have been next to the window, wouldn't it?"

"No, sir."

"He couldn't have been shot there if his back was to the house, could he?" Grider asked.

"I think so," Moore said.

"Did you go back to the house that night after you found that Conn had been hurt?"

"No, sir."

"There was twenty five of the party and you didn't go back and Conn died within 100 yards of the house?"

"He died as soon as we took him from his horse."

"Did you go back next day?"

"No, sir."

"Have you ever been back there since then?"

"No, sir."

"Is that house standing there now?"

"I do not know."

"You don't know?"

"No, sir."

"After you left that house that night you never have been back there since?"

"No, sir."

"Where did you take Conn that night?"

"To Mr. Williams'."

"Did the whole party go together?"

"No, sir. Eight or ten of them went with him."

"What became of the balance?" Grider asked.

"I don't know."

"Did you go with Conn?"

"Yes, sir."

"About 10 went?"

"Yes, sir."

"Did the balance of the party scatter and go to their homes?"

"Yes, sir," Moore said. "I suppose so."

"They scattered?"

"Yes, sir."

"Nothing further," Grider said.

One of the soldiers, people in the packed courtroom noticed, had fallen asleep while leaning on his weapon. He occupied a position near the railing that separated the increasingly sweaty crowd from the proceedings. Upon noticing, Captain Noel Gaines hurried to the sleeping militiaman and clapped him hard on the right shoulder, then escorted him from the room, a look of embarrassment on the young man's face. Soon another soldier replaced him.

The next two witnesses called by the Commonwealth—Joe Deaux, a forty-two-year-old white farmer and father of six, and William Townsend—confirmed the version of the story put forth by the first two: that theirs was a friendly mission, even though they'd gone at night and disguised their voices, and even though they were armed. That they were walking away from the house when they heard a commotion, that they turned and witnessed a shotgun blast from the second-story window, that Jodie Conn then reported: "Boys, I am shot." Both men denied going back to Dinning's house at any point after that night, even though Joe Deaux lived on adjacent property and could see Dinning's house from his front porch. They said they hadn't been drinking that night, and that if others were, they didn't see it. Deaux admitted to carrying a "little rifle." He also testified that he heard Doc Moore tell Dinning that he had ten days to leave Coffee Bottom, and that he shouldn't stop until he'd made it forty miles away. In one interesting exchange, Grider asked Deaux whether the committee had been instructed to visit Dinning at night.

"The committee arranged that," Deaux said.

"Who appointed the committee?" Grider asked.

"It appointed itself," Deaux said.

"What was the name of the organization?" Grider asked.

"We didn't call it anything."

"It was just a self-constituted committee?"

"Yes, sir."

"It took twenty-five men to confer with Dinning?"

"That many went."

"Went in the nighttime, armed with guns?"

"Yes, sir."

"They went on a friendly mission, did they?"

"They didn't mean anything else."

Townsend, who lived a mile and a half from Dinning, said Moore was the leader of the band, and recalled a slightly different version of the dialogue between Moore and Dinning.

"What did Moore say to Dinning when he said, 'You had better put me out tonight'?" Grider asked.

"Doc said, 'There is enough of us to do it, and just watch us as we go off if you don't believe it,'" Townsend said. In other words, *You'll see how many of us there are as we walk away and leave you alone.* It seemed preposterous to Grider.

Townsend added that the men waited two or three minutes to fire after George Dinning fired the first shot. Grider seemed astounded by this claim as well. "Two or three minutes?" the lawyer asked.

"Yes, sir," Townsend said.

"Was it that long?"

"Well, it wasn't long," Townsend said. "Just as soon as Doc Moore could give the command, 'Shoot boys, where you saw the blaze come from.'"

The other remarkable thing Townsend said was that the whole collective had met again since the night of the shooting. Perhaps, Grider assumed, that was why the language they all used to describe the night was so similar.

The fifth witness, J. H. Bloodworth, admitted that he went back to Dinning's house the following morning around nine o'clock, and that he observed bullet holes in the north door and two or three patches of blood inside the house, on the floor and on the bed that had been occupied by Dinning and his wife, Mollie.

The sixth, Bloodworth's brother, Tom Bloodworth, repeated the story from the first five, but said that Jodie Conn cried out, "I am shot," before anyone asked. And Tom Bloodworth admitted he was carrying a pistol that night, a Smith & Wesson, and he shot five times, unloading his gun at the upstairs window.

With that, court was adjourned for the day. Mollie Dinning, who was seated in the gallery, watched as soldiers escorted her husband away, his saturated suit clinging to his body.

Later that night, while on picket patrol outside the jailhouse where George Dinning would have been trying to sleep, a guard heard a noise and turned to see two men pointing shotguns in his direction. In terror, he aimed his own and squeezed off a round as quickly as he could, sending the assailants scrambling into the darkness. The shot aroused other soldiers, but by the time they arrived, all that remained of the men were boot prints in the dirt.

Chapter 7

"THERE WAS A GOOD MANY HOLES"

The witnesses called by the Commonwealth were decent men, according to the newspapers. They enjoyed the names of good, law-abiding citizens. So, too, did Jodie Conn, fatally injured by George Dinning's shotgun. Many had known Conn his whole life, and he was as much a part of southeastern Logan County as dark-fired tobacco. His grandfather Notley Thomas Conn was a farmer of Scottish descent, and around 1840 he moved to Logan County, purchased a large tract of land, and began raising a family. He amassed hundreds of acres of farmland and bought dozens of slaves. Notley Thomas Conn's offspring would long be numbered among the leading and representative men of southern Kentucky. The Conns owned the most fertile and level farmland on the Red River. They counted among their number the leading stockman in Logan County, a prominent tobacco dealer in Franklin, the vice-president of Peoples Bank, the owner of the South Kentucky Rabbitry, and the largest mule and horse trader in all of southern Kentucky. Jodie Conn's own father owned the most beautiful home in Logan County, which sat on about seven hundred acres in the Hickory Flat section. He had accumulated the best goods the world had to offer, and he spent all of his winters in Florida.

So it was perhaps fitting, then, that Jodie Conn's obituary accounted for the lost potential of the heir to an esteemed heritage, that it omitted certain facts and introduced for posterity a glorified version of the man's disgraceful final act. The lengthy column made no mention of his broad-brimmed black hat, his long black overcoat, or the rifle he carried at his side on that cold January night. The facts: he was born to Charles T. and Caroline J. Baird Conn on November 1, 1864, and died when he fell from his horse with squirrel shot in his cheek, neck, and ear on the moonlit night of January 21, 1897, the thirty-two-year-old scion of the wealthiest farm family in southwestern Kentucky.

"He was a descendant of honored ancestry, a son of most worthy parents, whose wise counsel and tender, loving care and commendable example he had continuously shared from infancy to his death, having spent his life in the neighborhood in which he had been reared," his flowery obituary read. "He was intelligent, honest, noble-hearted, amiable in disposition, generous, and in the fullest sense neighborly. By his deeds of kindness and helping service he drew men to him and around him in the strongest ties of affection and appreciation."

It continued: "Whatever may be the feelings of any who, without knowledge of his character and worth, or the circumstances connected with his tragical death, may to unkindly and harshly comment and criticise, the honest verdict of the last citizens about him who had known him for all his life, and who are entirely familiar with all the facts connected with his sad death, is, and will be, he gave his life for his friends, and the motive that led him to that cause which resulted in the sacrifice of his life was an honest and earnest desire that the rights and property of law-abiding citizens shall be protected, and if in his last act of

Jodie Conn, depicted by the Louisville *Times*.

kindness in behalf of his friends and at their solicitation for his help his judgement was at fault, it was an error of the head and not of the heart. His was an effort on behalf of the best interests of the best element in society."

"How far were you from Doc Moore when he was doing the talking?" J. B. Grider asked J. M. Phelps, who lived a half mile from George Dinning and had brought a double-barreled shot-gun loaded with squirrel shot with him to talk peacefully to a friend late that night in January.

"Some eight or ten feet," Phelps said.

"Did you see his face?"

"Yes, sir."

"Was his face disguised in any way?"

"He had a rag over his face."

"Did he make any effort to disguise his voice?"

"Yes, sir."

"You would have hardly recognized his voice yourself?"

"No, sir."

"You told Dinning to come out?"

"Told him to come to the door."

"That was said in a peaceable, orderly and quiet manner?"

"Yes, sir."

"Told him who you were?"

"No, sir. Told him we were friends."

"What was the purpose of keeping him from knowing who you were?"

"We didn't want him to know I guess."

"Why did you put that handkerchief over the mouth?"

"We didn't want him to recognize the voice."

"Who did you tell him you were?"

"Told him we were his friends that didn't want to bother him."

"You say the voice was disguised so he could not tell whether or not they were his friends?"

"No, sir," Phelps said. "I don't know."

"Did you tell him he must get away?"

"Yes, sir. Within ten days."

"Did you tell him within what distance he mustn't stop?"

"Within fifty miles."

"Did you see Conn where he was when he was shot?"

"Yes, sir."

"What part of the body?"

"Left side of the face and down below the shirt collar."

"He was shot in the face and the cheek?"

"Yes, sir."

"How much space was covered on his face?"

"He was shot in the ear."

"Was the shot thick?"

"Yessir, there was a good many holes."

"Has that committee met since that time?"

"Yes, sir."

"Did they discuss the facts that occurred there?"

Finn objected loudly. The judge called both lawyers to come closer and they had a short conference. Finn withdrew his objection.

"You say this party of twenty-five men discussed what had occurred there?"

"No, sir. Not twenty-five."

"How many?"

"Twenty-four."

"These twenty-four men have met and talked over what occurred there that night?"

"Yes, sir," Phelps said. "We met and talked with the lawyers."

Dinning's lawyer, John B. Grider, a forty-seven-year-old Presbyterian and lifelong Democrat, was widely known as the most absent-minded man in Bowling Green. He once put a lit cigar in his pocket and set his suit on fire, but then convinced an insurance company to reimburse him for the ruined clothing. Another time, while he was studying a legal case that was giving him fits, he pulled from his pocket a bottle of pills he'd received from a homeopathic doctor and munched the sweet pellets like candy for a half hour, until just 20 remained of the original 500. Only then did he realize his mistake and peril. He spent the night worried he had poisoned himself, but was otherwise fine.

He studied at Cumberland University in Lebanon, Tennessee, and launched his practice with a partner who rose to serve on the Court of Appeals. Grider was averse to the idea of public office, but he was so well liked that he was elected to serve as police judge, city attorney for Bowling Green, and county judge for Warren County, holding all three offices at once.

He was regarded as a good and fair lawyer. And he tried to shake the parade of the prosecution's witnesses off their agreed-to narrative with limited success.

He questioned James Wesley Flowers, and his brother Joseph Laranzy Flowers, both white farmers. Joseph Laranzy Flowers testified that he wasn't expecting any trouble but borrowed a Winchester rifle from a friend just in case, and when Doc Moore hollered for his boys to squat and fire, he did.

"How many times did you shoot?" Grider asked.

"Fifteen or sixteen times," Flowers said.

He questioned S. A. McDonald, a sixty-four-year-old farmer and Freemason; J. M. King; and Nick Williams, who testified that he stuffed Jodie Conn's large wounds with whiskey and cotton.

"You say these wounds were on the left side of his face and neck?" Grider asked.

"Yes, sir," Williams said.

"Ranged up or down?"

"Down."

"They showed that the man who fired the shot was standing above him?"

"Yes, sir."

A short time later, Grider asked Williams, who lived just a quarter mile away, whether he'd been back to Dinning's house since that night. Williams said he had returned a month or two later and noticed the house was no longer there.

"Do you know when the house was burned?" Grider asked.

"No, sir," Williams said. "I heard of it. I believe it was burned Saturday night."

"How far did you live from Dinning?"

"A quarter of a mile."

"You saw no signs of the flames of the burning building on Saturday night?"

"No, sir."

"Were you at home?"

"Yes, sir."

Grider questioned Pete Doss, John Webb, and Isen Hollis, who testified that during wheat threshing time he overheard George Dinning talking to another Colored man, saying that if Jodie Conn ever crossed his path he would kill him. Hollis couldn't remember details like where this happened or when it happened or who exactly Dinning was talking to, but, "I heard him say that if he ever crossed his path he would fix him," Hollis said.

"Did you ever tell anybody about these threats?"

"No, sir," Hollis said. "Not that I recollect."

Grider hoped the jury noticed the discrepancies in the stories told by the Whitecappers. Did Doc Moore have a bandanna over his mouth? Did they return fire immediately, or wait three or four minutes before shooting back? Were they truly walking away when Dinning threw open the shutters and fired? Was it even possible that Dinning fired first? Or did they all get together in the tense days before the indictment and decide that to avenge Jodie Conn's death in a court of law meant agreeing to all tell the same version of a lie?

Grider called the jailer at Bowling Green and the doctor who had visited George Dinning there, and both men testified that they had examined Dinning's wounds, on his arm and forehead; they testified with confidence that the wounds were created by bullets.

"Were they fresh looking wounds at the time he was brought there?" Grider asked Matt Christian, the jailer.

"Yes, sir."

"Did he have any trouble with this wound on his head?"

"He complained of it hurting him several days."

"Did you notice if it was swollen?"

"Yes, sir," Christian said. "It was swollen."

"Did you see the wound opened?"

"Yes, sir."

"Anything come out of it?"

"Yes, sir. Some blood and matter."

But Grider knew that his best chance of proving his case was to let the Dinnings tell the jury what had happened that night.

Though by the time of Dinning's trial this was no longer the case, it had long been illegal in Kentucky for a Black person to testify against a white person. Until the Civil War was decided, the same was true for other Southern states and five free states. Denying Black citizens access to the courts was a fundamental legal bulwark of institutional enslavement and white supremacy. But by the launch of Reconstruction, all Northern states had voluntarily changed, and the secession states in the Deep South were forced to make radical reforms, including granting Black people equal rights in the courts. By 1867, all the border states agreed that Black people could testify—all except Kentucky.

So as 1867 turned into 1868, Black citizens began to organize, primarily due to the deterioration of their personal security. They were being abused at every turn, and there was little they could do about it legally. If a white man punched a Black woman in front of a hundred Black men in Kentucky and no whites saw it, there was no evidence on which to base a prosecution because no witnesses could give admissible testimony. One commissioner for the Freedmen's Bureau told a colleague that in no other Southern state did such a fiendish spirit prevail as in Kentucky. "There are some of the meanest, unsubjugated, and unreconstructed rascally rebellious revolutionists in Kentucky that curse the soil of the country," he wrote.

The only place a Black man could seek justice was in federal court, where he was allowed to testify, and all agents were urged to encourage any freedman to take all cases to federal courts so they could be heard. Black leaders held well-attended meetings and passed petitions asking the state to grant them the right to vote and to testify. The conventions continued as 1868 turned to 1869, and the movement began to mature as the federal court docket grew burdened by cases brought by Black plaintiffs. The Fifteenth Amendment was ratified in 1870 and prohibited federal and state governments from denying a citizen the right to vote based on "race, color, or previous condition of servitude," and with their new right to vote, Black conventions began to organize forces for political contests. One convention that year charged that their wives, daughters, sisters, and mothers "may be debauched" and "outraged with impunity" if they weren't allowed to testify. Black women couldn't prosecute whites in state court for rape, couldn't sue for a share of their white father's inheritance, and couldn't sue whites for child support. More politicians came seeking Black support and agreed to campaign for changes to the law. When the legislature met in 1871, Kentucky governor John Stevenson declared that he was "in favor of making everyone equal before the law." There was one more factor at play that worked in favor of justice: federal prosecutors began indicting judges for failing to allow Black testimony. As word of the indictments spread, it didn't take long for lower-court judges to start allowing Black citizens to testify. And in 1872, six controversial years after the Civil Rights Act of 1866, a new Kentucky legislature passed a law granting Black men and women the right to testify against whites.

The upstairs courtroom in the Simpson County Courthouse as it appears today. (*Courtesy of the author*)

Twenty-five years later, a Black farmhand and laborer named Ben Conn took the stand to testify against a mob of whites.

"What is your age?" John B. Grider asked.

"Something near 65 years," Ben Conn replied.

Ben Conn didn't know exactly how old he was because he was born a slave, sometime around 1830, in Russellville, Kentucky.

In light of that fact, and the fact that Ben Conn would marry Matilda Hardin in 1866 and have a son they'd name Natley Conn, it's not a stretch to think that Ben Conn was at one time considered the property of Notley Thomas Conn, Jodie Conn's grandfather. In fact, the 1860 slave schedule shows that N. Conn of Logan County enslaved twenty-five Black people, and four of them were between the ages of twenty-four and twenty-seven. Ben Conn would have been about twenty-five then. Now he was something near sixty-five.

"Where do you live? How far from where George Dinning lived?"

"Between a quarter and a half mile."

"Did you hear anything of that difficulty which occurred there in which Jodie Conn was hurt?"

"Yes, sir," Conn said. "I heard the shooting."

"Did you see a party of men going towards Dinning's house that night?"

"Yes, sir. They came to my house."

"Who did they ask for?"

"Alexander Conn and Bob Lucas."

"They came up to your house?"

"Yes, sir."

"Did you go out of the house?"

"Yes, sir."

"What were they doing?"

"A lot of them were out in the road in front of the house, on their horses, and two or three of the party came into the yard, right at the door, and I was standing in the passage and one of them was standing there with his pistol up in my face that way," Conn said, showing the jury with his finger how the man held the pistol. "And another was on the other side with a gun at carry arms, and a white handkerchief over his face."

"One of them had a pistol?"

"Yes, sir."

"Pointed at your head?"

"Yes, sir," Conn said. "They were standing there just that way, and when they went off, they started in the direction of George Dinning's."

"What time of the night was this?"

"Between nine and ten o'clock."

"Did you hear any firing down towards George's?"

"Yes, sir."

"How long after these men left your house?"

"Between five and ten minutes."

"How did that firing seem to you?" Grider asked. "Was it guns, pistols, or what?"

"They first fired three shots," Conn said. "They sounded like pistols."

"What next?"

"Then a shotgun."

"Then what?"

"Then I heard a volley of shots."

"All turned loose?"

"Yes, sir."

When it was his turn, prosecutor G. T. Finn pressed Conn on whether it was possible he didn't hear the first shot.

"Were you in bed?" Finn asked.

"Yes, sir."

"Had you been asleep that night?"

"No, sir."

"How long had you been in bed?"

"I don't know."

"Door open?"

"No, sir."

"Window up?"

"No, sir."

"Windows down, doors closed and you're in bed and in the house?" Finn asked.

"Yes, sir."

"Covered up?"

"My feet were covered up, but my head wasn't."

"That was winter wasn't it?"

"I reckon so."

Finn left it at that, with confidence the jury wouldn't believe a Black farm laborer over the testimony of so many upstanding white men.

The defense called a key witness, Daniel Gilbert "Gib" Hackney, a fifty-nine-year-old white farmer who lived about a half mile from Dinning. Late on the night in question, Hackney heard a commotion and saw a party of armed men pass by his house, in the direction of the Dinning place. A short time later, he heard gunshots rip through the night.

He went to Dinning's house the next morning, around sunrise, and found Dinning's wife, Mollie, and most of her eleven children, awake and alone. Gib Hackney inspected the house, inside and out. He noticed bullet holes in the door that faced north. He looked at the wooden door from the inside and saw that three bullets had passed clean through. He looked around for about fifteen minutes, and from the yard he could see where the house had been shot in the gable, the part of the external wall that covered the end of the pitched roof. He saw that the picket fence palings were asunder, as if a bunch of people had stormed through.

Inside the house, near the foot of the bed upstairs, he saw a puddle of blood.

"I believe you said you heard the firing that night?" Grider asked.

"Yes, sir," Gib Hackney said.

"What kind of firearms was it that you first heard, Mr. Hackney?"

"I took it to be pistols," Hackney said. "I heard three or four shots that I took to be pistol shots from the report."

"Then what next?"

"Then I heard a much louder report, like a shotgun."

"Then what?"

"Then a good many guns went off," Hackney said.

"First you heard three shots that you took for pistol shots?" Grider asked. "And then a larger gun? And then a volley?"

"Yes, sir," Hackney said. "There were a good many when the last firing took place."

Grider showed Hackney the drawing of the Dinning house.

"Mr. Hackney, could a man standing here at the east end of the house—or anywhere around there—could he shoot into the north?"

"No, sir," Hackney said. "I couldn't stand at the east end of the house and shoot into the north door."

Grider next called Claud Hackney, Gib Hackney's twenty-one-year-old son, who sat uneasily at the witness stand and testified that he had planned to stay the night at his uncle's house, not far from the Dinning place. Sometime after nine o'clock, as he was fetching a drink of water on the front porch, he, too, heard gunshots coming from the direction of the Dinning homestead.

"There were three or four shots at first," he said, "and then the firing ceased. Those shots seemed like pistol or rifle shots, and then they ceased for a minute. And then there was a larger gun fired. And then there was a good many shots, what seemed like one hundred."

He, too, walked to the Dinning place the next morning, between daylight and sunup, and found Mollie and the children and his father. Another man, Arch Campbell, a white farmer in his late seventies, was there as well. The three men inspected the house, inside and out. Claud Hackney said it looked to him like four bullets had hit the door—three passed through and one lodged in the wood.

The house was dark inside. Only one of the windows was open. So Mollie Dinning lit a kerosene lantern and showed the three men upstairs. Claud Hackney noticed a trail of shiny, crimson-black blood on the stairs, and blood droplets upstairs, near the foot of the bed.

On cross-examination, G. T. Finn antagonized Claud Hackney.

"What did you take the lamp upstairs for?" he asked.

"I wanted to look at the room," Claud said.

"What for?"

"I wanted to see what had been done."

"What did you want to see that for?"

"I had curiosity to see how the house was shot."

"Just for curiosity?" Finn pressed.

"Yes, sir."

"Went up there looking for blood?"

"No, sir," Claud said. "Not particularly for blood."

"How much blood upstairs?"

"Just a little."

"How many drops?"

"I don't know," Claud said. "I never counted them."

"Blood on the steps?"

"Yes, sir."

"You took the lamp and looked at it closely?"

Finn hit him with a barrage of questions about the gunfire he'd heard. Where was he on the porch when he heard it? Was he tired? Was he thirsty? Was he certain what time of night it was? Claud Hackney was unshakable, testifying with certainty about what he'd seen and heard.

Grider called Robert Evans, a forty-six-year-old white farmer who lived in Middleton, seven or eight miles from the Dinnings. He happened to be staying the night at the Haddock farm, about two miles from Dinning's house, and he heard about the shooting early the next morning. He and Will Ballard rode over and found several other men inspecting the house. Evans said he wasn't looking closely, but he did see bullet holes in the east end of the house, around the windows, and in the north door and north window, plain as day.

Chapter 8

"A BULLET CAME
THROUGH MY HAIR"

George and Mollie Dinning married in 1875, when they were each twenty years old, and had their first son, Benjamin, nine months later. Four years passed before their second son, Hermann, was born.

In the early fall of 1896, Ben Dinning, twenty years old, was arrested, charged with grand larceny, and sentenced to serve two years in the state penitentiary in Eddyville, where he found that the majority of the inmates were Black like him, even though Black citizens made up just 16 percent of the state's population. In its case against his father, the prosecution had tried to float the theory that George Dinning blamed Jodie Conn for having his oldest son arrested, but the evidence was weak.

Hermann, the second-born and barely seventeen when his father defended their home, was called to testify. He wasn't home when the white men came to his house. He was sleeping at his paternal grandmother's about a half mile down the road. But he heard the gunfire that night and broke for home.

"When you got there, who did you find there?" Grider asked the boy.

"Nobody but the children and Mammy," Hermann said.

"Did you see any men there when you got there?"

"No, sir."

"Did you see your father?"

"No, sir."

"Did you stay there until morning?"

"Yes, sir," Hermann said, "and I got up, and I went looking for Pappy, and I couldn't find him anywhere. And I went upstairs to where Pappy was shot and I saw some blood on the floor."

Hermann told the jury that in the morning three men came by the house, including Bill King and John King, whom he recognized. He said that he did a thorough inspection of the inside of the house and found three bullets on the floor downstairs, and showed the bullets to the Kings. This evidence alone might have suggested that the men who claimed they had fired only at the upstairs window were lying.

"Mammy found one, too," Hermann said, "and gave it to Mr. King."

"Where was that one picked up?"

"Upstairs."

Hermann said that he, too, saw bullet holes in the north door, and that those holes hadn't been there the day before.

On cross-examination, Finn asked Hermann if he had picked the bullets up in front of the men who were there. Hermann said he found two before anyone arrived but picked up the third in front of Bill King and John King. Finn asked what he did with the bullets.

"I believe I give them to Claud Hackney and Bill King," Hermann said. "I give one to Claud, and Bill King took the other."

"You gave Claud one and Bill King two?" Finn asked.

"No, sir," Hermann said. "I had one and lost it."

"How old are you?"

"I don't know exactly just how old I am," Hermann said.

"About how old?"

"I reckon I am about fourteen," Hermann said. "Somewhere along there."

"Did your mother and father tell you how old you were?"

"Yes, sir," Hermann said, "but it has been so long."

All over Kentucky, men chose sides. Among them was Colonel William C. P. Breckinridge. His name was known across the state. He had power and clout and a distinguished heritage. His grandfather was John Breckinridge, a U.S. senator and cabinet minister. His cousin John C. Breckinridge served as vice president under James Buchanan and later ran for president. His father was a prominent minister and state superintendent for public instruction and a leader of the Union during the Civil War. Unlike his father and two brothers, William C. P. Breckinridge supported the Confederacy and rose to the rank of colonel in the Ninth Kentucky Cavalry. He rode with Morgan's Men on their Christmas raid in 1862. After the war, he practiced law and wrote editorials for the Lexington *Observer and Reporter* for a few years and became known for his then-progressive stance on racial issues. He was a sought-after speaker, and he later took over editorials for the *Lexington Morning Herald,* where he regularly pushed egalitarian ideas on race. His caustic column on the Dinning trial was remarkable, and several newspapers republished it.

"Some months ago 'an eminently respectable young gentleman,' in company with other 'eminently respectable gentlemen,' went to the house of a Negro man at midnight, and the Negro, in defense of his home, his family and himself, killed that 'eminently respectable young gentleman,' and the other 'eminently respectable gentlemen' in that community desired to hang that Negro for his lawful defense of his home. The Negro has been indicted, and is now on trial at Franklin. The Governor has sent parts of two companies to see that he is not hanged first and then tried.

"The officer in command asked that those attending the trial might be disarmed; the presiding judge refused to permit this; the prediction has been made that the Negro will be shot either in the courtroom or in going to or from the court. The Judge is Judge Reeves—one of the ablest and best Circuit Judges in the state. The grounds of his decision have not been given by authority. If this Negro should be killed by some one who would otherwise have been disarmed it would stick to this Judge closer and more fatally than the fabled shirt.

"It is an unseemly spectacle—the military guarding a prisoner under trial in a court of justice; it is a disgrace to Kentucky and to that county. But every sensible man knows that this Negro would be lynched if it were not for this guard; that if it were withdrawn he would be taken out of the custody of the officers of the law at once and hanged for an act that every brave man approves.

"In this county there has been a succession of really brave Jailers, and no man has been taken out of this jail by a mob for a generation or more. All this would be the history of all the counties if the Jailers had been brave officers and fit to hold their places."

As risky as it was, Grider then called Eva Dinning, George and Mollie's fifth, who was all of twelve years old. He spoke to her gently, starting with easy questions. Four men from the Conn family sat still in the hot courtroom, listening closely.

"What is your father's name?" Grider asked.

"George Dinning," the girl said.

"Were you at your father's house the night that Mr. Conn got hurt there?"

"Yes," she said.

"How old are you?"

"I don't know."

"Who was at your father's house that night but the family?"

"Nobody but me and Mammy and Pappy and the babies."

"How many children were there?"

"There was one sick and the babies and me."

"Which one was sick?"

"Viola was sick."

"Where were you sleeping that night?"

"Upstairs," she said.

"Where was your father and mother sleeping?"

"Downstairs."

"Did you hear any noise downstairs that night?"

"Yes, sir."

"What was the first thing you heard?" Grider asked.

"I heard someone call Pappy, and he asked who it was. And they said, 'Friends.' And they said, 'George, you get out, and don't you stop in fifty miles.' And the man said Pappy had been stealing, and Pappy said he could prove he hadn't. And then a man at the back door knocked on the door and said, 'Shut up, or I will tear your damn shack down!' And then I heard the shooting."

"When they said, 'Tear your damn shack down!'—then you heard the shot?" Grider asked.

"Yes, sir," Eva said. "And my father started upstairs and I heard another shot."

"You say your father started upstairs?"

"Yes, sir."

"And you heard another shot?"

"Yes, sir."

"Did you see your father come up into the room where you were?"

"Yes, sir, and he stood right at the foot of my bed."

"Was your bed near the window?"

"Yes, sir."

"Anybody sleeping in that room besides you?"

"Me and my sister."

"After your father came upstairs, what happened then?" Grider asked.

"Pappy shot, and then they began to shoot fast and a bullet came through my hair," Eva said.

"They began to shoot fast after your father shot?"

"Yes, sir."

"You felt a bullet go through your hair?"

"Yes, sir," Eva said. "The bullets just came through my hair and Pappy went downstairs."

"What did your pappy do when the shooting quit?"

"He went downstairs and went out."

"Did you get up and go down or stay up there?"

"I stayed up there until daylight, and then I got down."

Her father wasn't downstairs, just her mother and the babies. She told Grider that John and Bill King and John Webb came by the next morning. And that later John Bloodworth and Gib Hackney came.

Grider tried to ask about them being forced out of their home that evening, but Finn continued to object, saying that was irrelevant, had nothing to do with the crime of which George Dinning was accused. But Grider wanted the fundamentals on the record.

"What time in the evening did you leave?" he asked.

"Sundown," Eva said.

"When you left, who went with you?" Grider said.

"Objection!" Finn said.

"Withdrawn," Grider said. "Did anybody else leave when you did?"

"Objection!" Finn said.

"Withdrawn," Grider said. "When did your mother leave?"

"At sundown," Eva said.

"At the same time you did?" Grider asked.

"Yes, sir," Eva said.

"When did your little brothers and sisters leave?"

"Same time."

"Did you all carry away anything with you when you left?" Grider asked.

"Objection!" Finn said.

"Withdrawn," Grider said. "Where was your mother next day?"

"In Tennessee," Eva said.

"Did your mother go back to that house after that?"

"No, sir," the little girl said. "Didn't let her go back."

"Whose house did she go to?"

"Aunt Dixie's," Eva said. "Our cousins."

When it was time to cross-examine Eva Dinning, G. T. Finn was rough, and direct. He tested every memory. He challenged the little girl on minor inaccuracies. Where was the bed positioned? Who was sleeping where?

"Now, you didn't get up and go downstairs till the next morning?"

"No, sir."

"You stayed in the room upstairs all night?"

"Yes, sir."

"Your two little sisters stayed there all night with you?"

"Yes, sir."

"Which way was the head of that bed?"

"Towards you."

"Foot of the bed towards you?"

"Yes, sir."

"The side of the bed was next to the window?"

"It was next to the wall."

"One side of the bed was next to the wall?"

"Yes, sir."

"It didn't go as far down as the window?"

"No, sir."

"On which side of the bed were you?"

"In front."

On and on it went, the rapid back-and-forth, with Finn changing subjects and chronology often.

"That was winter time?"

"No, sir. It was warm."

"You didn't get up at all?"

"No, sir."

"Not until morning?"

"No, sir."

"When the shooting was going on did you raise up in bed?"

"I raised up."

"Just as you raised up a bullet brushed through your hair?"

"Yes, sir."

"How many bullets?"

"About a dozen came through my hair."

Finn pounced.

"You was not in front of the window, were you?" he asked.

"Yes, sir," Eva said. "The bed was in front of the window."

"You have just said to me that the head of the bed didn't come as far as the window," Finn said.

"No, sir," the girl said. "I was setting facing the window, just under the window."

"I think you said your bed was down here in the southeast corner of the room," he said.

"It was," she said.

"And didn't come out as far as the window?"

"No, sir."

"You were sitting in front of the window?"

"Yes, sir," Eva said. "I was facing the window."

"Where was the foot of your bed?"

"Setting right close to the window."

"You just said that the foot of your bed was down here!"

"Yes, sir."

"You say the head of your bed is in front of the window?"

"Yes, sir."

"And you just said the head of your bed didn't reach as far up as the window?"

"No, sir."

"The foot was away from the window?"

"Yes, sir," Eva said. "The head of the bed was in front of the window."

"Was the head of your bed or the foot of your bed closest to the window?"

"No, sir."

"Was the foot of your bed close to the window?"

"Yes, sir."

"Which was the closest?"

"Foot of my bed."

"You say that just as your father was going up the steps a shot was fired?" Finn asked.

"Yes, sir," Eva said.

"Well, go ahead," Finn said.

"I was asleep and the dog barked," Eva said, "and somebody came and knocked on the door and says, 'George, I will give you ten days to get away from here and don't you stop within fifty miles of here.' And Pappy said he hasn't been doing any stealing and could prove it, and a man at the back door fired, and Pappy started up the steps and they fired, and Pappy came upstairs to the window at my bed and shot, and then they shot fast, and the bullets came through my hair."

"You were upstairs in bed?"

"Yes, sir."

"Your father was downstairs?"

"Yes, sir."

"You knew he was on the steps when the shot fired?"

"Yes, sir," Eva said. "I heard him walking."

"You could tell where he was by the way he walked?"

"Yes, sir."

"You heard all those statements and you remember every word of it?"

"Yes, sir."

"You were not excited?"

"No, sir."

"You didn't get excited that night?"

"No, sir."

"You didn't get excited when the bullets whistled through your hair, did you?"

"No, sir."

"About a dozen went through your hair you said?"

"Yes, sir."

He was toying with her now.

"What time next morning did you go down?" Finn asked.

"Daylight," Eva said.

"Who did you say were there?"

"Mr. King and his son, and Mr. John Webb."

"Do you know them?"

"Yes, sir."

"Are you positive about that?" he said.

"No, sir."

"Are you certain they were there when you went down the next morning?"

"Yes, sir."

"Was Claud Hackney the first person there?"

"No, sir," Eva said. "Mr. Hackney and his son, and Arch Campbell."

"Were they the first ones there?"

"Yes, sir. I believe they were that morning."

"Mr. King was the first one there?"

"Mr. King came before any of them."

"Before Mr. Hackney?"

"Yes, sir."

"Mr. Hackney was there when you got up?"

"Yes, sir," Eva said. "He was there when I got up."

"Mr. King came before you got up?"

"Yes, sir."

"You were downstairs in the house before day?"

"Yes, sir."

"You say your father got shot upstairs?"

"Yes, sir."

"Whereabouts?"

"In the window."

"Did he get shot in the head?"

"Yes, sir."

"Got shot in the head and arm upstairs?"

"Yes, sir."

"Where was he when he got shot?"

"At my bed."

"Had he gotten to the window?"

"No, sir."

"Had not quite gotten to the window?"

"No, sir."

"He got shot in the head before he opened the window?"

"No, sir," Eva said. "After he had opened the window. The window was open that day."

"The window was open that night when you went to bed?"

"Yes, sir."

The banter went on like this for a long while. Finn was savage, challenging every answer.

"Was the shutter closed?" he asked.

"Yes, sir."

"Not open?"

"Yes, sir."

"Wasn't that a cold night in January?"

"No, sir," Eva said. "It was warm."

"Was it August," he asked.

"No, sir," she said. "It was warm inside in January."

He challenged the girl on what she heard, asking again and again if she could repeat the dialogue from that night more than five months ago. But she answered.

"Did they say there had been a lot of meat houses broken into in the neighborhood?" Finn asked.

"I never heard it," Eva said.

"Did you hear anything said about smokehouses?"

"No, sir."

"About meat having been stolen?"

"No, sir," she said. "I never heard it."

"How were those shots fired?" he asked, out of the blue.

"There was about three shots fired, and Pappy came upstairs," Eva said. "There was three fired at the back door and Pappy came up and shot."

"There were three shots fired at the back door downstairs before your pappy came upstairs and shot?" Finn asked.

"Yes, sir," Eva said.

"And then there was a lot of shooting?"

"Yes, sir."

"Was that all the shooting before he came upstairs?"

"Yes, sir," Eva said. "Before pappy shot upstairs."

Chapter 9

SON OF THE SOUTH

I n Louisville, Colonel Bennett H. Young was paying close attention to the trial through the city's daily newspapers, in which he was frequently lauded for this or that. He read the papers every day and the coverage of Dinning's trial was front-page news in all of them.

"Dr. Francis, jail physician of Warren County, testified as an expert, and gave it as his professional opinion that it was not an uncommon thing for a bullet to enter the skin of a man's head and pass entirely around the head between the skin and skull and come or pass out at the same place the ball entered, and there seems to be evidence that the ball that struck Dinning had gone this circuit," wrote a special correspondent for the *Courier-Journal* in Louisville on July 1.

"Ten witnesses have testified against Dinning," wrote a reporter for the Louisville *Times* in the same day's paper. "They all confess that they were members of the band and notified Dinning to leave the country. They conflict in their evidence in some particulars."

The fifty-four-year-old lawyer was at the apex of a legal career that would see him try more cases than any other attorney in the state of Kentucky. But the law wasn't Bennett Young's only concern. He was a storyteller, entrepreneur, author, antiquarian, orator, gardener, and vintner, and, perhaps most importantly, he was a humanitarian, even if he had fought for the South.

He stood just under six feet tall and had an oval face and a florid complexion. He parted his short hair neatly on the left and had a long graying handlebar moustache that seemed to be trying to hide his lips. He was a kind man with an excitable demeanor, and the intensity of his deep-set gray eyes and the slope of his moustache made him appear perpetually disgusted, as if he were holding a sour candy in his mouth and contemplating whether he should spit it out. He bore this expression even when telling stories to the children at the Kentucky School for the Blind, an event so routine that visitors regularly sat in to listen, and the newspapers often published the amusing parables. His favorites were about a large Chinese goose named Dr. Gander, who met Young routinely to update him on drama around the barnyard.

Young's office was in the seven-story Louisville Trust Company building downtown, at Market and Fifth Streets, and he lived in a palatial house on Fourth Street, halfway between his office and Churchill Downs.

Young was a devout Presbyterian and a member of the Filson Club, Kentucky's historical society, and had been unanimously elected president of the Polytechnic Society of Kentucky, which hosted lectures and was created primarily to fundraise for the preservation of the public library in Louisville. Morton and Company had just published Young's third book, *The History of the Battle of Blue Licks,* which drew upon recently released records to tell the story of a deadly 1782 ambush on Kentucky militiamen, one of the last battles of the Revolutionary War. The newspapers all praised the book, and Young was enjoying a small speaking tour that summer.

Col. Bennett Henderson Young. (*Courtesy of the Filson Historical Society, Louisville, Ky.*)

Just a few days before Dinning's trial, Young had boarded a special train car—he was a railroad investor—and traveled to Maysville in record time to give the commencement speech at the high school graduation ceremony. There he spoke of the courage of the pioneers who settled Kentucky, of the gift they passed down to the following generations, of the obligation of their descendants to take care of the place the Indians once called the Land of Blood. "Such an ancestry is a proud heritage, but it imposes great obligation," he liked to say. "To be degenerate sons of noble sires is one of the severest imputations that can be laid at the door of any race or generation." He encouraged the boys and girls to do right because it was right, and the local newspaper praised him for the speech, calling him "one of Kentucky's most eloquent orators" and "one of Kentucky's gifted sons."

He was a true son of Kentucky, and of his beloved Southland. His maternal grandfather, Colonel Joseph Crockett, fought in the Revolution under General George Washington and alongside Lafayette, then brought a young bride through the Cumberland Gap on the Wilderness Road and claimed a thousand acres in what would become Jessamine County, where he built a stone house and used slave labor to clear the land for a farm. President Thomas Jefferson appointed Crockett marshal of Kentucky, and he was so devout that he went to his grave wearing colonial attire—a long blue cutaway coat with brass buttons, knee breeches, shoe buckles, and black silk stockings. Young's father's grandfather also fought in the American Revolution and fired the shot that killed British major Patrick Ferguson at Kings Mountain. In 1789, three years before Kentucky became the fifteenth state in the Union, his grandfather John Young moved to Fayette County and settled on a farm to raise a family.

Half a century later, in 1843, Bennett Henderson Young was born in nearby Jessamine County. His father, Robert Young, an elder in the local church, owned a successful hat factory in Nicholasville and lived with his wife and seven children in a fine old two-story mansion boasting massive brick walls and tall columns. Robert Young also owned a plantation west of Nicholasville and claimed on the slave roster of 1860, when Bennett was seventeen, to own five slaves—three Black males, ages thirty-five, forty, and sixty; and two Black females, ages thirty-five and seventy-five. Robert Young's real estate holdings that same year were estimated at $125,000, and his personal estate was valued at $18,000.

The children went to Bethany Academy, a mile away. Bennett was in his last year at the school in 1861 when the Confederates fired on the U.S. Army at Fort Sumter in Charleston Harbor, prompting President Abraham Lincoln to declare a blockade of Southern ports and call for volunteer fighters to suppress the rebellion. The war had begun. Kentucky did not secede, but young men chose sides. Though Bennett Young never owned slaves himself, his family clearly benefited from free slave labor as his father amassed a fortune. Young was also connected by blood with many in seceding states, and his sympathies were with the Confederacy. Late that spring, when someone at the school ran the Stars and Stripes up the flagpole, Bennett Young demanded it be taken down unless a Confederate flag could also fly. As he was shinnying up a ladder to remove the flag, another student jerked the ladder from under him. Bennett Young fell upon his foe and started throwing punches—the Civil War had reached Kentucky.

Early the next winter, at age nineteen, he enlisted as a private in the Eighth Kentucky Cavalry under General John Hunt Morgan, and a few months later began a raid into the heart of Kentucky's Bluegrass region, fighting scattered Yankees and the bitter cold. The following summer, Young rode with Morgan and twenty-five hundred men on a raid north through central Kentucky. Near Burkesville, the second brigade had to cross the Cumberland River at Turkey Neck Bend, and that meant stripping down and loading their arms and saddles into a rickety ferryboat and swimming alongside their horses across the river. Alas, as they emerged nude on the north bank of the Cumberland, the Federals were waiting and the naked rebels came under fire. They didn't have time to dress. They grabbed their cartridge boxes and guns and, following a bare-assed Bennett Young, charged the boys in blue. The Union soldiers—amazed, bewildered—gave up the resistance and fled.

Morgan's men commenced one of the longest raids in the Civil War—and the longest nonstop cavalry march in American military history—that summer, through Kentucky, Indiana, and Ohio, burning bridges, looting towns, stealing horses, and disrupting railroads. They were at times pursued by no fewer than twenty-five thousand Union soldiers. When the Federals finally overtook Morgan near Salineville, Ohio, the northernmost point ever reached by uniformed Rebels, they sent Young to the Ohio Penitentiary, then Camp Chase near Columbus, then Camp Douglas in Chicago.

Young paid a willing Union soldier $100 to help him escape from Camp Douglas in the winter of 1864, and he fled to Canada, then caught a ride on a British ship to the Bahamas. From there, he sailed on a blockade runner to Fort Fisher on the Cape Fear River, at Wilmington, North Carolina. Young sent word to James A. Seddon, the Confederate secretary of war, that he had a scheme to harass the United States on its northern border. He was dispatched back to Canada and began crossing the border in civilian clothes on a series of spy missions to investigate whether Confederate soldiers could be freed from Camp Douglas, Camp Chase, and the Rock Island Prison on the Mississippi River near Davenport, Iowa. He spirited thousands of dollars in a valise into New York State in the fall of 1864, delivering the money to John Yates Beall, the Confederate privateer, at the Genesee Hotel in Buffalo.

Seddon sent a cipher to Young instructing him to reconnoiter towns along the northern U.S. border, and to pick a few to sack and burn. "It is but right," he wrote, "that the people of New England, and Vermont especially, some of whose officers and troops have been foremost in these excesses and whose people have approved of their course, should have brought to them some of the horrors of warfare." Young began strategizing. "If nothing else," he wrote to a friendly superior, "may I destroy the northern border of Vermont and New Hampshire for 150 miles?"

Young set his sights on St. Albans, Vermont, a town of about five thousand people, fourteen miles south of the Canadian border. He promised his superiors he would not plunder or rob, but if he could take funds from a bank that would benefit the Confederacy, he'd do it in a heartbeat.

On October 15, 1864, Young and two of his men made their way from Canada to St. Albans and checked into the Tremont Hotel on Main Street. Soon, two more disguised Confederates arrived at the American House down the street. The next day three more of his men showed up. They passed themselves off as hunters and inquired around town about guns and horses. They were well-received tourists. One of them, maybe Young, could be heard reading his Bible aloud through an open window for an hour each day, and was soon observed walking around the town green with a young white woman, engrossed in conversation about religion. The audacious Young even visited the home of Vermont governor John Gregory Smith with permission to inspect his horses. More Confederates showed up on October 18, and more the next day. No one in town suspected they were anything but travelers.

They conferred quietly and set their plans. On Wednesday, when the clock struck three, Bennett Young rode on horseback up to a group of men in front of the American House.

"Gentlemen," he said. "I'm a Confederate officer and I've come to take your town."

Just then, his men—twenty-one in all—entered each of the three banks on Main Street, pulled the revolvers from beneath their coats, and pointed them at the heads of the tellers. They stuffed their leather satchels full of cash. A local merchant entered one of the banks with nearly four hundred dollars to pay off a note. "We'll take that," said one of the Confederates. When the merchant asked whether private property would be spared from the robbery, the soldier replied that Grant, Sherman, and Sheridan did not respect private property, and neither would they. One of the robbers launched into a red-eyed diatribe about the Yankee ravages on the Southland and the need for vengeance, and when he was finished, he made all of his prisoners in the bank raise their hands and swear allegiance to the Confederacy and to Jefferson Davis. At another bank, the robbers pulled their guns on the teller and one of them said, "We are Confederate soldiers. There are hundreds of us. We have come to rob your banks and burn your town. We want all your greenbacks and property of every kind."

They funneled their prisoners toward the town green. "We'll treat you like you do our people in the South," one of the raiders shouted. "We'll show you how it feels."

Meanwhile, they stole horses from the livery and hitchracks on Main, and cut teams loose from wagons and buggies. An alarm sounded around town, and angry residents began running toward the green with their squirrel rifles and cap-and-ball pistols. "Keep cool, boys!" Young shouted. He ordered his men to burn the town down, and they began throwing bottles of a combustible cocktail called Greek fire against buildings, but the liquid was impotent and just one outhouse burned. His men began riding out of town, firing warning shots to keep the townsfolk back. As they left the northernmost land action of the Civil War, a railroad conductor found a document in the muddy street, titled "A Proclamation." It seemed as though the Confederate leader meant to read it aloud but didn't have time.

The conductor called it "a high-falutin address to the people of Vermont in the style of Southern chivalry."

They fled to Canada, and a number were captured. They'd dropped most of the stolen money. Authorities returned some $80,000 to the banks. Young turned himself in and they spent long months in custody near the American border, waiting for trial. The rebels were treated cordially by their Canadian captors, and they feasted and drank fine wine. The aggrieved residents of St. Albans streamed through the garrison daily, and they were surprised to find a bunch of handsome, gracious young men from the best families in Kentucky—chivalrous raiders. A reporter for the *Toronto Globe* noted that the men were singing love songs and appeared to have little concern about the serious charges they faced, that they seemed rather proud of what they had done. Sympathizers came bearing gifts of beer and fried chicken.

The United States tried to have them extradited to face charges, but Young, now in Montreal, argued that they were Confederate soldiers and had conducted themselves as such, and that what they did at St. Albans was to "retaliate in some measure for the barbarous atrocities of Grant, Butler, Sherman, Hunter, Milroy, Sheridan, Grierson, and other Yankee officers, except that I would scan to harm women and children under any provision, or unarmed defenseless and unresisting citizens— even Yankees—or to plunder for my own benefit."

While he waited for a ruling, Young wrote to the manager of the hotel in which he had stayed in St. Albans.

"You will probably remember that I was a guest in your house," he wrote. "I regret I neglected to settle my hotel bill. Nevertheless I am inclosing five dollars drawn from the St. Albans Bank."

He wrote, too, that he hoped those who had pledged allegiance to the Confederate states were living up to their vows. He also asked about the woman he had met, who had joined him on the walks around the green. "Make to her your best bow," he wrote.

Neutral Canadian courts determined that the men were, in fact, soldiers, and had simply obeyed orders, then released them to the cheers of a courtroom packed with Confederate sympathizers. Before Young could flee Canada, he was again arrested, and this time charged with robbery, on the presumption that a single criminal conviction would secure extradition to the United States. Vermonters testified against Young and his men in court, telling the judge how they'd robbed the banks and the livery barns and tried to set fire to the town. The judge let Young defend himself. The soldier displayed his commission in the Confederate Army and the instructions he had received from the secretary of war, making the case that the raid was an act of war.

"I have left friends, luxury and ease to battle for a cause endeared to me only as the cause of right," Young told the court. "I have espoused the cause of a people whose blood fills my veins and those whose feelings and interests are identical with my own. I will never look back, but rather than yield, I will pour out my blood as a sacrifice at the altar of the noblest cause that can call forth the efforts of man."

The "noblest cause" was slavery, a word he never uttered.

"I have faced death many times ere this and should I, contrary to precedent, be extradited, I am perfectly well aware what my fate shall be. I can die as a son of the South, and the agony of ten thousand deaths will never cause me to regret what I have done and the part I have borne in the struggle for right against might."

His attorney read off a long list of atrocities committed by Union soldiers in the South, as reported in Northern books and newspapers. He argued that the St. Albans raid was mild by comparison, and not an act of uncivilized warfare. The judge ruled that Young and the rest were in fact Confederate soldiers, and that they were following orders, and that they should be freed.

Young lingered around Toronto after his release in the fall of 1865. Even though the war was over, Young was not granted amnesty like most other Confederate soldiers, so he couldn't return to Kentucky. He spent much time with Reverend Stuart Robinson, a respected Presbyterian minister from Kentucky who had moved to Canada to avoid arrest for sympathizing with the Confederates. Young fell in love with Robinson's daughter, Martha, and married her in July 1866 at Niagara, Ontario, Canada.

From the pulpit that year, Robinson had preached on Mosaic slavery in the Old and New Testaments, and, at the prompting of several Canadian Christians, he was working on a book that argued that perpetual slavery as an institution was not deemed sinful in the Bible. Young would have been part of discussions with Robinson about why Jesus never repudiated slavery, and why the apostle Paul seemed to offer implicit approval when he commanded bond servants to "be obedient to them that are your masters according to the flesh, with fear and trembling...." It is unknown which side of the debate Young was on, and no clues are found in the vast public record of his writing and speeches. What we know is that he fought hard for the South, and the South fought to preserve slavery, and he therefore fought to keep slavery intact.

He moved to Europe and lived for a time with former vice-president General John C. Breckinridge, a fellow Kentuckian and Confederate veteran. Young studied law at the Queen's University of Ireland, and in 1868, around the time President Andrew Johnson extended amnesty to all former Confederates, he moved back to Kentucky. He was admitted to the bar that autumn and began practicing law. By the time he was thirty years old, Young was regarded as one of the best lawyers in Louisville. In summing up his arguments before a jury, he had few equals, and crowds of onlookers would pack the courtroom to hear him speak.

He also began to establish himself as someone who was interested in helping Black people across Kentucky.

In 1877, Young took the lead in establishing an orphanage for Black children in Louisville, and he served for two decades on the board of the Colored Orphans' Home Society, often as its president, always as a donor and major fundraiser. There were many occasions when impoverished people of color were charged with a crime and Young defended them in court without asking for compensation.

"Often I have heard him say that he appreciated no position he ever held more than presidency of the Colored Orphans' Home that he served," wrote the editor of the *Courier-Journal*. "He appreciated the progress of the colored people along all lines. He was foremost in crushing unjust laws against the colored people. He touched almost every phase of uplift of the colored people and was always easy to approach.... How often has he said: 'Let us live in love, for there is no difference up yonder, why should there be contentions here?'"

It's hard to know whether this philanthropy was a departure from a belief in white supremacy that compelled Young to take up arms during the war. If he betrayed a belief that slavery was acceptable, it can't be found in the historic record. Young would go on to make hundreds of speeches and write a handful of books and papers, and only once address institutional slavery: he would admit the South was wrong and remove the reference to slavery from the Kentucky Constitution. His biographer, fifty years after Young's death, barely acknowledged the astonishing conflict. Young would devote time and money to memorializing his dead Confederate comrades, to building monuments and lore supporting the Lost Cause, but he would also go out of his way to help a person of color in hard times, with no motivation of any explicit benefit to himself.

Maybe he faced some kind of moral reckoning and changed his ways. Maybe his benevolence was coupled with white supremacy, the notion that a certain kind of power came from kindness. Or maybe his power enabled his kindness. Maybe he believed when he signed up to fight, still a young man, that secession was fundamentally an issue of the rights of the states to self-governance. Or maybe when the war was over and enslavement was ended, he sought ways to help his fellow man regardless of color.

So when he read the stories about George Dinning—when he saw on July 2, 1897, a headline in the *Courier-Journal* that said Dinning would be taking the witness stand on his own behalf— it piqued his interest. He knew how these things played out.

The same edition of the newspaper carried a good example of the typical trial. A Black man named Tol Stone was tried, convicted, and sentenced, all within an hour. Stone was accused of abducting a white girl who had voluntarily climbed into his carriage trunk to be shuttled through Kentucky to a free state. Following his arrest, he'd been protected by a militia on Governor Bradley's orders, likely the only reason he was still alive. He'd been sentenced to nineteen years. When the trial was over and Tol Stone was safely transported to the state prison in Eddyville, the townsfolk got together to rant.

The newspapers called it an "indignation meeting," and it was held at Jewell's Hall when the trial was over. One reporter estimated that five hundred men attended. They passed resolutions expressing their indignation over the judge, prosecutor, and sheriff, calling upon the governor to send armed troops into the county to protect a criminal. Baptist preachers and the editor of the local paper spoke. "The greatest indignation is felt because of the escape of Stone from the vengeance of an outraged people," the *Courier-Journal* reported. "It was the almost universal opinion that his life should have paid forfeit for his crime."

Franklin was just thirty miles from Glasgow, where Tol Stone was tried, and the public sentiment was familiar. Young would have known the odds of Dinning's being convicted and sentenced to prison. He would have known how unjust that would be.

Bennett Young, Confederate war hero and the best lawyer in Kentucky, started thinking of ways he could help.

Chapter 10

A BAD MAN

The sun burned hot on the afternoon of Thursday, July 1, when George Dinning was called to the stand to try to save his own life, not with bullets this time, but with a story. A heat wave had moved over the South and stalled out, and this was day ten of oppressively high temperatures. The mercury climbed to 96 degrees in Atlanta, 98 in Jacksonville, 94 in New Orleans, 96 in Vicksburg, 95 in Little Rock. They registered highs of 101 at Helena, Arkansas; Hernando, Mississippi; Decatur, Alabama; and Milan, Tennessee. A laborer and a wealthy shoe dealer were dead from heat prostration in Memphis, where the high was 96 degrees. The temperature reached 98 in Nashville, where organizers were busy preparing for the Independence Day parade and fireworks show at the Exposition Grounds. A Nashville mail carrier succumbed to heatstroke and wasn't expected to return to his duties for a few days, and J. Rice Wilson, an ex-Confederate soldier from Paducah, was found dead in his bed at the Pullman House on College Street—the coroner listed his cause of death as heat prostration. In Kentucky, the weathermen were calling it a "superheated atmosphere" and praying for thunderstorms to bring brief relief. Across Louisville, more people fell prostrate that Thursday than on any previous day of the heat wave. Patrolman Melville Lapaille collapsed in the middle of Lafayette Street and had to be carried home by carriage. Miss Frannie Hodges succumbed to the heat at the First-Avenue Hotel and began having convulsions. Dave Owsley, forty, passed out at Taylor Brothers lumberyard and was taken by ambulance to City Hospital, where he was listed in serious condition.

The crowd filed into the sweltering Simpson County Courthouse in Franklin, each submitting to a pat-down from the soldiers. They climbed the stairs to the second floor and found seats on the hard wooden benches, and when those were full, they filed into the balconies above, on both sides of the courtroom. Reporters noticed that the same four male members of the Conn family took their regular seats behind the prosecution. Mollie Dinning, who had sat through the proceedings the day before, was not in the courtroom. Colonel E. H. Gaither was there, watching closely, as always. The reporters noted that two jurors and a soldier were ill, possibly from the heat.

George Dinning, wearing his donated three-piece suit with brass buttons and an ascot, put one hand on a Holy Bible, raised the other, and swore before God to tell the truth.

John B. Grider stood as Dinning took his seat at the front of the courtroom. The soldiers flanking him scanned the room like ospreys.

"How old are you?" Grider asked.

"Forty-two years old last Monday," Dinning said.

"Where did you live at the time this difficulty came up?"

"At the state line between Tennessee and Kentucky," Dinning said. "Simpson County."

"How long did you live at that place?"

"Fourteen years last Christmas."

"Do you claim that land there?"

"Yes, sir."

"Lived there for fourteen years?"

"Yes, sir," Dinning said. "It was my home in my name."

"And that was your home for yourself and family?"

"Yes, sir."

"George, when did this difficulty occur in which Mr. Conn was hurt?"

"In January."

"1897?"

"Yes, sir."

"Do you remember what day of the week it was on, George?"

"On a Thursday."

"What had you been doing that day?"

"Hauling wood after dinner and before dinner I went down to Mr. Babb's."

"What time did you and your family go to bed that night?"

"Directly after sundown," Dinning said. "About dusk."

"Were you disturbed in any way that night?"

"Yes, sir."

"I will get you to go ahead and tell in your own way everything that occurred that night as you remember it."

"The first thing I know about," Dinning said, "it was my wife woke me up, and about the time that I woke up somebody knocked on the door. Knocked on both doors—one on one door and another on the other door, and the one at the front door says 'George, get up and come out!' And I says, 'Who is that?' And he says, 'It's friends.' And I says, 'You ain't much friends if you won't tell me who you are.' And he says, 'Come out! I want to see you!' And I says, 'I ain't got any business out there.' And he says, 'George, is Bob Lucas here?' And I says, 'No.' And he says, 'I will give you just ten days to get away from here, and don't you stop within forty miles, and you tell Bob Lucas to do the same thing.' And I says, 'Why, gentlemen? What have I done?' And they says, 'You have been stealing and you get away from here in ten days and don't you ever come back.' And I told him I hadn't been doing any stealing and could prove it by respectable white people and neighbors.

"And then this man at this other door says, 'Don't you say anymore or we will take you out now and burn your house up!' And I says, 'I haven't done anything for you men to take me out for.' And about this time the man at the back door fired, and so I ran and got my gun, and as I went up the stairs I was shot as I passed the window, and I went on upstairs."

"There is a window in that room downstairs?" Grider asked.

"Yes, sir."

"On which side?"

"North side of the chimney," Dinning said.

"On the east end of the house, downstairs?"

"Yes, sir."

"Now, that shot that struck you in the arm, where did that come from?"

"Through that window on the lower stairs, on the east end of the house."

"You had started up those steps and you say the shot came through the window and struck you on the arm?"

"Yes, sir."

"How many shots were fired at you on the head on the steps?"

"They never stopped firing after the first," Dinning said. "I had no time to count them. I was scared."

"Go ahead," Grider urged.

"I went on upstairs and opened the window—the window was on the north side of the chimney upstairs—and I throwed open the window and shot into a whole gang of men standing down there. And when I shoved the window back there was a shot struck me there."

The jury watched him point to his forehead.

"And when that shot struck me," Dinning said, "I fired down into the crowd."

He paused.

"They were all standing there in a bunch and then they commenced going away and kept shooting, and some of them kept shooting after they had gotten away from the house. And then they went up about a hundred yards from the house, and I came out of the house and I heard them talking and I went out and laid down in the field. And, directly, I heard two of them ride off down the road."

"When these men rode off, did you go back to the house?"

"Yes, sir."

"What occurred when you got back to the house?"

Finn objected and Grider withdrew his question.

"Did you get your boots, hat, and coat?" Grider asked.

"Yes, sir."

"Did you get them yourself or did someone hand them to you?"

"Someone handed them to me," Dinning said. "My wife."

"At the time, did you say anything to your wife about where you were going?"

"No, sir."

"What did you do?"

"I went over to Mr. Hackney's and called him, but I never raised him," Dinning said. "And then I went to Mr. Murray's and called him and Mr. Murray come and opened the door."

"You went to Gib Hackney's and he was not at home?"

"I don't know," Dinning said. "I bellowed a time or two and didn't raise anybody, and I went on to Mr. Murray's and called him."

"When did you go?"

"I went right on there."

"Who did you see at Mr. Murray's?"

"I didn't see no person except him and his lady."

"Did Mr. Murray see those wounds on your body?"

"Yes, sir. He came out with his lantern and looked at them."

"How long did you stay at Mr. Murray's?"

"All night," Dinning said.

"How far is Mr. Murray's from your house?"

"About a mile. Not much over a mile."

"What time did you get up next morning?"

"About five o'clock."

"Where did you go from Mr. Murray's?"

"To Mr. Lum Babb's."

"Did you go home next morning?"

"I started home and got nearly to the house," Dinning said. "About 100 yards of the house."

"Meet anybody?"

"Yes, sir."

"Who was the person you met?"

"Bob Lucas."

"Where did you go then?"

"To Franklin."

"How long did you stay there?"

"I reckon I was there about an hour."

"Where did you go to?"

"To Bowling Green."

"How long did you stay there?"

"Three or four days."

"Where have you been since you left Bowling Green?"

"Louisville."

"Where did you go when you got to Franklin?"

"I gave myself up to Sheriff Clark."

Grider thumbed through his notes. Sweat streamed down his forehead.

"The men at your house, they asked you to come out?" he asked.

"Yes, sir."

"You asked them who they were?"

"Yes, sir."

"Did you know who any of those parties were out there?"

"No, sir."

"Did they tell you who they were?"

"No, sir."

"When you went upstairs and shot out that window, did you know who those parties were out there?"

"No, sir."

"Did you see Mr. Jodie Conn out there?"

"No, sir."

"Was the window standing open or shut when you went upstairs?"

"Shut."

"Did you open it?"

"Yes, sir."

"Did you see any men down below there?"

"Yes, sir," Dinning said. "I saw some men standing under the window."

"Men at the east end of the house?"

"Yes, sir. As far from the house as you are from me." Grider was standing five feet away from his client.

"Did you shoot at any particular person?"

"No, sir," Dinning said. "I shot at the bunch."

"You didn't know who was down there when you shot?"

"No, sir."

"When did you first learn that you had shot somebody?"

"Next morning, when I was nearly back home."

"You say that when you got back within about 100 yards was the first time that you learned you had shot somebody?"

"Yes, sir."

"Did you then find out who you had shot?"

"He said I had shot Mr. Jodie Conn."

"Did you, at the time, know you had shot Jodie Conn?"

"No, sir. Not before that man told me."

"When you first found out that you had shot Jodie Conn you went to Franklin and gave yourself up?" Grider asked.

"Yes, sir," Dinning said. "I went to Franklin right straight."

"When you opened that shutter upstairs," Grider said, "how long after you opened the shutter before you fired?"

"As quick as I could get ready," Dinning said, "because when I opened the shutter I was shot and I shot into the crowd just as quick as I could."

"What kind of a load was that you shot?"

"Bird shot."

"Who loaded the gun?"

"My boy, Bob Lucas."

"Now, at the time these men came to your house I want you to give me the names of everybody in your house."

"No person except me and the children."

"Give me their names," Grider said.

"Mollie and Eva."

"How old is Eva?"

"Next to the oldest child."

"Go ahead."

"Viola."

"How old is Viola?"

"Ten years old."

"Next one?"

"My little son," Dinning said. "George is his name. Eight years old."

"How old is the next one?"

"Next one is six years old—Mertrude."

"Girl?"

"Yes, sir," Dinning said. "Next is Nannie, four years old."

"Any more?"

"Yes, sir. Oh! I have got em'."

"How many children you got?"

"Twelve," he said. "Next one is three years old—Emma."

"Got any more?"

"Next is the baby," Dinning said. "Four months old."

"You and your wife and these little children were there in the house that night?"

"Yes, sir."

"Anyone else there except you and your children and wife?"

"No, sir."

"All of you sleep in the same room?"

"Eva slept upstairs."

"When you shot from the window upstairs, did you believe that you and your family were in any danger?" Grider asked.

"Yes, sir," Dinning said. "Because they shot me first and of course I knew I was in danger."

"Would you have shot if these men were leaving your house at that time?"

"No, sir."

"When you got to the window you saw them standing right below the window?"

"Yes, sir."

"How many men do you say was out there?"

"I didn't count them," Dinning said. "I was scared. I don't know how many. A good big crowd of them."

"You was frightened at the time?"

"Yes, sir."

"Did you see any of them in the yard at the time you shot?"

"Yes, sir," Dinning said. "Looked like the biggest part of them. There was a whole crowd of them standing at the paling fence in the yard. The fence was down."

"How far is that fence from the house?"

"About twelve feet."

"Did you see any of the men go out of the yard as soon as you shot?"

"No, sir. They vanished as soon as I shot."

"How many times did you shoot?"

"Once."

"Did you have another load in that gun?"

"Yes, sir."

"Did you make an effort to shoot any more?"

"No, sir."

"You saw they were leaving?"

"Yes, sir."

"What did you do with that gun?"

"I left it with Dick Henry, a colored man here in town."

"Do you know where the gun is now?"

"No, sir."

"Whereabouts does Dick Henry live?"

"Out here on the Springfield road."

"How far from town?"

"About half a mile."

"You heard the testimony of Isen Hollis," Grider said. "Did you tell them at any time that you were going to fix Mr. Jodie Conn the first chance you had?"

"No, sir. I never did."

"Did you say anything against Conn in their presence?"

"No, sir."

"Did you have anything against Conn?"

"No, sir."

"Did Conn have anything against you?"

"Not that I know of," Dinning said. "We always spoke and I worked for him by the day."

"Did you have any grudge against Conn for having your boy arrested?"

"If he had him arrested, I didn't know it," Dinning said. "And I was working there at his house."

"You never knew that Mr. Conn had anything to do with having your boy arrested?"

"No, sir."

"Did Conn talk to you about the boy being arrested?"

"No, sir."

"You say you had nothing against Conn and liked him up to the time you killed him?"

Finn objected and Grider rephrased the question.

"Did you have anything against Conn till the difficulty occurred?"

"No, sir."

"If he had anything against you, you didn't know it?"

"No, sir."

"When you shot, you didn't know that Conn was in the party?"

"No, sir."

"These witnesses said you threatened Conn at the wheat-threshing," Grider said. "How long after the wheat-threshing before he got hurt?"

"It was from wheat-threshing until January," Dinning said.

"Can you show the jury your wounds?" Grider asked.

Dinning stood and walked to the jury, leaning forward so they could see the scar on his forehead. He removed his overcoat and rolled up his sleeve so they could inspect the scar on his arm. When they'd had a long look, he returned to the stand while the prosecutor, G. T. Finn, prepared his questions.

"Where did you get that shot in the arm?" Finn began.

"Just as I started upstairs," Dinning said.

"How far up the steps had you gotten?"

"I was on the bottom step."

"Had you gotten up the first step?"

"My feet were on the first step."

"Your back was to the East?"

"Yes, sir."

"Where did that shot come from?" Finn asked. "What window?"

"East window."

"Right from your back?"

"Yes, sir."

"Where is that wound?"

"On my arm."

"How could your arm ever be shot there?"

"What is to hinder it?" Dinning said, showing the lawyer with ease how his arm was positioned.

"You were going up the steps and your back was to the window and it hit your arm on the inside?"

"Yes, sir."

"How did you get shot going upstairs by a shotgun?"

"I don't know."

"Don't know whether it was a shotgun or pistol?"

"No, sir," Dinning said. "Something like a bullet."

"Did that cut your arm?"

"Yes, sir."

"Did it go in?"

"Yes, sir. But not much."

"How did it go in?"

"Well, it cut a place there."

"Did it lodge in there?"

"No, sir. It cut across."

"You say that was made by a ball?"

"Yes, sir."

"Went in and then come out?"

"Yes, sir."

"Never struck the bone?"

"No, sir."

"Dived in and dived out?"

"Yes, sir."

"Now, George," Finn said, "where were you when you got the wound there in the head?"

"At the window."

"In front?"

"Not exactly," Dinning said. "At the side of the window."

"You opened the window?"

"Yes, sir."

"You were standing at the window?"

"Yes, sir."

"Which side of the window were you standing?"

"South side."

"You were standing on the South side of the North window?"

"Yes, sir."

"How did you shoot?" Finn asked. "From which shoulder?"

"Right shoulder," Dinning said.

"Were you standing right square up in front of the window?"

"No, sir."

"How could you shoot the gun from your right shoulder on the South side of the window?"

"Easy," Dinning said, and he illustrated what he had done.

"You didn't shoot from the center of the window?"

"No, sir."

"You shot from the right shoulder?"

"Yes, sir."

"Was your body before the window?"

"No," Dinning said. "Not all."

"Your right side was to the window?"

"Yes, sir."

"Your right side never was in front of the window?"

"No, sir."

"You were standing back from the window?"

"No, sir," Dinning said. "I was standing pretty close to the window."

"Now, George, how long did you stand there before you shot?" Finn asked.

"From the time I opened the window?" Dinning said. "Just as quick as the gun could fire."

"You threw the window open and got shot in the forehead?"

"Yes, sir."

"Yet you stayed in the window and still shot?"

"Yes, sir," Dinning said. "As quick as I could shoot. I turned the window loose and fired."

"They were firing incessantly at you but you still fired?"

"Yes, sir."

"You didn't fire the second shot because you saw they were going away?"

"Yes, sir."

"Just as soon as you fired they stopped firing?"

"No, sir."

"Why didn't you shoot the second time?"

"Because they started away."

"They were still shooting?"

"Yes, sir."

"Why didn't you shoot the second time?"

"Because I saw them leaving."

"You were still in danger?"

"Yes, sir."

"What did you get shot with?" Finn asked. "A pistol or shotgun?"

"I suppose it was a shotgun," Dinning replied.

"And only one shot hit you in the face?"

"No, sir. There was one that hit me in the face."

"There was not more than one unless two or three hit in the same place?"

"No, sir."

"Did two or three hit in the same place?"

"I don't know."

"How many wounds were there up there?"

"One."

"There was one shot in your head you say?"

"Yes, sir."

"How close were they to you when that shot was fired?"

"I reckon it is about fifteen feet from the ground to the window," Dinning said, "and they were standing down on the ground."

"Right close to you?"

"Yes, sir."

"Shotguns wouldn't scatter much in that distance, would they?" Finn asked.

"No, sir," Dinning said. "But the biggest portion of the load went in the window I reckon."

"It wouldn't scatter much in that distance?"

"No, sir."

"One shot hit you on the forehead?"

"Yes, sir. I reckon it did."

Finn considered his next line of questioning. He had

testimony from the first men Dinning saw after the shooting, the men he first told what had happened. They testified that Dinning said the mob threw dynamite at his house. This was incorrect, clearly. But could dozens of volleys of bird shot hitting a wooden house and a tin roof and a wooden tongue-and-groove floor—could that have *sounded* like dynamite to a man in fear for his life, a man whose sudden stress would have triggered a surge of adrenaline, which slows cochlear blood flow and causes hearing loss?

"Now, George," Finn said, winding up, "wasn't that dynamite thrown in there?"

"I don't know whether it was dynamite or not," Dinning said.

"When were those bombs thrown in there?" Finn asked coyly, hoping to make him sound like a fool.

"I don't know whether it was bombs or guns," Dinning said.

"Your recollection was better then than it is now," Finn said, toying with him.

"I told you I didn't know whether it was bombs or guns," Dinning said.

"Didn't you say it was bombs or dynamite?"

"I don't know."

"Do you say it rattled over the floor like hail?"

"Yes, sir," Dinning said. "It rattled over the floor and bed and all in the house like hail."

"The house was shot in the gable end?"

"Yes, sir."

"How come the shot to rattle on the floor in the house when the shooting was done from the ground?"

"Why, there is nothing to hinder it when they had got way off from the house," Dinning said.

"When did you throw the window open?"

"As soon as I got up the steps."

"Now, hadn't they started to go away before you shot?"

"I don't know."

"They were shooting all the time?"

"Yes, sir."

"And you thought it was bombs or dynamite?"

"Something," Dinning said. "I don't know what it was."

"Didn't you receive the wound in your arm and head after you had shot out that window?" Finn asked.

"No, sir."

"Didn't you receive that wound in your arm at that window?"

"No, sir—not in my arm."

"You were hit in the head there?"

"Yes, sir."

"What kind of shot was that?"

"I don't know," Dinning said. "A gunshot or something of the kind."

"Did you see any bombs?" Finn asked again.

"I don't know what it was," Dinning said. "I was scared."

"Now, you stated to this jury you were shot there with a pistol or gun?"

"I reckon that is what it was."

"Didn't you tell Mr. Grider that you were hurt with a gunshot when you passed that window going upstairs?"

"Yes, sir. Some kind of shot."

"I will ask you, George, if you didn't tell Mr. Zack Murray that they threw bombs in your house?"

"I told him I didn't know what it was," Dinning replied.

Finn wouldn't let it go. His voice grew louder, his questions sharp.

"Didn't you tell Murray that they threw bombs or dynamite in your house?"

"I told him I didn't know what it was," Dinning said, his

frustration building. "Something like dynamite. I didn't know what it was."

"Didn't you tell him it was dynamite of some kind?"

"I told him it seemed to be dynamite or something of the kind. I didn't know what it was."

"Didn't you tell him that it rattled over the floor like gravel?"

"No, sir."

"Didn't you further state to him that you went upstairs and shot as they were leaving?"

"No, sir."

"Didn't you also tell Mr. Lum Babb that they threw some kind of dynamite in your house and then you went upstairs and shot as the crowd was leaving?" Finn asked.

"No, sir."

"And that the dynamite rattled like gravel over the floor?"

"No, sir."

"Will you state to this jury whether or not there were any dynamite or bombs thrown on that occasion?" Finn asked.

"I couldn't tell you what kind of guns it was," Dinning said, trembling. "I was so scared. I was scared badly. Some guns were shooting—I don't know what it was. I was frightened."

"Dr. Francis said that the wound was here on the forehead and came out above there at the edge of the hair," Finn said. "I would like for the jury to examine this man's head and see if they think there is any evidence of the ball coming out there?"

Dinning ambled to the jury box and the men leaned in to inspect his head. Then he returned to his seat.

"Did you see John Lovell the day after the shooting?" Finn asked.

"Yes, sir," Dinning said.

"Did you have a talk with him?"

"Yes, sir."

"Did you tell John Lovell there was dynamite used there that night?"

"I told him like I told Mr. Murray."

"Answer my question," Finn said.

"I told him they were shooting some guns or dynamite," Dinning said.

"Did you tell Mr. Babb that one of them fired a gun and then the others of the party dynamited you or threw bombs in your house?"

"No, sir."

"Didn't you tell him when you fired the gun they were leaving?"

"No, sir."

"Didn't you tell Mr. Bud Clark that they dynamited you?"

"I told him that they shot some guns or threw dynamite," Dinning said.

"Didn't you tell Mr. Grider when he examined you that they shot you instead of throwing any dynamite or bombs?"

"I don't know what they were," Dinning said. "Seemed to me at the time that it was bombs or some kind of guns."

"When you received that wound on the arm, did you have on any clothes?"

"Yes, sir. I had on an undershirt."

"Did the bullet tear your undershirt?"

"Yes, sir."

"Where is that undershirt?"

"In my valise."

"What kind of a hole did it make in the shirt?"

"It just tore a hole in it," Dinning said, motioning in the direction of his scar. "Sorta across this way."

Finn visited his notes again, then rested. Grider stood to cross-examine his client.

"You are left-handed are you?"

"Right-handed."

"You were going up the steps with the gun and there was a gun fired and made that mark on your arm?"

"Yes, sir."

"Now hold up your arms," Grider said, and Dinning did. "Now, in that position, don't you think a man could have shot through that window and it would've made that wound?"

"Yes, sir."

"A nail couldn't have made that could it?"

"No, sir."

"Any nails there around that window that you could have scratched that on?"

"No, sir."

"You say they continued to shoot as they were leaving the house and after you shot?"

"Yes, sir."

"You were scared and didn't hardly know what it was they were shooting but it sounded to you at the time like big guns or dynamite?"

"Yes, sir."

"What is that house covered with?"

"Boards."

"Any plastering?"

"No, sir. Lathes were nailed on the boards."

"How far were the lathes apart?"

"An inch," Dinning said. "Or an inch and a half."

"Bullets would make a right smart rattle on the room wouldn't they?"

"Yes, sir."

"You saw no guns?"

"No, sir."

That was the last question. Without ceremony, George Dinning stepped down from the stand and returned to his seat at the defense table. He had done what he could, and now he would watch and wait.

Grider wasn't quite finished making his argument. On the morning of July 2, the defense called Zack Murray, the first man Dinning saw after the shooting. He lived a mile away, and he'd been asleep when Dinning woke him with a bellow. He got up, leaving his wife in bed, and went to the door.

"Did he make any complaint of some wounds that he had received that night?" Grider asked.

"Yes, sir."

"Did you examine him?"

"Yes, sir."

"Tell the jury what you found."

"I found a place on his arm—I don't remember which arm," Murray said. "His shirt was torn across and there was a scratch or sore on his arm."

"Did it appear to be a fresh wound?"

"Yes, sir."

"Was it bleeding at the time?"

"No, sir."

Murray said he didn't hike up Dinning's sleeve to inspect it closely, but he saw a "sore place and it looked white."

"Did you notice his head?" Grider asked.

"Yes, sir," Murray said.

"What was the matter with his head?"

"When he first came to my house, I suppose it was something like a half hour before he had me to examine him," Murray said. "There was a swollen place in the center of his head—about the size of the end of my finger—and I looked at it the next morning and it was swollen a good deal more, and there was a little ridge running up his head to another place, I suppose about a half inch broad."

"Not swollen so much when you first saw him?"

"No, sir."

"You say it was swollen considerably next morning?"

"Yes, sir, and there was a ridge running from the center of his head on up."

Finn, on cross-examination, cut to the chase.

"Mr. Murray, that scratched place there on his arm," Finn said, "what was the nature of that wound? Is that a scratch or a gunshot?"

"I don't know that it was a gunshot."

"I will ask you if that shirt was torn the way the wound ran?"

"No, sir," Murray said. "It was torn across the wound."

"Did George tell you that somebody had been over there throwing dynamite and bombs at him?" Finn asked.

"He said that they had been throwing dynamite and bombs at him and I tried to reason with him and told him if they had they would have killed him," Murray said.

"What did he say to that?"

"He never claimed that there was any guns that were shot," Murray said. "He said it was dynamite and bombs."

"Did he say it rattled?"

"He said it hit the floor like gravel."

"Did he say it hit on the upper floor?"

"Yes, sir. And he said the first one struck him on the arm."

"Where did he say he was when it struck him?"

"Downstairs."

"Where did he say he was when he shot?"

"He said he grabbed his gun and ran upstairs, and he said there was six or seven of them down there below and he shot into them after he was shot in the head," Murray said. "And I asked him if he hit any of them and he said he shot some of them if the gun was loaded right."

"Do you live in the neighborhood of George Dinning?"

"Yes, sir. Pretty near."

"Do you know his general reputation for truth and honesty."

"The neighbors say it is not good."

"You have heard what the neighbors say?"

"Yes," Murray said. "I have heard them say it was not good."

"Did George tell you that night that they threw some dynamite in the window and struck him on the arm?" Finn asked.

"I never understood him to say that."

The prosecution's next strategy was to impeach the character of all the defense's key witnesses. This tactic had been used before, ad nauseam. Say enough times that the defendant was a bad man and the jury might believe it. G. T. Finn, the able prosecutor for the Commonwealth, had grown up with live-in Black servants, and his father, a lawyer, former circuit judge, and former member of the Kentucky Legislature, was opposed to the antislavery movement, Abraham Lincoln, and the "Black Republicans." Finn still lived with his mother and brother, L. B. Finn, on College Street in Franklin.

A white man, John King, from Logan County, testified that he had gone to the Dinnings' house around sunrise the morning after the shooting. He testified that Mollie Dinning gave him a single bullet, which he had in his pocket, but her boy, Hermann, never found or produced any bullets in John King's presence. He said he saw no signs of shots or bullet holes around the downstairs window. King said he saw blood upstairs, but none downstairs or on the steps. He saw no signs of dynamite or bombs exploding in the house.

"Do you know the general reputation for truth and honesty of Claud Hackney in the neighborhood," Finn asked.

"It doesn't seem to be very good," King said.

"Is it bad?"

"I would certainly regard it as bad."

Next came John Webb, who visited the house with John King. He said he saw one bullet, the one Mollie Dinning gave to John King, and no more. He said he saw no signs of dynamite or bombs in the house.

"Do you know Claud Hackney's general reputation for truth and honesty in the neighborhood?" Finn asked. "Good or bad?"

"Very bad," Webb said.

"Do you know George Dinning's general reputation for honesty and truth?" Finn asked. "Was it good or bad?"

"Rather bad," Webb said. "Very bad, I would call it."

John King's son Bill followed. He had seen a single bullet. No sign of dynamite or bombs.

"Do you know George Dinning's general reputation for truth and honesty there in the neighborhood?" Finn asked. "Good or bad?"

"Bad," Bill King said.

"Do you know the general reputation of Claud Hackney?"

"That is bad, I suppose."

"Ben Conn?"

"Bad."

Grider shot up when Finn finished.

"You have a good many *bad* fellows down in that country, haven't you?" he asked.

"It seems that way," Bill King said.

"Did you ever hear of Claud, or George here, or old man Ben Conn riding around at night and scaring people?" Grider asked.

"Objection!" Finn said.

"Withdrawn," Grider said.

The prosecution next called W. P. "Lum" Babb, who testified that he had heard what sounded like a shotgun first that night, followed by a volley from smaller arms a few moments later. He said that Dinning came to his house that night and told him that "someone had been there and thrown dynamite or something like it and it scattered over his floor like gravel." He testified that Dinning told him there was but one gun there that night—the one Dinning was holding.

"Do you know the general reputation of George Dinning for truth and honesty?" Finn asked.

"I think I do," Babb said.

"Good or bad?"

"Bad," Babb said.

"Do you know the general reputation in that neighborhood of Ben Conn for truth and honesty?" Finn said. "Good or bad?"

"Bad," Babb said.

And so it went, a parade of George Dinning's white neighbors besmirching his character, one after the other.

Was George Dinning's reputation for truth and honesty good or bad?

Robert Angel: "Bad."

Benjamin Ferguson: "I would call it bad."

Pete Doss: "I would say bad."

R. P. Kelley: "Bad."

E. H. Dilliard: "I should call it bad."

W. H. Samuels: "Bad."

T. McDonald: "Tolerably bad."

J. S. Ray: "I would call it bad."

"Do you think from his reputation that he is entitled to credit on oath?" Finn asked Ray.

"I don't think he is," Ray said.

*   *   *

As afternoon turned to evening, John B. Grider had two more tricks, and the first was literally up a sleeve. He introduced into evidence the undershirt George Dinning wore the night he was shot and called Dinning back to the stand.

"Is that the shirt you had on at the time you were shot?" Grider asked.

"Yes, sir," Dinning said.

"Has that shirt been washed since the shooting?" Grider asked.

"Yes, sir," Dinning said. "Several times."

"How long have you worn it?"

"I have worn it ever since I was shot."

"Was the hole in that shirt before the shooting?" Grider asked.

"No, sir," Dinning said.

At this point, due to the controversial nature of the next witness Grider wished to call, the judge excused the jury. They retired with the sheriff to private chambers. Grider called L. G. Berry, who lived in southwestern Simpson County, not far from the Dinning place.

"Do you know Nick Williams?" Grider asked. Williams was in the party, had stayed back at the road with the horses, and it was Williams's house to which they had taken a dead or dying Jodie Conn. Williams had stuffed his wounds with whiskey and cotton.

"Yes, sir," Berry said.

"How long?"

"You might say from infancy," Berry said. "I knew his father well."

"Did you have any conversation with him at Mr. Charley Conn's on the day his son, Jodie Conn, was buried, in regard to who fired the first shot or what gun was fired first?" Grider asked.

"I had a conversation with him in regards to the circumstances," Berry said.

"What did he say in regard to the first shot that was fired?" Grider asked. "Did he tell you on that occasion that the first gun that was fired was one that was accidentally fired in the hands of his own party?"

"Yes, sir," Berry said.

The courtroom observers were stunned as Grider sat and Finn stood to question this late witness.

"Mr. Berry," Finn said, "Mr. Williams didn't claim he was there, did he?"

"No, sir," Berry said. "I asked him the question and he told me he was not there."

"He told you he was not there?"

"Yes, sir."

"And he didn't know, by his own knowledge, which gun fired first?" Finn asked.

"No, sir."

Finn was done. He sat once more. Grider rose to follow up.

"Did he say at the same time that he didn't know of his own personal knowledge how it occurred?" Grider asked.

"No, sir," Berry said. "He seemed to give the details so clear that I asked him whether or not he was there and he told me that he was not there, and that the parties told him."

"When you asked him if he was there," Finn said, "did he hesitate before answering?"

"Yes, sir," Berry said. "I thought he did, and I regretted having asked the question."

"Did he say what parties told him that?"

"No, sir," Berry said. "I didn't ask him."

"So, some of the parties down there that night told him that the first shot that was fired was one that was accidentally discharged in the hands of his own party?" Grider asked.

"Yes, sir," Berry said.

The judge weighed Berry's testimony. It was the definition of hearsay: an unsworn statement made out of court. As jarring as the information was, and as helpful to George Dinning, the judge could not allow it. Besides, it was getting late. He ruled that the testimony was incompetent in contradiction to the sworn testimony of Nick Williams. The jury could not hear it. He remanded the jury to the sheriff for the night. Grider had no choice but to accept the ruling, unless he could find Nick Williams and put him back on the stand.

Chapter 11

"THE PRAISEWORTHY ACT OF KILLING"

On the morning of Saturday, July 3, the courtroom was over-flowing. Colonel Gaither was there, overseeing things. "Sweltering spectators," one reporter called the onlookers. The heat wave would not abate. Nor would interest in the case. The dirty streets of Franklin buzzed with activity, and gunfire echoed sporadically in the night.

Overnight, Grider had prepared a motion to continue the trial during the next session. He filed it that morning, along with an affidavit that explained his thinking. Nick Williams had been in the mob at George Dinning's house that night in January, and Williams had testified against Dinning, swearing that Dinning had fired the first shot. Only after Nick Williams was excused did Grider become aware that L. G. Berry—"a reputable man," as the newspapers called him—would swear that Williams had told him the first shot was an accident, and that it was fired by one of the Whitecappers. Grider wanted to call Nick Williams back to the stand to contradict him, but Williams could not be located. A group of militiamen had gone in search of him the night before.

Judge Reeves allowed the affidavit to be filed but overruled the motion for continuance. The lawyers agreed that each side would make three closing arguments, then send the case to the jury by Saturday evening.

The standing-room-only crowd heard the men go at it, making their cases. The speeches dragged on for hours. All day. Back and forth they went, rehashing the testimony and evidence, arguing for and against a man's life. When they had finished, there was no time for the jury to come to a verdict, so the jurors were again placed in the custody of the sheriff, who had sworn to keep them together until Monday, July 5, at 8 a.m. The court would observe the Sabbath.

Gunfire echoed down the streets of Franklin that Saturday evening, and the soldiers were on edge. It seemed like the boys of Simpson County were trying to annoy the militiamen. The guards were called out four times before midnight to keep the peace.

After midnight, in the early hours of Independence Day, Lieutenant F. L. Gordon and Captain Noel Gaines went out on a patrol. They spied three suspicious men loitering near the stone Simpson County jail, where George Dinning was held. The soldiers quietly approached, and Captain Gaines heard the men plotting. He heard them say they were going to throw a stick of dynamite against the jail.

"Halt!" Captain Gaines shouted.

The three men halted, until they discovered that they had the numbers. Then they attacked. Two of the men jumped Captain Gaines, striking him three times. He collapsed to the ground, his head bleeding from a gaping wound. Gordon got the best of his man, striking him several severe blows and locking him in a bear hug. The man then escaped his grasp, and Gordon pounded him with his revolver. The man fell, then scrambled to his feet and

Capt. Noel Gaines, depicted in the Louisville *Times*.

tried to leap a fence nearby. Gordon struck him with his gun, breaking it at the lock. Gordon swung his gun again but missed the man and smote the fence, bending the barrel of his gun.

The other two men began beating Gordon. They had him on the ground. By the lamplight Gordon saw one of the men pull a gun and aim. He swung his arm and knocked the pistol away as a sharp shot rang out. The bullet sailed through his coat, pantaloons, and underclothes and grazed his left side. Blood spread across his uniform. One of the men pulled and fired on

Gaines as well. The shot split the ventilators on the left side of his cap and passed through the seam on the right. The shots stunned the soldiers, and their assailants scrambled into the darkness. Gaines drew his sidearm and fired as they fled, and he heard one of the men cry out.

Somewhere, fireworks exploded in the night sky and lit up the eyes of little children. Somewhere, patriotic songs left the lips of the free. In Franklin, Kentucky, two shaken soldiers stumbled back into camp, lucky to be alive.

The story of the attack ran in newspapers across the country the next day, from San Francisco to Savannah, a reminder of the violent chaos orbiting George Dinning's trial.

"KENTUCKY SOLDIERS ATTACKED," read the headline on the front page of the *New York Times*.

"It is believed the assassins wanted to kill Col. Gaither," the story said, "as he has been zealous in preventing the friends of Conn from killing Dinning during the trial. It was known that he made nightly visits to the jail to see if the negro was guarded properly."

The jury filed into the courtroom on the morning of Monday, July 5, and they were sworn in as a group. The judge gave them instructions, explaining the technicalities of the law and the charge against George Dinning: willful murder. Then Sheriff Clark ushered the group of five Democrats and seven Republicans—all men, all white—into the privacy of a small room to consider the case.

It was anyone's guess which way they'd decide. A reporter diligently covering the trial for the *St. Louis Daily Globe-Democrat* noted as much. "Before the trial began it was freely predicted that the testimony would be so severe on Dinning that the jury could do nothing but find him guilty, but under the cross-examination of Dinning's attorneys the testimony of Conn's confederates is

A photograph of a crowd near the Simpson County Courthouse at the turn of the century. (*Courtesy of the Simpson County Historical Society*)

severely punctured," he wrote. "Dinning may get a light sentence for manslaughter. The witnesses confessed on the stand that they had warned Dinning to leave, thus showing that the negro naturally expected to receive great bodily injury at their hands when they came to his house on the night of the tragedy."

"The people of Simpson and Logan counties are greatly worked up over the affair, and the feeling is very strong against the darkey," wrote Will C. Perry for the *Ledger* in nearby Russellville. "If a verdict for the death penalty is not rendered it is likely that there will be trouble. At any rate it looks like Dinning's days on this planet are numbered with small digits."

In other papers, there were explicit calls for a pardon.

"If the negro George Dinning is convicted at Franklin the governor ought to pardon him without a day's delay," wrote the editor of the *Owensboro Inquirer*. "A lot of low down scamps fell out with him and went to his house after night to whip him and run him out of the country. He performed the praiseworthy act of killing one of them... Dinning ought to be given forty acres of land and a mule for his action in protecting himself and his family."

Soldiers escorted George Dinning to a cell in the county jail to await the verdict. What that must have been like for him is lost to time. Maybe he found sleep, and dreamed of hiding in the folds of his mother Mary's skirt, or of sitting in the tall grass and listening to a cacophony of frogs chirping on the banks of the Red River, or of kissing Mollie's lips for the first time, or of welcoming a baby into the small world of Simpson County, Kentucky. Maybe he sat upright, staring straight ahead, his sweaty face twitching from fear, as the reporter had noticed in the courtroom. Maybe he peered through the narrow lancet windows in the limestone walls of the cruciform, medieval-style county jail, watching free men and women hustle by on the street outside.

As the sun began to fall, the sheriff returned for him, and the armed guard led him down the street to the courthouse. He turned into the heat of the courthouse, greeted his lawyers, and took his seat at the table. After a bit, the members of the jury filed in and took their seats, and Judge Reeves called the court to order. He asked if the jury had reached a verdict, and the foreman, John Snider, indicated that they had. The judge asked him to read the verdict and he spoke thus:

"We, the jury, find the prisoner not guilty as charged in the indictment..."

Maybe there was a gasp, maybe not. Maybe hearts jumped in chests. Maybe they sank. Maybe someone let out a cry. What is known is that George Dinning sat motionless, the eyes of the crowd upon him. The foreman continued.

"...but guilty of manslaughter, and we fix his punishment at seven years in the penitentiary."

Manslaughter, not willful murder. Seven years, not death. But *manslaughter,* and *seven years,* all for defending his home.

Immediately, John B. Grider and his team filed a motion to set aside the verdict of the jury and the judgment of the court and grant the defendant a new trial. Judge Reeves overruled the motion, and Grider immediately objected, announcing he would appeal the ruling. Judge Reeves gave Grider until November 5 to prepare and present a bill of exceptions.

The judge asked Dinning if he understood the nature of the verdict, and if he had any legal cause to show why the guilty verdict should not be pronounced against him, and Dinning said he understood, and that he had none. Judge Reeves then commanded the sheriff to take George Dinning to the state penitentiary at Eddyville, Kentucky, and confine him to hard labor for a period of seven years.

Soon, he was loaded onto a train with another man convicted of murder.

Soon, he was leaving Simpson County for the last time.

Soon, he stepped off at Eddyville, and was taken to the massive, imposing state penitentiary. By noon on July 6, he was wearing prison stripes.

"The verdict fails to give entire satisfaction," reported the *Courier-Journal* in its front-page story the next day. The people of Simpson County weren't happy, even if others around the state disagreed. "Public sentiment says that the punishment is too light," the reporter wrote. "The political complexion of the jury favored the defendant."

The only hope Dinning had left was a pardon by the governor.

Chapter 12

"MAY THE LORD PROTECT US, OR THE DEVIL TAKE US"

The verdict was outrageous.

Readers of the *Lexington Morning Herald* picked up their newspaper on July 7 and found an editorial occupying the center of the front page of the newspaper, above the fold, under the headline "OPEN LETTER TO LT. GOV. WORTHINGTON."

> The Herald prays your Excellency to at once issue a pardon to George Dinning, lately convicted in the Simpson County Circuit Court of manslaughter and sentenced to the penitentiary for seven years. It was established in the testimony that about midnight a band of regulators composed of citizens—said to be eminently respectable—went to the home of George Dinning, in which he and his family, some of them being females, were residing, to order him to leave his home and find residence elsewhere; that these regulators were armed; that guns were fired, and one of them was shot by Dinning with a load of bird-shot, and from that shot died. It is certain that Dinning fired from his own house, that it was after midnight, that those who were at his house were an organized band of regulators, and the man killed

was one of the band there to aid in carrying out whatever purpose that band had in going there at that hour.

The foundation of our civilization and liberty is the family, and the home is the basis and hope of the family; that home is sacred from assault and has been in our civilization since the memory of man runneth not to the contrary. In its defense a man, a citizen, has a right to shoot, to kill; it is his duty to shoot, to kill; and he who attacks it and is killed "dies as the fool dieth."

It has been said that the man killed was a "citizen of eminent respectability." If he had been humble, ignorant, or brutal; if he had been inflamed by liquor; blinded by ignorant prejudice, the act might have palliation. But Your Excellency owes to the State to have it settled that the home of the humblest is sacred from the lawless assault of the "most eminently respectable citizens;" that no station can excuse the brutal conspiracy to raid a home where men, women and children sleep; that the law is as tender of the homes of her citizens as against the gentlemen of Kentucky as against the lowest.

Dinning is a negro; he is poor; he was a slave; he may be unworthy; but he is a citizen, a man, a husband and a father, and it was his home and he was its defender. There are six whites in Kentucky to every negro. The whites have been free, rich, educated for centuries; the negros have been slaves, poor, illiterate. Manliness, courage and charity unite to make outrages on them cowardly and unspeakably base. And they need to be taught the value of home and to realize the inestimable preciousness of all the pregnant and hopeful meaning of that blessed and unique word "Home." Kentucky, through you, its honored Chief Magistrate, ought to proclaim to these humble citizens, struggling, striving to better light and greater advantages, that their homes are as sacred as the homes of the wealthiest Kentuckian—aye, if possible, more so—for the wealthy can protect their own homes. For God's sake draw the line of safe ruffianism before the door of the poor and humble, and if the law be powerless elsewhere, make the nights of the humble in their own homes safe from the marauder and regulator.

The Herald has no criticism to offer upon the action of the court and jury, nor is it necessary. The constitution entrusts the unlimited power and duty of pardon to the Chief Magistrate for such cases as may not escape the technical sentence, or where the ends of justice are satisfied without the infliction of the assigned penalty, or where for any cause justice has miscarried, or where clemency is wiser than punishment. This is such a case, and illustrates the wisdom of the provision imposing this duty upon the Governor. For these and other good reasons which will occur to your own generous, manly nature, The Herald prays for the exercise of this lofty and benign power, and it will ever pray.

The editorial was written by William Campbell Preston Breckinridge, who had served Kentucky ten years in the U.S. House of Representatives and was following the Dinning case closely. He was called a "silver-tongued orator," and though his reputation had been tarnished by an infidelity scandal, his forceful editorials were persuasive.

Other readers in other sections of the state found similar editorials. The newspapers—most of them—had begun to rally for Dinning.

"Acting Governor Worthington should not hesitate a day about pardoning George Dinning," read a column in the *Owensboro Inquirer*. "He is a poor negro, it is true, who found it necessary to shoot a white man who was engaged in an unlawful attempt to drive him away from his cabin home, but he performed a meritorious act, and it is a shame that he was ever brought to trial."

"His conviction and sentence to the penitentiary for that act were a travesty of justice," wrote the editor of the *Courier-Journal*. "If a man can not protect himself and family from lawless bands of night raiders, then, indeed, is the spirit of the mob supreme and law is a mockery."

"The Negro, George Dinning, who exercised the God-given and law provided right to defend his humble castle from cowardly midnight raiders by shooting one of them dead, after he had been shot himself, was given seven years at Franklin, after a trial held in a court-house fortified with bayonets, to protect him from lynching," wrote the editor of the *Interior Journal* in Stanford. "The verdict is a parody on justice and ought to be set aside without delay."

The editors seemed to believe that the future of the state was riding on the outcome. A pardon was a strong rebuke. To do nothing was fuel on the fire of hate.

The sense of outrage at the verdict transcended racial bias to a large degree. Defending one's own property against attack was one of the oldest and most deeply held principles in Anglo jurisprudence. It had legal roots as far back as the Roman republic and English common law. Its champions were great philosophers and thinkers and lawyers like Sir Edward Coke, who famously said in 1604 that the "house of every one is to him as his castle and fortress, as well for his defence against injury and violence as for his repose." Eighty-five years later, John Locke tried to outline a theory of civil government in his *Second Treatise of Government* by suggesting that all men exist in a *state of perfect freedom* and also a *state of equality*. He established the right to own property in pursuit of survival, and to defend that right with force. The influential writer William Blackstone carried the principle farther seventy-six years later in *Commentaries on the Laws of England,* in which he wrote that the "law of England has so particular and tender a regard to the immunity of a man's house, that it stiles it his castle, and will never suffer it to be violated with immunity."

Colonists carried the English common law to the shores of the New World, where it became known as the castle doctrine, and in time, state after state codified a version into law, giving homeowners the right to use deadly force to defend their homes from attack. This was true in Kentucky, where each iteration of the state's developing constitution gave citizens the right to bear arms and also the right to "be secure in their persons, houses, papers and possessions from unreasonable seizures and searches." The principle was so deeply American that it formed the fabric of the Fourth Amendment to the U.S. Constitution, which protects citizens and their homes and property from un-reasonable search and seizure by the government. And while it's true that private patrols and early Southern law officers often did not extend the same protection to enslaved African Americans before Emancipation, the War Between the States seemed to settle any question of whether a free Black man, too, could defend his home. Editors and politicians often supported this fundamental idea, even if the local legal systems didn't.

"If in defending his humble home from an attack by midnight marauders the negro Dinning violated any statutory or moral law, his punishment is already in excess of his offense," wrote the editor of the Louisville *Times.* "For months he has been deprived of liberty and held in peril of his life. His house has been burned over the heads of his wife and eleven children; shifted from jail to jail, he has finally immured within penitentiary walls at harder than slave labor for a period of seven years. Even if released he must ever remain an exile from his old home and whatever friends he had there."

"Prompt action in the Dinning case would prove of incalculable importance in the way of showing the mobs that they can not invade the homes of citizens of the state and secure their conviction when they repel by force their assaults," wrote the editor of the *Louisville Commercial*. "If Dinning is pardoned it will show people in the North and East that in Kentucky there is a chief executive who has the courage to see that a friendless negro obtains justice, even after a jury failed to return a fair verdict; that in Kentucky all citizens are treated alike."

Even the *Paducah Sun* called on Worthington to pardon Dinning. "He was only a negro, had no influential friends, but he was only exercising that divine law that says that every man's house is his castle and he has a right to defend it," the editor wrote. "As the particulars of the case are becoming known, sympathy is being aroused everywhere for the unfortunate man whose color alone denied him the right in the eyes of the mob to protect his home and family."

Governor Bradley returned to Kentucky that day, July 7, earlier than expected, from his vacation to Colorado, and when he walked into the statehouse the reporters barely recognized him because he had shaved off his fiery beard. Acting Governor Worthington immediately surrendered the reins of government, and Bradley was ready to get back to work. A growing stack of mail was waiting for him, and he was surprised to see that so much of the correspondence had to do with the Dinning case.

It was not just the newspaper editors pushing for pardon.

The state's preachers and religious leaders began calling for action from their pulpits. "Every man has a right to defend himself, no matter what color he is or in what country he lives," said the Reverend John P. McFerrin, pastor of the Methodist Episcopal church in south Louisville. "If Dinning had been a white man he would have been cleared on the evidence without question," said Adolph Moses, rabbi of Temple Adas Israel. "If he had done nothing which made him liable to the law he had done nothing that justified a mob attacking him in his own house."

Doctors called for action, too. "I am a rip-roaring, rearing, democrat, and ex Rebel," wrote Dr. Ben P. Earle, a well-respected doctor from Charleston, Kentucky. "And I know nothing of either Dinning or Conn, but it is sufficient to know that he was defending his home, be it ever so humble. It was his. His castle. A place too sacred for any outside interference."

And lawyers: "This is the worst outrage on law, justice, decency, and manhood that ever our poor old state has had to suffer," wrote Lexington attorney Suydam Scott. "Kentucky is indeed far on the road to perdition if any of her citizens, of any color, is to be imprisoned and disgraced for defence of his house against any man or mob."

And bankers: "There is not a Kentuckian anywhere who, under similar circumstances, would not have done as he did," wrote William Myall of the Citizens Bank in Paris, Kentucky.

Carriage builders: "I feel that the verdict in sentencing Geo. Dinning to the penitentiary is an outrage and I therefore ask that you will promptly pardon him," wrote B. P. Grigsly, president of Fulton, Conway & Co. in Louisville.

Dealers in fancy groceries and fruits: "He did nothing more than any of us would do under the same circumstances and should be commended for his fidelity to his home and family instead of being punished," wrote wholesaler A. J. Ross.

Dealers in dry goods, notions, and shoes: "In the name of all that is sacred an holy," wrote E. H. Cox of Kaye, Carter & Cox, "pardon the negro Dinning!"

Notary publics: "An impartial jury could not be obtained from among a people so prejudiced that a battalion of soldiers backed up by a battery of cannons had to be placed around the jail to protect the prisoner," wrote Thomas Marion of Ninth Street in Louisville. "Praying in this case not for 'mercy,' but justice, pure and simple."

The mayor of Louisville: "I am convinced that said Dinning was justified in pursuing the course he did," wrote Mayor George Todd. "I know that you will agree with me in the opinion that the Afro-American race has as much right under the law to save the honor of their families, even at the risk of shedding blood, as any other race which esteems virtue—the first requisite to a happy home life."

One entire newspaper: "We have carefully investigated the Dinning case and hope with thousands of other people of the state that you will promptly pardon him," wrote the staff of the *Louisville Commercial*.

Letters and telegrams also came from the expected quarters, of course—like the 350 members of the S. S. Frye Republican League Club of Danville, the Black teachers of Logan County, and the Central District Association of Baptists in Kentucky, embracing a membership of eleven thousand: "We decided that the verdict is unrighteous and degrading to the Commonwealth of Kentucky," wrote the Reverend C. P. Bates, president, "and in view of the fact that he was defending his own home, life and family and guilty of no crime, we earnestly petition for his immediate pardon, and will lay a formal application for the same before the Governor."

Pastor L. M. Hagood and ninety-five members of the Ninth Street Methodist Episcopal Church in Covington, whose petition did not mention the race of Dinning, nor of Jodie Conn. The entire Grand Lodge of Odd Fellows in Kentucky. A sizable chunk of the citizens of Versailles, Kentucky. The leaders and members of the A.M.E. Zion Church in South Carrollton, Muhlenberg County. A committee of ten men appointed at a mass meeting of Black citizens at the Alpha Baptist Church in Franklin, Simpson County.

"If a man cannot legally defend himself and family in his own house and home, where on earth can he do so?" the committee asked.

Hoteliers, college professors, housewives. Members of the State Board of Equalization. Members of the Afro-American League of Jefferson County. Tom Hall, an ex-Confederate and reporter for the Louisville *Evening Post*.

"I have served every court in the confines of Louisville, and have hundreds of times been appealed to, to sign pardon documents, and have always refused," Hall wrote. "The reason that I intercede for this negro is that his duty was to protect his home and life, and he did it."

The case had struck a nerve. A letter arrived carrying dozens of signatures and purporting to be from the "colored Citizens of Louisville." Another arrived from the tiny town of Stephensport, Kentucky, on the Ohio River, and it bore the signatures of the town's marshal, police judge, merchant, postmaster, druggist, ferryman, and railroad agent. Petitions arrived with hundreds of names attached. One came from Lexington bearing the name of the mayor, the city councilmen, and some 250 residents.

"Just think if George Dinning had been a white man," wrote J. W. Overstreet, who owned a general store in Little Hickman in Jessamine County.

"Is not this a case where you have it clearly in your power to rebuke the lawless element that is bringing the fair name of our state into contempt in the minds of civilized people?" wrote

Charles E. Craik, dean of Christ Church Cathedral in Louisville. "In granting pardon to this man you will be making some atonement for the wrongs he has already unjustly suffered, and I am convinced you will have...the calm judgement and most hearty approval of our very best people."

"I do not write to you because I am a sentimentalist or a crank," wrote lawyer John H. Early from Chattanooga, Tennessee, "but the law of self defense should be upheld."

The Louisville Board of Aldermen, who were Republicans and Democrats and ex-Confederate soldiers and ex-Union soldiers, asked Governor Bradley to "vindicate the right of the humblest citizen to defend his home from lawless men, even if they are high above him on the social scale."

Even the troops who had guarded Dinning during his trial believed he was innocent. "The soldier boys are in sympathy with Dinning and say he should not have been convicted," reported the *Courier-Journal* on July 7. "Dinning, they say, was not proven to be a bad character and so far as the evidence showed was never involved in any lawlessness."

Citizens far and wide were passing resolutions in favor of a pardon. "Resolved," one said, "that the colored citizens of Junction City, Kansas, extend to Governor Bradley of Kentucky their hearty approval of the manly, and perhaps unprecedented, act taken in prevention of the lynching of the colored hero, George Dinning, who so bravely defended his family against the outrageous 'White Caps,' who wantonly determined to drive him from the county and his home."

One letter stood out to Bradley, and he read it with great care. It came from Augustus E. Willson, who would later become governor of Kentucky. Willson was orphaned at a young age and lived for a time with his older brother, Forceythe, a poet, in Cambridge, Massachusetts. It was there he was exposed to men of letters who visited his brother: Emerson, Holmes, Lowell, and Longfellow. Willson graduated from Harvard and made his way back to the Louisville law firm of renowned attorney and future U.S. Supreme Court Justice John Marshall Harlan, who described Willson as "one of the brightest young fellows I ever met."

My dear Governor,—

I beg leave to join those who petition the Governor to pardon Dinning, the man who defended his own home. I make this request not only because of the honor that is due to the poorest man for defending his own home and family against mob violence, but because the position which this case occupies in the public mind is such that regardless of the merits of the case, it would be an injury to the character of the state not to pardon him. The public feeling is almost universal regardless of race lines or party lines; a strong wave of high humanity has swept over the country, beyond all State lines, and in the public mind, the question has passed beyond all personal or party consideration. The good name of the State is involved, and would be hurt if he were not pardoned, even if the case were in fact really less meritorious than it seems to the popular mind to be.

I do not wish, however, in this expression of the policy of the State to overlook or in any way lessen my expression of my deep-seated conviction of the great merits of the application for the pardon of Dinning. We should feel that a man able and free to take care of himself was an unspeakable craven if he did not, when a threatening mob with fire arms surrounded his home where his wife and children were sleeping at midnight, try to shoot to kill.

When a man thus called upon to defend his home, is poor, helpless and friendless, his act in defending his home under such circumstances raises him to the grade of a hero, and without any personal knowledge of any other fact in Dinning's life, this one fact, under the circumstances, is an act of high courage and heroism.

Every man who takes the law in his own hand and especially every man who is a member of a lawless band that goes with the double cowardice of those who enter upon lawlessness with the protection of night and of overwhelming numbers against one poor and helpless man, be the written and un-written law, takes his life in his hands, and if the victim in despair kills him, no one has any right to complain. It is what the man who entered upon that lawlessness in that double cowardly way had a legitimate right to expect and should not complain of if he meets his doom, so that the act of Dinning was heroic on his part and strict unfailing justice to Conn. I have made very few recommendations to Executive Clemency in my time during nearly thirty years of active business life under the circumstances, which have brought hundreds to me to join in such petitions. I believe not more than three or four in nearly thirty years, and never from any interest but that of justice and humanity, and I have never made an application of this kind without a stronger feeling of its justice.

I write this letter, of course, without any request from any-one. It is the impulse of humanity unsought and unexpected. I have read with the greatest interest the magnificent and nobly humane utterances of Col. Breckinridge on this subject. I have read with warm appreciation of the humanity of it the names of the signers of the petition that was forwarded from City Hall yesterday, the old Confederate soldiers, former slave holders, earnest, sturdy partisan Democrats, and some of

*known color prejudice, whose humanity and veneration for
the thought of home has risen nobly above every prejudice.*

*I write this letter personally and not for publication, al-
though I have no doubt it accords with the sentiments of
almost everybody. Of course I expect to be on record as one of
the justifications for the pardon, if you shall deem it your duty
to grant it, but I sincerely wish not to figure in any public way
and simply write this to uphold the Governor's hand, if the
formal application for pardon and the record which accom-
panies it when received, contain nothing which makes the
Executive Clemency contrary to your convictions of duty.*

Yours respectfully,
Augustus E. Willson

The *Courier-Journal* reported that petitions for pardon were
coming from everywhere, "and are more numerous than those
received in any case of recent date." The following day an even
more important letter came to Bradley, this one from Colonel E.
H. Gaither.

Governor—

*During my stay in Franklin, in command of the detail sent
there to protect George Dinning during his trial, I attempted
to acquaint myself with all the facts and circumstances connected with the case, and from my investigation I obtained
some information that was not produced in evidence. Before
the beginning of the trial I became convinced, and so wrote
Governor Worthington, that the parties engaged in this attempt to kuklux Dinning had abandoned the idea of taking
his life by force and expected to secure a conviction by the*

testimony, and that they intended to swear to whatever facts were necessary to secure a conviction. I have no question that they were informed that if they could establish the fact that at the time Dinning did the shooting he knew that they were about to do him no harm, but were leaving his premises, that he had no right to shoot, and that a killing under such circumstances would be murder, and to establish this fact the entire party swore to identically the same words that they said were spoke to Dinning, although they were scattered about the yard, and it had been some months since the conversation took place. The substance of this statement that was so exactly remembered by these people was that Dinning defied them to make him leave at that time, their leader stated that they were strong enough to do so. "And if you don't believe it, George, watch us as we go away." Each of these men swore that no shot was fired until after Dinning had shot Conn, and yet quite a number of prominent and excellent citizens, among them some of the County officials, told me that it was universally stated by these men the day after the killing that there would have been no trouble if some of their men had not taken "too much tea" and let a gun or guns go off accidentally. It was the statement of all of these witnesses that all of the shooting done by them was from one point and into the front and gable end of the house, while there was uncontroverted proof that there were bullet holes through the back of the house. I haven't the remotest doubt that at the time Dinning fired into the crowd he was absolutely sure that an attack had been made upon him, and that the life of himself and his family depended upon his ability to repel this attack. And I believe that the action of these men, their appearance there after midnight, armed and demanding his appearance in disguised voices, and the firing of a shot, whether accidental or purposely, gave Dinning reasonable grounds for such belief.

I do not believe it is possible that this negro could get a fair and impartial trial in Simpson or any adjoining County, nor do I believe that his conviction was warranted by evidence. While in Franklin, quite a number of prominent citizens expressed to me, under a pledge of secrecy, their full belief in the innocence of the man and his right to act as he did; but the fact that they felt constrained to pledge me to secrecy is the strongest evidence of the state of public feeling.

My investigation in this matter was absolutely without prejudice, and only a feeling that a gross injustice has been done this man induces me to make these statements.

I am, Sir, most respectfully,

Your Obedient Servant,
E. H. Gaither

Kentucky, like a lot of the South, had entered a brief chapter of progressive politics, as editors at urban newspapers pushed for reforms and politicians realized the negative economic impact of racial violence. This wasn't the case in some of the state's isolated rural sections, where politics were personal.

The local Simpson County newspaper objected to Dinning's pardon, of course, but the argument was flat. *We can take care of ourselves,* it seemed to say, *and your cities are troubled.* The *Franklin Favorite* editorialized:

THE FAVORITE had labored under the delusion that the discussion of the Dinning case would cease with his sentence. It was an instance where the wish may have been father to the thought, for it has been the conviction of this paper since the tragedy occurred that the case was receiving undue prominence, and was on the lips of too many people distant from the scene of its enactment, who knew nothing of the matter they so flippantly discussed; and it has endeavored for the first to wring a tale of truth from this babel of tongues. We shall have to surrender the undertaking. But we would have a parting word with the thoughtless long-distance critics who have turned their batteries of denunciation, ignorance and prejudice against the court that tried and convicted Dinning. The negro's pardon is asked for by W. C. P. Breckinridge, who undertakes to discuss the case with as little knowledge of it as any one could well have. The people of Lexington have petitioned the Governor for his pardon, as have the officials of Louisville. All the Louisville newspapers ask it, except the *Dispatch*, and so the mad carnival of idiocy continues and the fool-killer nowhere appeareth upon the scene.

Every intelligent and unprejudiced man in Simpson county knows that the negro was tried by a jury of honorable and substantial citizens and intelligent and unprejudiced men. He was ably defended and afforded every protection by the court. The jury found him guilty of manslaughter and his sentence was seven years in the penitentiary. Yet we find men hundreds of miles away who question the justice of that verdict. The *Courier-Journal* says it was a travesty on justice. Breckinridge ditto. The Louisville *Times* says it was a verdict of ignorance and prejudice. We should like to be accorded the liberty—without having the militia called out to discipline us—to inquire where'n thunder they get their information; by what right they set their mouths to going, and by what peculiar process they are enabled to have a clearer conception of the affair than those who knew all its surroundings and heard the evidence; under what particular code of ethics or of law they justify the killing of a man who had assured his slayer that he did not desire to injure him and was leaving him as fast as he could go; what Breckinridge and the *Courier-Journal* and the *Times* expect to gain by this cheap bid for colored votes; and we should be particularly pleased with a tender of information that would explain the presumption of virtue, the arrogant assumption of superlative goodness and pre-eminent moral qualification with which Louisville and Lexington have essayed to put Simpson county morals and manhood on the rack of condemnation. If we mistake not, the pious Sam Jones has said that Lexington was not more than six inches from hell, and if that be true, we can well imagine that the temperature in Louisville is too near the top of the scale to admit of that burg advertising itself as a summer resort.

When we have descended in the moral scale to the low level that obtains in those ungodly towns, may the Lord protect us, or the devil take us. We leave Dinning with his God and his Bradley. If the weaker of these judges errs, we may depend upon the other. And with this THE FAVORITE hopes to dismiss the Dinning case forever.

Bradley was still reticent with reporters. Back in Franklin, the court stenographer was hurrying as fast as he could to produce a transcript of the proceedings. Bradley wanted to read it. He'd been gone during the trial, so he wanted to consider the evidence for himself, rather than take anyone's word for it. Asked on July 8 if he would grant the pardon, he said he could not tell. Asked if he was favorably impressed with the petitions for the pardon, he said that he had really formed no impression about it, except from the rumors that he had read and heard. He said he would have to have the evidence and some real reasons before he would undo the work of any court of law, or of any jury.

A Western Union telegram reached Bradley that evening. Short and terse, it came from one of the best lawyers in the Commonwealth, a former Confederate who had marched with Morgan's men, who had suffered in Camp Douglas and Camp Chase, who had led a raid from Canada into Vermont and robbed three banks of more than $200,000 in the northernmost action of the Civil War, and who after the war had raised money for blind children and an orphanage for African American children.

The telegram said simply:

DINNING VIOLATED NEITHER HUMAN NOR DIVINE LAW.
YOU WILL HONOR KENTUCKY AND YOURSELF BY
IMMEDIATE PARDON. OPEN THE PRISON DOORS
BEFORE THE SUN GOES DOWN.
　　　　　　　　　　　　　—BENNETT H. YOUNG

Chapter 13

"I WILL NEVER COME BACK TO KENTUCKY"

George Dinning looked out the train window as the sun set on Saturday, July 17, 1897, and big, beautiful, oblivious Kentucky blurred by. To think this was once the First West, the frontier, the first state west of the Appalachian Mountains, the land of tomorrow, the edge of the rest, the cradle of the corps of discovery. "What a buzzel is amongst people about Kentucke?" asked a minister in 1775. "To hear people speak of it one would think that it was a new found paradise." One early pioneer said the trees were fifteen feet in diameter and grew so close together that a man could barely squeeze through. Some said the elk wore horns ten feet wide, tip to tip. This was the hunting ground of Daniel Boone and Benjamin Cutbirth. Lewis and Clark met here, hired Kentuckians for their squad, before droves of settlers began trudging through the Cumberland Gap in search of the promised land.

That morning's surprise was fresh in Dinning's mind. He had been sitting in his cell inside the Eddyville penitentiary, the limestone Castle on the Cumberland, when Warden Happy arrived and told him he'd been pardoned by Governor Bradley. Dinning had felt sure it would happen, but he had never expected it to be so soon. He'd been in prison just two weeks.

Bradley had wired Warden Happy to warn him to be cautious about releasing Dinning publicly. He still feared the mob. If word got back to Logan or Simpson County in time, it wouldn't be out of the realm of possibility for the outlaws to intercept and board the train and go car by car searching for Dinning. Bradley wasn't going to make his decision public until the following day.

Warden Happy gave Dinning five dollars, a new suit of clothes, and a train ticket to Louisville, and at three-thirty that afternoon, a group of officers escorted him to the depot and watched him board. He stowed his small grip and found a seat inside. He'd been locked in the penitentiary for thirteen uneventful days and was happy to be out. And he was happy to be leaving southwestern Kentucky.

The train departed the station at 4:11 p.m., leaving the Eddyville prison behind.

One day earlier, on July 16, Governor W. O. Bradley received a letter by express mail from John B. Grider, Dinning's lawyer. Grider wrote that he had sent the trial transcript by express as well, in a great hurry to get it to the governor. "We think the testimony of the prosecuting witnesses should be taken with many grains of allowance," Grider wrote. "They were all members of the mob which went to Dinning's house, or men directly under their influence. These 25 men composing the mob are related in some way, either by blood or association, to all the witnesses against Dinning." Grider wanted Bradley to pay particular attention to the fact that Dinning had always claimed that the first shots fired were those that came through the door on the north side of his house. "We prove conclusively that there were four bullet holes through this door that were not there the evening before the difficulty, but were there the next morning, and certainly Dinning had no opportunity to shoot them in there."

He pointed out that none of the night raiders has ever been indicted, though they admitted they were kukluxing. Grider wrote that he believed the mobsters had been promised immunity in exchange for agreeing to testify.

He asked the governor to pay special attention to the testimony of L. G. Berry, even though the judge had excluded it. Berry testified that one of the men had told him that none of it would have happened had one of their party not accidentally fired at the house.

"The gun was not fired accidentally, but intentionally, and this proof would have accounted for the bullet holes in the north door," Grider wrote.

What upset Grider badly was that the prosecutors had attacked the character of old Ben Conn, but none of the twenty-five men took the stand to contradict what Conn said. They attacked the character of Claud Hackney, but Claud's father, Gib Hackney, presented the same facts and was unimpeached. They attacked the character of George Dinning, who had never in his life been in trouble with the law or anything but kind to his neighbors.

"This gang, in order to exculpate themselves, could tear down the character of any man in their neighborhood if necessary for their purposes," Grider wrote.

He also pointed out that Lum Babb, who had testified that Dinning told him he fired as the mob was leaving, was kin to one of the members of the mob. Everyone in that section, it seemed, was related in some way.

"The mob had three or four men on the ground all the time during the trial, who talked to all our witnesses as fast as they were learned, and in several instances got them to change or modify their testimony before they came on the stand," Grider wrote. "You will observe that only 10 or 12 of the mob testified, and I believe they did not put the others on the stand because they feared that we would find out who burned the house and probably something about the gun accidentally fired."

Perhaps the letter went out before evening, but another odd thing happened that very night, of which Grider made no mention. His cocounsel, Virgil Hagerman, a promising twenty-four-year-old attorney, died unexpectedly, just ten days after the biggest trial of his life had ended. Born and raised in Bowling Green, Hagerman was an 1896 graduate of Cumberland University in Lebanon, Tennessee, where he'd been a member of Beta Theta Pi and the Kentucky Klub, motto: "Our greatest enemy is whisky, and our highest ambition is to surround the enemy." The official cause of Hagerman's death was typhoid fever, a bacterial infection that wrecks the organs. The symptoms of typhoid fever—diarrhea, rash, dry cough— are similar to those of poisoning. The death shocked those who knew him.

The clean-shaven governor sat at his desk, pulled out a few sheets of official stationery, and jotted "July 17, 1897," at the top of the first. Then he penned a statement that would set him apart from the Kentucky governors who came before him, and many who would follow. It would earn him a place of respect among many citizens, Black and white, and lead historians to puzzle over the building blocks of a short period of progressivism among Southern governors at the end of the nineteenth century. What he wrote would be emblazoned on a plaque that would hang in the governor's mansion. It would be the reason offered when a Black leader later bent to kiss Bradley's hand.

The people in many sections of the state seem to feel a deep interest in this case and petitions and letters from many localities have been sent, asking Dinning's pardon. The decision has been delayed in order to obtain a copy of the evidence, and a statement from some of the persons present as to what was done and proven in the trial.

Having inspected the evidence and other papers connected with the application, a most remarkable state of case is disclosed.

In January last, between 10 and 11 o'clock at night, a band of twenty-five men, more or less armed, the leader of whom was disguised with a handkerchief over his face, went, as they say, on a "peaceable mission" to the humble home of Dinning and notified him to leave the country in ten days, it having been charged, as they said, that he was guilty of stealing. He denied the charge and stated that he could prove by his neighbors that it was false. This did not appease or satisfy the mob, and he was again peremptorily ordered to leave in ten days and to get as far as fifty miles. The evidence up to this point is without contradiction. The members of the band say they assured him that they came with no intention to do him harm, and started away, when he, without any provocation, fired from a window upstairs and killed one of their number: that their captain then ordered them to "squat and fire in the direction from which the shot came," which they did, and that they then retired with their dying comrade, who lived only a few minutes.

On the other hand, Dinning says, in which he is corroborated by one of his children, that after the notification to leave, shots were fired by the mob into the lower story of the house, one of which struck him in the arm; that he then rushed up the stairway and threw open the window of the second story, at which time he received another glancing shot in the forehead, and fired into the crowd.

The testimony shows that an examination of Dinning

disclosed the two wounds. Witnesses living in the neighborhood say that they first heard three shots, which sounded as if they came from pistols or rifles, then a shot, apparently from a shotgun, and then a fusillade.

It also appears that an examination the next morning disclosed the fact that as many as three shots had been fired through the door below.

On the day following the shooting, after Dinning learned that he had killed one of his assailants, he went to the county seat and surrendered to the officers of the law; an examination was waived on account of the prevailing excitement, and he was sent to Bowling Green, and afterward to Louisville for safe-keeping. From the latter place, accompanied by two companies of the State Guard, he was taken back to Simpson county, the scene of the killing, tried and sentenced to confinement in the penitentiary for seven years, and taken to the Eddyville penitentiary.

In a day or two after the killing Dinning's house was burned by incendiaries. When it is known that no indictment was ever found against any member of the band, or against any one who burned the house, and that the grand jury indicted Dinning mainly upon the evidence of these self-confessed outlaws, the conviction is easily accounted for. Indeed, his conviction was procured almost entirely on the evidence of his assailants, and yet they swear that when he asked who they were they answered through their disguised leader, and in a disguised voice, that they were his friends.

I have no doubt that the first shots were fired by the mob. Because, first, according to their statements, no shots appear to have been fired by them into any part of the house except the window above. The holes in the door downstairs are a flat contradiction of their evidence. They were not fired through *the door after the shot from the window was fired, hence they must have been fired before that time.*

Second. It is clearly shown that the moon was shining so that men could be almost recognized, and that all of the twenty-five men, except four who remained in the road, were very near the house. It is not reasonable to suppose that Dinning with a shotgun, loaded small shot, would have fired upon twenty-five armed men, except in the case of extreme necessity, and when he had been previously assaulted.

Third. Although the defendant was an humble negro, without friends capable of giving him material assistance, and although he had killed a member of a prominent and influential family, he voluntarily surrendered the next day.

Surrounded by his wife and six small children, this poor and friendless man was ordered, without warrant of law, to leave his little home, after which his house was fired into and he wounded. He defended himself as every dictate of reason and humanity demanded and justified. In protecting himself he did no more than any other man would or should have done under the circumstances, and instead of being forced to wear a convict garb, he is entitled, not only to acquittal, but to the admiration of every citizen who loves good government and desires the perpetuation of free institutions.

Too long have mobs disgraced the fair name of Kentucky, and while I am Governor of the Commonwealth, no man, however obscure and friendless, shall be punished for killing a member of a mob who comes to take his life or drive him from his home.

Dinning stepped off the train in Louisville at 10:55 p.m., holding a grip containing his three-piece suit. He didn't know where he would go or what he would do. The streets were dark, and he wondered about his wife and children, but he was free, finally, after six months of confinement in Bowling Green, Louisville, and Eddyville. And he was back at Louisville, a city with two hundred churches, fifty public school buildings, three gorgeous public parks, and a streetcar system connecting them all for a nickel a ride. What's more, it was a city with forty-four thousand Black citizens, the largest cluster of African Americans in the state, where Black men were accredited teachers and physicians, where Black men owned boot shops and barbershops and lived in stately two-story Victorians on broad boulevards. He was only 130 miles from Coffee Bottom, but it felt like a different universe.

Louisville was an old city, born in war, from the 1778 invasion by the British settlements north of the Ohio River. Louisville was the supply base for General George Rogers Clark's army, and though he had no intention of founding a town, the place was platted and named Louisville and the first lots were sold in 1779. The city's development was tied directly to the Ohio—and the Falls in particular. A series of rapids that descended some twenty-six feet over two miles, the Falls was the only obstruction on the nine-hundred-mile river between Pittsburgh and New Orleans. The geography represented a dichotomy. Kentucky had been a slave state, but Louisville was always a two-sided coin spinning on a tabletop. And as such, the argument would later be made that Louisville, positioned as it was like a kind of purgatory between liberty and subjugation, was the birthplace of the blues. Or *a* birthplace of the blues, because the blues didn't come from any one particular place. But singing commonly on streetcars around town when Dinning showed up was Ophelia Simpson, a moaner and shouter who some early-music collectors believe was the first true blues singer. And born in Louisville just a few days after George Dinning stepped off that train was Sylvester Weaver, who twenty-six years later would make the very first recording of a country blues song.

This was a town of enterprise, for Blacks and whites alike, where men didn't just grow things, they made things. American Standard was born here, as were the Kentucky Wagon Manufacturing Company, the Louisville Textile Mill, and the Mengel Box Company. None were divisions of some far-off corporation, but all came up from the spirit and sweat of Louisville residents. The houses here were larger and statelier than any Dinning had seen, built in architectural styles foreign to him, like Gothic and Italianate and Richardsonian Romanesque and Queen Anne. And the grand churches were worthy of postcards.

A free man with five dollars in his pocket could paint this fascinating town red. He could buy custom cabinets from Gustave Bittner, or delicious chocolates from Frank J. Menne, or brick ice cream from George W. Cuscaden, or a city directory from Charles K. Caron, or a Falls City bicycle from Prince Wells on Third near Walnut. Or he could mosey into one of the city's smoky pool halls or stroll through the stench of open sewers and rancid meat to a brothel at the Chute or on Green Street, or pop into any number of bawdy saloons where men with pistols on their hips grated on one another. The city police were well on their way to arresting 3,759 people on charges of drunk and disorderly conduct that year, so maybe *Ruined By Drink*, the new drama showing at Music Hall in the West End, was a safer bet. If he wanted, a man could also pick up a copy of that day's *Courier-Journal* and flip over to the front page of the second section and read the following account of yesterday's news, just a bit behind:

Copies of about three-fourths of the evidence in the Dinning case reached the governor to-day at last, and the

Executive began at once a consideration of the case, which he says will be thoroughly and completely gone over. He has already let drop expressions that indicate he is impressed in Dinning's favor, and those about the Executive office are convinced he is going to pardon the man.

A reporter from the *Courier-Journal* caught up to Dinning not long after he'd come off the train and asked him if he'd be open to a short interview. Dinning was happy to talk.

"I am at last a free man," he said. "I have had several narrow escapes from being lynched and am glad to get in Louisville."

The reporter asked him when he got the news about his pardon.

"I was sitting in my cell this morning when Warden Happy came to me and said that I had been pardoned by Gov. Bradley," Dinning said. "I knew all the time that this would be done, but I was not expecting it to be quite so soon. They told me to make preparations to go to Louisville. Warden Happy at first said he would accompany me to the city, but he changed his mind and said there would be no danger for me to make the trip alone. I left the prison at 3:30 o'clock this afternoon. Before I left they gave me $5, a new suit of clothes and a ticket to Louisville. I was taken to the depot by several officers. The people at stations along the road did not know that I was on the train, and, of course, there was not trouble."

The reporter asked what he expected to do now.

"I am going to stay here until Wednesday," Dinning said. "I am then going to Indianapolis, where I expect to live all the rest of my days. At any rate, I will never come back to Kentucky. I will wait here to see that my wife and children are removed to a place where they will be safe."

He was right to be worried about their safety.

"I am afraid my enemies will take out their vengeance on

them," Dinning said. "Just as soon as I can make money enough I will remove them to Indianapolis."

He wasn't sure where he was going to stay in Louisville, but five dollars was plenty to cover room and board for a few days.

"I will find a cheap lodging house somewhere," he said.

The reporter observed that Dinning possessed "unusual intelligence," and that he said he'd never again feel safe in Kentucky.

But he had to stick around, at least until he got his bearings and was able to find his wife and children.

If the newspapers are to be believed, the white people of Simpson County, generally, felt indignant over the pardoning of George Dinning, according to various reports. They said it made other Negroes insolent. They warned there would be more trouble.

Outside Simpson County, Bradley was roundly praised. The same newspapers that had urged him to action took time to thank him for the pardon.

"WELL DONE, GOVERNOR BRADLEY," said a headline in the *Hartford Courant* in Connecticut.

"There is a refreshing directness in his statement of reasons why he granted a pardon to George Dinning," wrote the editor of the *Boston Globe*. "The straight-out talk will not please all Kentuckians, but there is no doubt that Gov. Bradley speaks his mind fully and frankly. Nor is there the slightest reason to suppose that he does not mean precisely what he says when he declares: 'While I am governor of this commonwealth, no man, however obscure and friendless, shall be punished for killing a member of a mob who elect to take his life or drive him from his home.'"

"An act of Gov. Bradley's which deserved commendation is his pardoning of the negro Geo. Dinning, who was sentenced to the penitentiary for a long term," wrote the editor of the *Ohio County News* in Hartford, Kentucky. "It will be remembered the neighbors suspected Dinning of being a bad character and warned him to leave the community where he owned property. He was never proven guilty of any offense, but nevertheless a mob attacked his home and the negro repulsed them. During the fusillade, Jodie Conn, a young white man and member of the mob, was killed by a bullet from Dinning's gun. The negro had a perfect right to protect his home against the depredations and unwarranted attack of a lawless mob, and Gov. Bradley's pardon in this instance will be greeted with applause."

"Every citizen who is not hopelessly blinded by race prejudice, every Southern man who retains a spark of the old American spirit, will acknowledge the justice of Gov Bradley's point of view," wrote the editor of the *Brooklyn Times* in New York. "The man who makes so brave a fight against overwhelming odds as Dinning made for his family and his home ranks as a hero in the estimation of every manly man, no matter what the color of his skin may be."

As Dinning waited to reunite with his family, and to finally find a new place to live, he accepted an invitation to speak at the Fifth Street Baptist Church in Louisville. Someone told him he was the first Black man ever pardoned by a Southern governor for killing a white man, and that the people wanted to hear his story.

The following night, he waited onstage as the Reverend John H. Frank made introductory remarks, reminding the crowd that they weren't gathered to criticize the authorities, but to allow the Colored people of the city to signify their disapproval of mob law.

When it was his turn, Dinning stood behind a podium at the

church and told of the entire ordeal. He was neatly attired and spoke clearly and distinctly about the night of the raid, never wavering from the story he had told on the witness stand. The church was packed. A reporter noted that about a dozen white people showed up to listen.

"How many of those who were in the mob were allowed to testify?" asked a member of the audience.

"Well, boss," Dinning said, "I don't know exactly, but I think all of them testified except the man that I killed."

He told the crowd that some of the jurors approached his lawyer after the trial and said they believed that Dinning was innocent but would not acquit him because they were afraid. Dinning told them all that he owned 125 acres of fertile farmland in Simpson County, and it was now for sale. He mentioned that he was searching for a new home, and that he was considering living in Indianapolis.

The audience was stunned when a man mentioned that Dinning was considering filing a lawsuit against the mob for damages. The newspaper coverage of the event doesn't give the man's name, but it was most likely Bennett H. Young. Young was close friends with the Reverend John H. Frank, the activist preacher who bought Dinning his suit for trial and invited Dinning to speak. Reverend Frank and Colonel Young had served for years together as president and vice president of the Colored Orphans' Home Society, and Frank found no shame in asking his white friends for help. "I think white people owe us something more than a word of commendation," he once said.

Before the service was over, Frank called for the collection of an offering for George Dinning, and ushers passed baskets down every pew as men reached for their wallets and women dipped into their purses. When it was tallied, they had collected $37.50 (the equivalent of $1,162 today). The man who had lost his home and nearly lost his life had found a community in Louisville. And no one was surprised by that. He had been convicted on color, not crime, and his people therefore saw the courts as instruments of oppression, and those convicted they saw as martyrs.

Dinning went on a well-attended speaking tour after that, visiting churches and clubs in and around the River City, telling his story. They were packed. In a single speech, he addressed more people than he had ever met in his life.

At a meeting at Odd Fellows' Hall at the corner of Thirteenth and Walnut Streets, he stood and spoke before an audience of three hundred. That such a meeting took place is in and of itself remarkable, since any act by Black citizens that threatened the status quo was often viewed as militant by whites. Occasionally, Dinning would conclude a story by saying, "Well, I believe that is about all I know," and one of the auditors would walk across the stage and whisper something in his ear. Dinning would then say, "I forgot about that, but will tell it now," and he'd again commence to lecturing. At the end of his talk at the Odd Fellows' Hall, which took all of two hours, he told the crowd that if he had not made all his points clear, he would be willing to answer any other questions. A stream of questions poured in, and he spent another solid hour answering them. The Odd Fellows took up a collection for him as well. He told them he was going to use it to invest in a home in Jeffersonville, Indiana, just across the Ohio River, and that the money would help his family along until he could get a regular paying job. He had picked out a house already and was eager to make a down payment and move in.

Jeffersonville was an interesting town in which to settle, for it had been the first and largest Underground Railroad route for escaped refugees crossing the Ohio River into Indiana. Once a slave had crossed the Ohio, he was out of the South—not completely safe, but well on his way to freedom. Jeff, as they called it, was a gateway. Free Black men from Louisville would row runaway slaves across the river and pass them off to friends or abolitionists on the Indiana banks. This was where George Dinning would finally feel secure.

A reporter for the *Courier-Journal* noted Dinning's growing fame.

"Dinning is a lion among the colored people, both in this city and in Jeffersonville," the reporter wrote. "They follow him around as if he were a superior being, and greedily devour his slightest utterances. In fact, Dinning is living in clover. He has more money than he ever had in his life and is decidedly a 'gentleman of leisure.'"

That story appeared in Louisville's paper of record on August 6.

Two days later, a similar story ran on the front page of the *Russellville Ledger*, the paper covering the seat of Logan County, home to the Conn family.

"MOVED TO JEFF," read the headline.

George Dinning, the brutal murderer of poor Jodie Conn in Simpson County, has now located in Jeffersonville. He has moved his wife and family to that city and will try to get work on one of the farms in the suburbs of the city. It is not likely that he will ever come to Kentucky again. He has gotten a cottage on Prison Hill, and all ready his story is known to all the people. The negroes have made friends with him, but the whites look upon him with suspicion. He also gives lectures in Louisville by telling the history of his wrongs and makes some money this way.

In one short news article, the paper managed to besmirch George Dinning, portray Jodie Conn as a victim, suggest that

Dinning was profiting off "his wrongs," and offer readers, to include Conn's friends and family, information about where the "brutal murderer" George Dinning, recently pardoned, had finally found another home for his family. The article seemed to be encouraging violence, and even though Dinning was out of Simpson County, he was not out of danger.

Chapter 14

INDIANA

In those first few weeks in Jeffersonville, Dinning sometimes sat beside the front window of his little house at 706 Broadway, watching the road outside. He had a lot of lives to protect. At just forty-two years old, he had ten children living at home, ranging from nine months to seventeen years. Two more grown children lived elsewhere. His wife, Mollie, and his mother, Mary, ran the house.

On August 26, shortly after he'd moved in, a reporter from the Jeffersonville *National Democrat* appeared on his porch and knocked on the front door. Dinning rose and let the white man inside.

The reporter noted immediately that Dinning was smart, clean, and good-looking, as if that was a surprise. He also noticed that Dinning didn't appear overly concerned about someone attacking him in Jeffersonville. The fact that the reporter mentioned it shows the danger Dinning was in.

He had been making "a good living lecturing to his race, telling of his experience," the reporter noted. And he was willing to talk. He told the reporter things about his experience that night that had never been printed before, things that hadn't surfaced in court.

Dinning said he bought his farm at a tax sale for $150, that he was born and raised in those parts, and that he had always enjoyed a good reputation. In fact, he told the reporter that he spent the day before the attack working alongside the same men who made up the mob, and they treated him in the friendliest terms, as they always had. He went to sleep that night not knowing anything was amiss.

After the shooting, when he turned himself in and was confined in the cold stone Simpson County jailhouse, with narrow vertical slits for windows and a hole in the floor to piss in, he overheard Sheriff Clark begging the mob outside to hold off until the next day, when Dinning would be given a preliminary hearing. Then they could have him. When the Whitecappers rode off, satisfied, the sheriff spirited Dinning away to Bowling Green in a carriage.

One other thing, Dinning said. After he squeezed the trigger that night, after the white men retreated, after Dinning fled the house, he was close enough—and the night was quiet enough—that he could hear the men talking. He heard them angrily laying plans to burn the house over the heads of his wife and children. It was a pregnant moment of terror, for he wasn't sure what he could do to defend his family if the mob set to carrying those plans out. He lay there in the field, his chest rising and falling, flumes of his breath rising in the moonlight. Then he heard them retreating, their bootfalls growing distant on the frozen ground.

"He says he is afraid to go back to Simpson county but intends holding on to his farm as it would bring nothing at a forced sale," the reporter noted. "It is possible that at some future time, when the trouble quiets down, a damage suit will be filed against the individual members of the mob for burning the house."

Chapter 15

"MASS OF BLOOD AND BONES"

His assailants found him in the opaque darkness of the city's West End, near the stock pens on Thirteenth Street, on the cool night of Monday, September 20, 1897. They found him just six weeks after the newspaper in Logan County broadcast his routine and new address and hinted that he was getting rich from the death of one of their favorite sons. The stench from the city's open sewers and the nearby livestock corrals hung thick as the ceaseless thumps and moans and boot scuffs rose into the air—as punches and kicks landed on the face and head and ribs of a free man. It is hard to know whether George Dinning tried to defend himself, or whether they caught him unaware, then shattered his skull, then gouged out his right eye. What is known is that an ambulance was called to the No. 18 engine house at Thirteenth and Maple Streets, near a mammoth pork-packing plant, to take to the hospital an unconscious Colored man who had been seriously wounded in an attack and was bleeding profusely from trauma to his head, clinging to life. When the man was examined, it was found that his right eye had been knocked out, and that his skull had been cracked open, possibly by a brick or stone. The newspapers would report in the following days that the man's head had been "battered into a mass of blood and bones."

The Louisville City Hospital logged him into the patient admissions book under the name George Denning and noted that he was "colored," age forty-two, male, a laborer, a native of Kentucky, and a "non-resident," for he had recently established his home across the river on Jeffersonville's Prison Hill. He was admitted with "Contused Wound of Eyeball" and was wheeled over polished floors to one of many metal-framed beds in a long row.

The rare condition for which he was treated would come to be called traumatic globe luxation, or traumatic avulsion of the globe, in modern medical parlance, but doctors of the day often referred to it as exophthalmos, and two of them, George M. Gould and Walter L. Pyle, had written a section on the condition in a book called *Anomalies and Curiosities of Medicine*, which was published the year before, 1896. In the book they describe cases in which the eye was jolted out of its socket but the eye muscles and optic nerve remained intact. In those cases, the eye was successfully replaced, the injury fully healed, and normal sight restored. Patients weren't so fortunate in cases in which the optic nerve was severed and the eye muscles detached. Dinning's medical records might have indicated the severity of his injury, but they have been lost. What is known is that the outlook was not good.

Because of the misspelling of his last name, the reporters didn't catch wind of the assault for three days. When they finally did, the news spread across the country, and stories of the attack ran in newspapers in Pittsburgh, Buffalo, Brooklyn, St. Louis, and beyond. Each reported that Dinning said he could describe his assailants. Some warned that he would die if inflammation set in. Several noted that Dinning had recently announced plans

The stretch of abandoned road in Louisville where George Dinning was attacked in 1897. (*Courtesy of the author*)

to sue the mob and speculated that there might be a connection between the lawsuit and the assault. The *New York Sun*, in fact, had published a story just a few weeks before about the possibility of Dinning's bringing suit, referring to him as "the first negro pardoned in the South for killing a member of the mob that attempted to lynch him." The newspaper suggested there was precedent for instituting civil action against a mob, and pointed to the case of Ben Holton v. the Duncans, filed in 1882.

American Lawyer, a publication dealing with legal news, wrote about the Dinning case as well, offering more details on the precedent-setting suit. The Duncans were wealthy distillers who had accused Ben Holton of petty theft and tried to lynch him three times. He eventually escaped to another state and sued the Duncans for damages. The Duncans, on the advice of their attorneys, settled the case by paying Holton $7,500.

"Dinning's action will be followed by other negroes whom mobs attempt to lynch," read the article in *American Lawyer.* "Eminent Southern lawyers are of the opinion that in the prosecution of these suits lies the solution of the mob problem in the South. Dinning is backed by some of the most influential men in Kentucky. He will move to Indiana and reside there for one year, in order to become a citizen of Indiana, thus giving jurisdiction to the United States Court."

Those influential men included Colonel Bennett H. Young, the rip-roaring lawyer in the prime of his practice. Young, in fact, was already at work preparing the lawsuit. He'd been studying the case for months through the Louisville newspapers, reading and rereading the articles, and insatiable was his desire for justice. Especially now that his client was clinging to life. Young wanted a fight. He knew where to attack, and that was in the court of law.

Since the Civil War, African Americans in the South had successfully litigated a range of cases in federal courts—cases dealing with inheritance, work, custody, money, and property. Historian Melissa Milewski found that the majority of Black litigants won their suits against whites in the highest courts of eight Southern states during this period and into the twentieth century. It may seem as though the scales of justice in federal court leaned toward correcting the imbalance in criminal courts, but part of Black litigants' success could be ascribed to the fact that white juries and judges didn't always see civil cases brought by Black plaintiffs as dangerous or as having the potential to upset the social structure. In fact, suits over personal injury or fraud in which Black men and women testified about being beaten or driven off their land strengthened whites' ideas about Blacks' ignorance and dependence on them. And so long as the courts offered the veneer of impartiality, and Black plaintiffs could access the civil courts to seek justice, they might not revolt or boycott or march or protest other areas of discrimination. Nonetheless, limited as it was, the courts' focus on legal precedent provided a level of access and equality that Black citizens did not enjoy in other white Southern institutions. Blacks could sue whites, and they did with regularity, and sometimes they won.

The history of such cases extended all the way back to the days of enslavement, when slaves whose masters had left wills emancipating them occasionally appealed to Southern courts to win their own freedom. And in 1864, the U.S. Congress passed a law that permitted Black citizens to testify in federal courts to the same degree as whites. In the next decade, African Americans celebrated their new legal rights. A *New York Times* reporter who visited Louisiana to investigate an uptick in racial discrimination lawsuits observed in a how-dare-they tone: "There is no class of people here that are fonder of the pleasures of court proceedings, and of becoming parties to controversies in them, than the newly-enfranchised citizens. For every trivial matter wherein they believe their rights assailed or threatened, a rush is made to some court or other for redress. They think it is a glorious privilege to make an appearance in a law-suit, and will spend the last cent they can get to obtain what they consider and believe to be 'justice.'"

The nature of the cases brought by Black litigants changed over time, morphing from cases over wills and estates to cases against whites or white-owned companies for personal injury. According to Milewski, the number of personal injury cases brought by African Americans against whites skyrocketed during the two decades after Reconstruction, 1877 to 1897. Even so, Black residents had trouble getting legal representation. Lawyers weren't interested in taking on civil cases that didn't offer the possibility of big payouts, and it was often hard for Black litigants to pay lawyers' fees. Another deterrent was the constant threat of violence against white lawyers who would dare to represent Black citizens suing whites.

Bennett Young wasn't worried about violence, but if George Dinning was dead, there would be no lawsuit. Young was a praying man, and while there is no record of this, it's safe to say that he prayed for George Dinning.

The details of the police investigation, if one was launched, are unknown. No man was ever brought to trial for the assault that left George Dinning with one good eye and a cracked skull. The newspapers speculated that Governor Bradley would announce a reward for information leading to the arrest of the men who had attacked Dinning, but no reward was publicly announced. Just thirty-five police officers manned the Louisville force in 1897, fighting crime and keeping the peace in a city spread out over roughly twenty-one square miles, with its spires and smokestacks and pool halls, and a population exceeding 230,000. The officers were underpaid, and some months they went unpaid, because the city's budget was such a mess that the mayor couldn't afford the gas bill for street lighting.

Staffing issues were just one item on a long list of concerns plaguing Louisville's police chief. The city had no mounted police, no bicycle squad, crumbling jails, just three patrol wagons, and no electrical alarm system, which meant police often weren't even alerted to a major crime like rape or assault or murder until the information could be relayed by word of mouth at the next shift's roll call, eight or ten hours later. What's more, no detectives were on duty from midnight until 6 a.m., unless they were working a case that had occurred before midnight. All this came at a time when arrests by the detective bureau were skyrocketing, up more than 200 percent from the year before.

"There are several stories as to how Dinning was hurt," reported the *Courier-Journal*. "One is to the effect that he got into an argument with a crowd of young white men about the outcome of the coming election." (The election pitted a Democratic challenger against Mayor George Todd, a Republican who was promising to appoint his Black friends to white-collar positions in government.) "It is said that Dinning told the white men that Mayor Todd would be re-elected and that he would then be their boss, whereupon one of the men threw a brick at him," the *Courier-Journal* reported. But Dinning said he was assaulted without provocation, for unknown reasons.

The syndicated story that circulated widely took a different stab at motive: "Some time ago, Dinning prepared to file suit for damages against the Franklin [sic] county mob that attempted to lynch him, and it is thought that the men who assaulted him were from that section of the state."

A completely different story emerged in the Louisville *Evening Post*, in the form of a letter to the editor—signed with the pseudonym EQUAL RIGHTS—whose author claimed to have been given an eyewitness account. The person reported that a group of young white men commonly loafed around the corner of

Thirteenth and Delaware and made a practice of throwing things at Colored people when they passed. "I have known of two being injured by them," the correspondent wrote. "They chased the man Dinning down Delaware to Fourteenth, throwing as they went, and after a stone had struck him and knocked him down they gathered about him and beat him in the face until they had knocked out an eye and well nigh killed him." The person went on to say that there might not have been any words exchanged at all, that this was simply an unprompted act by racist thugs. "All respectable, justice-loving people would like to see the crowd of toughs punished for that and other outrages inflicted upon passersby, and if it is not done it will be a disgrace to Louisville," the person wrote.

But the assailants went unnamed, and the attack on George Dinning—one of seventy-two assaults in Louisville that year—was folded into the statistics of a lively, violent, dangerous city.

As George Dinning languished in City Hospital, Governor Bradley accepted a rushed invitation to speak at a gathering of the Kentucky Conference of the African Methodist Episcopal Church in Frankfort, and he was greeted by robust applause when he walked into the room. In introducing him, one minister expressed the sentiment of the crowd. "There are monuments and monuments—monuments to Lincoln, Washington, Grant and Garfield—but in the future there shall rise one higher and grander than them all," the minister said, recalling the governor's recent pardon of George Dinning. "And on it shall be inscribed the words: 'No man, while I am Governor, shall ever be punished for killing a member of the mob that goes at night to murder him or drive him from his home.'" Bradley was introduced to Bishop Salter, who shook his hand several times, then asked permission to kiss the hand that had signed George Dinning's pardon.

Bradley congratulated the ministers on their good work for their people and posterity, and urged them to teach their congregants that honest lives and good citizenship should be their first ambition because the merits of the race would be measured on its conduct in favor of law and order and against crime.

He thanked them all for their friendship and confidence.

"I am glad the colored people are my friends," Bradley said. "I have never looked into the face of a Black man who had acted the hypocrite with me, or who had stabbed me in the back. This is more than I can say for the people of my own race."

Chapter 16

THE TRUE SITUATION

As fall turned to winter and winter to the spring of 1898, an earthquake in California crumbled bridges and buildings, an avalanche at Chilkoot Pass in Alaska killed 160 people, the United States entered into a war with Spain at Cuba, and reports of great gold strikes in the Yukon Valley found their way to Seattle on the steamship *Portland*. Closer to home, the Colored troops demanded at Springfield, Illinois, to ride in Pullman chair cars rather than the condemned old coaches provided by the Chicago and Alton railroad.

Bennett Young, meanwhile, stitched together a case against the mob that had attacked the Dinning home that night in January 1897 and then returned to drive George Dinning's wife and children away and to burn the house to the ground. The criminal trial had produced the names of a good many of the men.

Young's partner was St. John Boyle, a noted railroad lawyer. Besides being lawyers, the two were entrepreneurs. They united in building the New Albany and St. Louis Railroad, and Young, soon after construction of that line was complete, bought the near-defunct Louisville, New Albany and Chicago Railway and reconstructed it; the railroad resumed operation in 1883, but Young resigned after a dispute with stockholders.

He then became president of the second Southern Exposition in Louisville, which was a massive world's fair held on nearly fifty acres on the outskirts of town for one hundred days. The first was so important that President Chester A. Arthur was on hand for the opening. The exposition showcased Louisville's manufacturing capabilities and helped strengthen business relationships with Northern and Southern cities. The main Exposition building covered thirteen acres and was said to be the largest wooden building ever built in the United States. It housed exhibits from many states; machinery that produced barbed wire and silk; an annex displaying sawmills and one displaying wagons and carriages; an art gallery containing masterpieces by world-famous painters; theatrical performances; floral displays; and concerts. There were coal and iron and six hundred carloads of machinery from Eastern states. All of it was lit by 4,600 electric lamps, the largest display to date of Thomas Edison's new invention: incandescent lights.

Journalists called it "one of the largest and most important exhibitions of human industry ever made in the world," and wrote, "It is not an easy task to even attempt to do the display justice."

The surrounding grounds of the second Exposition featured examples of farming advances and of Kentucky's finest crops, such as hemp, tobacco, flax, peanuts, and a variety of cotton. And if managing all that wasn't enough, Bennett Young could occasionally be found displaying his own handsome grapes, for he was a vintner by hobby and he delighted in fine grapes. He raised them for pleasure and conducted experiments on them— for example, covering them with paper bags until they ripened to protect them from the extreme elements.

Young's next ambitious adventure was to promote and fund-raise for a bridge over the Ohio River, stretching from Louisville to New Albany, Indiana, connecting the North and the South. After five years of effort, the $2.5-million Kentucky and Indiana Bridge opened in 1886, and it was mammoth. The cantilever bridge spanned 2,453 feet and included a 370-foot drawbridge. It supported a railroad track, a track for streetcars, a road for wagons, and a footpath. Young was the head of the venture, and he lost a ton of money on it, "but it did much good for Louisville and Kentucky and I am content," he said later.

At the same time, Young endeavored to build a line of railroads—to be called the Louisville Southern Railway—to compete with the Louisville & Nashville Railroad. His intention was to break up the L&N monopoly and open new shipping channels to the South. To complete the massive task, Young had to pay $276,000 for twenty-two miles of right-of-way between Versailles and Lexington, but the new line sparked an era of rapid industrial development in Louisville and established its commercial importance.

When Young was chosen as a delegate to redraw the state's constitution in 1890, he put together a reference manual for his colleagues, to help in the reframing. This manual, printed by the *Courier-Journal,* contained all three prior state constitutions along with important founding documents, such as the Bill of Rights and the Magna Carta. In its preface, Young was forced to reckon with the problem of slavery, which had been written into two previous constitutions, establishing that "the right of the owner of a slave to such slave and its increase is the same and as inviolable as the right of the owner of any property whatever."

"Slavery, then considered the most important of all the issues involved in the discussion of our present constitution, has been blotted out by a higher, stronger and wiser power than man's," Young wrote. The constitutional section on slavery, he wrote, "has been nullified by the edict of a great civil war, and that paragraph, then deemed so essential, so ably demanded, will now, by common consent, be stricken out, and its elimination is even urged as one of the reasons for calling of a Constitutional Convention."

Over the next few years, besides marrying Eliza Sharp in 1895 (his first wife died in 1881), Young began working on a complete history of Jessamine County, Kentucky, where his mother and father had settled and where he had spent his boyhood. The *Courier-Journal* published his book a few years later, and it's a racially inclusive history: in a section on churches, Black churches are praised, and included in the biographical sketches of prominent citizens of Jessamine County is one on Andrew McAfee, a city councilman who "is one of the younger generation of colored men who by his conduct and character has done much to dissipate the prejudice against the education of his race." By that time, Young's home in Louisville had become something of an antiquarian junk shop. He'd taken a keen interest in collecting artifacts that told the stories of the prehistoric men of Kentucky, and he aimed to someday write a book about them.

The Dinning case was a welcome diversion. It seemed noble to Young, especially since Dinning had been assaulted. His attackers had left him for dead, but the man refused to die. In fact, as time ticked by, he recovered. He was missing an eye, yes. And he would carry a scar the length of his head. And he would forever have a mark where the bullet entered his forehead. But his heart was still beating in his chest, and he had relocated with his young family to the safety of Jeffersonville, Indiana, across the Ohio River. He was even appointed to a temporary job by the Collector of Internal Revenue in Louisville. Dinning was a civil servant now.

Young wanted to lend all his energy to righting this terrible wrong. He was working for free. Dinning had no money to pay him, anyhow. The only way his court costs would be covered was if he won.

The first draft of Young's federal petition listed as defendants every man he could tie through testimony to the attack on Dinning's home. Young sat with Mollie and George and Eva and Hermann and the other children and they cobbled together a list of every white man they could remember who had come to their home that night or the following day with hate in his heart.

The list of names grew and grew.

The lawsuit, filed in federal court at Louisville on August 6, 1898, one year after George Dinning established residency across the river in Indiana, was simply styled.

The plaintiff was a resident and citizen of Clark County, Indiana, and a citizen of the United States. And the defendants were all residents and citizens of the state of Kentucky. And the plaintiff would be asking for more than $2,000 in damages.

Young laid out the facts of the case:

Fact: On or about the 21st day of January 1897, George Dinning was in possession of and owned a farm in Simpson County, Kentucky, about ten miles from the county seat of Franklin, containing about 125 acres; the land had on it then a residence, stable, and outhouses, and was used and occupied by Dinning as a home for himself and his family: his wife, Mollie, and their children—six of whom were in the house at the time of the trespass.

Fact: The farm was stocked with horses, hogs, chickens, and turkeys, and the home was "well and comfortably furnished for a man in his position of life."

Fact: On that date, the defendants, including Jodie Conn, maliciously confederated, conspired, and agreed to take his life, to destroy his property, to burn his house, and to run Dinning's family away from his home "and to otherwise maltreat plaintiff and his family;" and for those reasons they entered upon George Dinning's land with force and arms, and in pursuance of that purpose, at or about the hour of midnight, the defendants maliciously with threats and oaths demanded that plaintiff should open the door of his house and let the defendants and Jodie Conn come in. "And upon his refusal, the defendants and said Jodie Conn then and there fired into the house of plaintiff and wounded him twice, and plaintiff then fired upon the defendants and mortally wounded said Jodie Conn, who afterwards died."

Fact: After the wounding of Jodie Conn, who with the others were clearly trespassing and greatly endangering the safety of Dinning's wife and children, the defendants retired for a short while and Dinning fled from his home and left his wife and children alone in the house and has never been able to return thereto.

Fact: Most of his children were young—one was just three months old, another two, and the oldest about fifteen.

Fact: His family stayed in the house alone until early the next morning, when the defendants, except Jodie Conn, "returned to his farm and surrounded his house—all being armed—and that they remained during the entire day, threatening, cursing, and abusing his family, and late in the afternoon ordered plaintiff's wife and children to leave the house and farm of plaintiff, informing them that they intended to burn the house of plaintiff and all the furniture in said house."

Fact: Dinning's infant daughter was "dangerously ill with fever and unable to walk," but the defendants, "with guns in their hands and with threats and cursings, ordered the wife and children of plaintiff to leave the house." The men "forced the wife and children of plaintiff to depart from home and did maliciously destroy the house of plaintiff and burn it to the ground, together with all the furniture contained therein, and did expel and drive the family of plaintiff away from his home and farm before mentioned, and did maliciously destroy and drive off his stock; and that his wife and children were forced away and driven from his farm and home; that the weather was cold and the roads muddy, and that a part of his infant children were compelled to walk barefoot through the cold and mud a long distance before they found shelter and rest, and that his sick daughter was forced to leave her bed and to ride on horseback for several miles before a place of lodgement could be found for her, thus giving her great pain and distress and greatly imperiling her life."

Fact: George Dinning's farm was ruined, his home broken up, and his property destroyed, and he has never been able to return to his home and farm since that cold, moonlit night.

"By all of which plaintiff has been damaged in the sum of $50,000, for which sum he prays judgement, and for all proper relief."

The suit was signed by Bennett H. Young and George Dinning.

News of the lawsuit spread quickly. Deputy Marshal Moses Dixon was dispatched to the borderlands to serve the fourteen defendants, and he executed the summonses on August 19 and 20. It was sensational, and many newspapers pointed out that it was the first time in history a Black man in the South had brought suit for damages against a white mob.

"The men sued are prominent white farmers of Logan and Simpson counties," reported the *Daily Leader* in Lexington, "and the suit has caused intense excitement there."

In Simpson County, the newspaper's response was predictable.

"In the petition Dinning alleges all kinds of silly things which can not, of course, be proven," wrote the editor of the *Franklin Favorite*. "He says the 'mob' came to his house, shot him, ran him from home, returned again and abused his family, drove them from home and then burned his residence. One of the allegations is true—the men in question did go to George's cabin and tell him to clear his skirts of a certain piece of devilment, or leave the country. The brute replied to this by shooting into the crowd and killing Jodie Conn. Realizing his dastardly deed he fled to Franklin for protection, which was given him."

The editor then made a remarkable leap in defense of the mob.

"As to the burning of his 'residence,' it is the usual belief that George had the torch applied to this $25 structure, to destroy the stolen goods secreted therein," he wrote, not bothering to draw any assumptions as to how a man in custody of Sheriff Clark could have had his own home burned down. "Of course his family was 'driven away' before his smooth piece of work was consummated," he continued. "But George neglects to say that he had them driven away—to his kinfolks, a few miles distant."

In one last stab, the editor pointed his pen at the ex-Confederate soldier who had filed the suit.

"The friends of Col. Bennett Young express some surprise that he would take such a case and cherish the belief that he will yet see the error of his ways and wash his hands of the whole affair," he wrote. "He would certainly do so if he was familiar with the true situation."

The defendants hired G. T. Finn, who had prosecuted the criminal case for the Commonwealth, along with his partner G. W. Roark, and W. M. Smith, all of Franklin. Finn made a motion requesting that the case be relocated to federal court in Owensboro, Kentucky, about forty miles closer to Simpson County. When the motion was denied, he filed a general demurrer to Dinning's petition, saying it failed to state facts sufficient to constitute a cause of action, and on grounds that the action was for conspiracy and injuries resulting from conspiracy, all of which occurred more than twelve months before the suit was filed, which would mean they were barred by the statute of limitations.

In response Young made the case that while an action merely for conspiracy would be barred by statute in one year, the actions for trespass to real or personal property, and for trespass upon a person, were only barred in five years. "It would be absurd to say that an action for trespass on real property can only be barred in five years, but if alleged to have been done jointly by two or more, shall be barred in one," he wrote. The judge overruled Finn's demurrer.

The defense's next strategy in answer to the petition was to deny much of what Dinning claimed. The lawyer for Doc Moore, the leader of the mob, in his response, denied that Dinning owned a farm in Simpson County, denied that Moore had maliciously, or at all, confederated, conspired, or agreed with Jodie Conn or anyone else to take Dinning's life, or to destroy his property or to burn his house down or to run off his family or to otherwise maltreat Dinning or his wife or children. He denied that he had entered Dinning's premises with force or arms, denied that he had made any threats or oaths, denied that he had demanded that Dinning open the door. He denied that he had come back early the next morning, or at any other time, and he denied that he had driven Dinning's family away.

"He admits that (Dinning) was in possession of a poor and unenclosed tract of land which had upon it an old cabin, stable and smokehouse, all of which were greatly out of repair and of very little value, to wit; not exceeding $100," his answer stated. "He denies that said farm was well stocked with horses. Avers that plaintiff had two horses, which were old, not well cared for and worth not exceeding $25. He avers that from the number of hogs, chickens, and turkeys which had mysteriously disappeared in the neighborhood, no doubt, plaintiff's farm was well stocked with chickens, turkeys and hogs."

Moore, his attorneys wrote, said that he and the others "quietly and peaceably" went to Dinning's house "with no purpose to hurt or harm him and so informed him...that the neighborhood believed that he was instigator and principal participant in all the thievery and smokehouse breaking going on in the neighborhood and that his place was the repository for stolen property and that unless he proved himself clear of this charge he must leave the neighborhood in ten days." After that, he claimed, he and the others "quietly and peaceably left" and then "without provocation" Dinning, "secreted in his house fired upon the defendant and mortally wounded and ruthlessly killed Jodie Conn, and thereafter in necessary self defence some shots were fired by some of the parties at the said Dinning which perhaps struck his house."

A similar answer came from King, listing many of the same denials. King admitted that he had heard of the killing the next morning and had gone to the scene—as had numerous others, both from the neighborhood and from all over the county. He said "many, perhaps hundreds, as is perfectly natural, went to the premises and viewed the place of the tragedy of the night previous." King claimed he was unarmed, quiet, and peaceful, and entered the property without any objection from Dinning's wife, and "did no harm to person or property."

As all the answers were filed, Young noticed they each contained the same lines about Dinning being the "instigator and principal participant in all the thieving" and that his home was a repository for stolen turkeys, chickens, and pigs. He filed motions to strike that and other incriminating language from the answers, and the judge agreed. He would limit testimony to events on the night of the shooting and the night of the burning.

Young filed suit in federal court in Tennessee as well, since more than a dozen of the farmers lived across the state line. Many he named in that suit were not present the night Jodie Conn was killed but had shown up the following day. That expanded the lawsuit to include a total of thirty men: Doc Moore, Monroe White, John Felts, James Flowers, Joseph Flowers, Albert Freeman, William Ragsdale, William Ballard, Pluitt Copeland, Joseph Copeland, John Webb, James King, Samuel Randolph, Charles T. Conn (as administrator of Jodie Conn's estate), all of Kentucky; and Henry Jenkins, Lum Babb, Elbert McDonald, William Rainwater, Jesse Cook, George Cook, Stephen Walker, Gibbs Powell, Mayberry Powell, Jasper Powell, Arch McDaniel, Nick Williams, Joe Deaux, W. T. Bloodworth, J. H. Bloodworth, and Samuel McDonald, all of Tennessee.

Chapter 17

"A NEGRO'S LIFE IS A VERY CHEAP THING"

In late April 1899, on the eve of the hearing of George Dinning's case against his would-be lynchers in a sterile federal courtroom in Louisville, a crowd of people 220 miles south abducted a Black man named Sam Wilkes on an Atlanta-bound train and accused him of killing an aristocratic white farmer named Alfred Cranford and assaulting his wife. A reporter present said the mob was composed of citizens from Newnan, Griffin, Palmetto, and other little towns in the area. They dragged Sam Wilkes to Newnan and handed him over to the sheriff, who gave them a receipt so that they could claim a reward of $50. Someone sent notice to Mrs. Cranford that she was needed in Newnan to identify the suspect.

Word spread like wildfire, and soon a mass of people gathered at the jail and demanded that the sheriff turn him over, and he did. The sheriff quickly sent word to former Georgia governor William Yates Atkinson, who lived in Newnan. Atkinson hustled to the scene, hoping his presence might dispel the mob. He stood in a buggy and shouted at the crowd.

"The law will take its course!" he shouted to the red-faced and bloodthirsty barbarians on the street. "And I promise you it will do so quickly and effectively. Do not stain the honor of the state with a crime such as you are about to perform!"

As if the state's honor hadn't already been stained. In fact, this event was preceded the month before by a terrible slaughter. In mid-March, a mob of one hundred masked white men, armed with Winchesters, pistols, and shotguns, rode into Palmetto, kicked open the doors of a warehouse, and unloaded their arms into four Black prisoners accused of setting fire to two business blocks in town: Tip Hudson, Bud Cotton, Ed Wynn, and Henry Bingham. The prisoners were tied up and cowering when murdered. The *Atlanta Journal* reported that the Black population of Palmetto fled from town, "and it is believed the Negroes are now congregating on the outskirts and will make an assault on the town tonight." The assault never happened. But the whites were scared.

"The place is in the wildest excitement and every citizen is armed, expecting an outbreak as soon as night shall fall," the *Atlanta Journal* reported. "The Negroes left the town in droves early this morning, weeping and screaming and dogged and revengeful."

That was March, and the Atlanta dailies were full of sensational headlines such as "NEGRO WILL PROBABLY BE BURNED." This was April, a month later.

A local judge who had some sway spoke, too. He pleaded with the mob to stop, to go home, to let justice run its course. As soon as he finished, the mob roared.

"On to Palmetto!" they said.

"Burn him!" they shouted.

"Think of his crime!" they roared.

They whisked the Black man away and had started for Palmetto when word spread that the train inbound from Atlanta contained a thousand people. The mob assumed this to be a militia and decided to burn Sam Wilkes at the first wide spot in the road. More people joined the crowd as they marched, and the mob soon numbered fifteen hundred, Sam Wilkes in shackles being marched forward at the front of the pack. A mile and a half outside Newnan, someone spotted a strong pine tree, and they pushed his back against it. A hush fell over the crowd, and for the first time Sam Wilkes was allowed to speak.

"I am Sam Wilkes," he said plainly. "I killed Alfred Cranford, but I was paid to do it."

The newspapers reported the following, which was later disputed.

"Lige Strickland, the negro preacher at Palmetto, paid me twelve dollars to do it."

The mob roared.

"Let him go on!" someone shouted. "Tell all you know about it."

Sam Wilkes shook with fear and adrenaline.

"I did not outrage Mrs. Cranford," he said. "Somebody else did that. I can identify them. Give me time for that."

The mob would hear no more. They stripped Sam Wilkes naked, and someone wrapped a heavy chain around his body and secured him to the tree. He did not speak then, but when he saw the flash of knives in the hands of the members of the mob, he stifled his cries. A man sliced off one of Wilkes's ears and caught it in his hand. Another white man cut off the other ear. Wilkes asked for them to kill him quickly, to no avail. They sliced off his fingers, one by one, and passed them around to those in front. Someone cut off his penis, a trophy. Through it all, he never cried for mercy.

"Come on with the oil," someone shouted.

A huge can of kerosene was produced and placed at the feet of Sam Wilkes, who was covered with blood from head to feet. He was silent but struggled against his chains. Three men lifted the kerosene can and poured it over his head. Others hauled dead twigs and branches to his feet. Someone struck a match and the flames climbed up his legs. The smoke went into his mouth and eyes. He shouted, "Oh, Lord Jesus," and drew his fingerless hands up to the tree behind him and heaved against the chains, and those around his torso broke, leaving just his legs attached to the tree at the thigh. A man ran up and pushed him back and lashed him again to the pine.

"Get back into the fire," the man said.

The road for a half mile in each direction was choked with people. After Wilkes had burned for an hour, his head hung limp to one side. The crowd took turns slicing hunks of flesh off Sam Wilkes, souvenirs, and when there was no more of him left, they carved pieces out of the tree.

Then they went after Elijah "Lige" Strickland. They found the sixty-year-old preacher on the farm of a man called Major Thomas, in his little cabin in the woods with his wife and five children. They stole him away and took him out to the road for torture.

"I have told you all I know, gentlemen," Strickland said. "You can kill me if you wish, but I know nothing more to tell."

The mob, hearing this, took a vote, and they agreed to let him live. They took him to Palmetto, to the town square, and staged a trial. It was after midnight. There was no judge or jury. The crowd of whites had swelled to two thousand. Everyone who knew Strickland was called to testify about his character, and several Black men were brave enough to step forward to say he was an upstanding citizen, law-abiding and good-natured. Some in the crowd favored turning him over to the sheriff to allow justice to run its course, but they were overwhelmed by those who sought to move the trial to the woods outside town.

They strung the preacher up two or three times in the woods, trying to get a confession, but he would not say he had any connection to Sam Wilkes's crime and denied he had paid Wilkes to murder Cranford.

Major Thomas, having been aroused by the earlier commotion, came upon the scene in a buggy, jumped down, and asked for a hearing. He asked the crowd to let him speak on behalf of Strickland, and they agreed to let him talk.

"Gentlemen, this Negro is innocent," he said. "Wilkes said Lige had promised to give him twelve dollars to kill Cranford, and I believe Lige has not had twelve dollars since he has been on my place. This is a law-abiding Negro you are about to hang. He has never done any of you any harm, and now I want you to promise me that you will turn him over either to the bailiff of this town or to someone who is entitled to receipt for him, in order that he may be given a hearing on his case. I do not ask that you liberate him. Hold him and if the courts adjudge him guilty, hang him."

Major Thomas retired some distance, and someone said: "We have got him here. Let's keep him." They sent a messenger to tell Major Thomas to leave town for his own good. He couldn't help but speak up.

"I have never before been ordered to leave a town and I am not going to leave this one," he said. "Tell them that the muscles in my legs are not trained to running. Tell them that I have stood the fire and heard the whistles of the Minies from a thousand rifles and I am not frightened by this crowd."

The mob seemed split over Strickland's guilt. They decided to carry the preacher to jail in nearby Fairburn, Georgia. This was the last time Elijah Strickland was seen alive. Sheriff's deputies found his body hanging from a tree the next morning, his ears missing, a placard pinned to his chest stating WE MUST PROTECT OUR SOUTHERN WOMEN.

The series of events was so outrageous that a group of Black people in Chicago took up a collection and hired a white detective to go to Georgia to investigate the murders. He spent a week in the South, and his report was shocking.

"I did not talk with one white man who believed that Strickland had anything to do with Wilkes," he wrote. "I could not find any person who heard Wilkes mention Strickland's name. I talked with men who heard Wilkes tell his story, but all agreed that he said he killed Cranford because Cranford was about to kill him, and that he did not mention Strickland's name. He did not mention it when he was being tortured because he did not speak to anybody. I could not find anybody who could tell me how the story started that Strickland hired Wilkes to kill Cranford."

The detective also found the claim that Wilkes had assaulted Mrs. Cranford to be untrue. She never made the claim, but the papers had reported it as indisputable truth.

Of the four men shot dead while in custody, he wrote: "Nothing was done about the killing of these men, but their families were afterward ordered to leave the place, and all have left. Five widows and seventeen fatherless children, all driven from home, constitute one result of the lynching. I saw no one who thought much about the matter. The Negroes were dead, and while they did not know whether they were guilty or not, it was plain that nothing could be done about it. And so the matter ended.

"With these facts I made my way home, thoroughly convinced that a Negro's life is a very cheap thing."

Against the backdrop of this saturnalia of bloodlust and violence and sadism, George Dinning mounted the national stage.

Chapter 18

DERBY DAY

Morning broke on May 4, 1899, and Louisville was buzzing as on no other day of the year. The bourbon began flowing at sunup as the hotels rattled awake and the street sweepers quickly cleaned up debris from the previous day's festivities. Twenty-five thousand people had been on hand the evening before, at Preston and Oak Streets, to bear witness to Buffalo Bill Cody's Congress of Rough Riders of the World, the stunning and exciting shoot-'em-up show, complete with reenactments of an attack on a mail coach at Deadwood and the taking of San Juan Hill by the Rough Riders. They cheered a dazzling shooting stunt by Miss Annie Oakley, and were taken by the multiculturalism of the cast of Rough Riders, which included Filipinos, Mexicans, cowboys, Cossacks, whites, Blacks, Indians, and Cubans. The talent threw lassos and pranced horses and sang a medley of "Dixie" and "Old Folks at Home" and "The Star-Spangled Banner." The newspapers called the show "patriotic," and the whole shebang was a compendium of 1899 America. The revelry continued through the night and into the next morning, when the city waved her rosy garlands at her visitors.

Each new locomotive that puffed and chawed into Union

Station dumped a new quota of revelers wearing their finest clothes into the boulevards: the chumps with just enough weight in their pockets for a bet or two, the plungers from Tennessee with their poolroom earnings, the dashers from Lexington with their congested pocketbooks. The trains were followed by carriages and buggies and brakes and traps, all funneling toward Churchill Downs. There were bookmakers and grandstand philosophers and women wearing hats smothered in roses and shirtwaists with lace in just the right places. The railbirds clicked their stopwatches as the three-year-olds strode by in warm-up. They had all come to bet on blood and pray for luck.

If the Kentucky Derby was religion, this was the Sabbath, the High Holy Day. The General Council, had, in fact, declared it a sanctioned holiday.

Every Derby Day enjoyed the expectation of being the best-ever Derby Day, but this, the Twenty-Fifth Kentucky Derby, the last running of the nineteenth century, really did seem special. And what a time to be alive, at the end of the Gilded Age and the start of the Progressive Era. Teddy Roosevelt and his Rough Riders, wearing their slouch hats and flannel shirts and handkerchiefs knotted around their necks, had ousted Spain from Cuba. General Arthur MacArthur's army was heavily favored to win the war in the Philippines, the extreme edge of westward expansion, and seemed sure to claim the Peal of the Orient for Uncle Sam and to open new trade possibilities with Asia. New York was buzzing about a new motorized contraption called the automobile. The German chemical company Bayer had just patented a pharmaceutical called Aspirin, which was said to be a wonder drug that would alleviate pain and reduce fever.

Only the day before, at the Chickamauga battlefield in Chattanooga, a large delegation from Kentucky had unveiled a new kind of monument that stood apart from all the other markers dedicated by other states: the towering shaft was for the fallen Kentuckians on both sides of the Civil War, blue and gray, and veterans from both armies stood shoulder to shoulder to honor the dead. That important symbol was not lost on Bill Bradley, governor of a state that had given the country both Abraham Lincoln and Jefferson Davis, born just one hundred miles apart. Bradley marked the occasion, there in the shadows of Missionary Ridge and Lookout Mountain, by acknowledging the roots of the conflict. "For years preceding that period we had two civilizations. One, founded on the justice of slavery and the sovereignty of each state, espoused by a brave and impetuous people. The other, founded on the declaration that all men were created equal, and the sovereignty of the nation, espoused by a conservative and chivalrous people. For years, antagonisms and bitterness increased between the sections until the dispute, by force of circumstances, was submitted to the arbitrament of the sword," Bradley said. "And now, after the mists of prejudice have been torn from our eyes, and we are enabled to see the bright stars of truth and reason which shine beyond, all can plainly divine the sentiments which inspired the actors in that bloody drama. That the Union should have been preserved and slavery abolished, all are ready to concede. That the victors won in honorable fight, no one will dispute. But while this is manifest, it is equally true that those who were fortunately defeated were inspired by sincere devotion to principles conscientiously believed to be just."

In Louisville, the revelers began filling the grandstand at Churchill Downs before eleven o'clock. They were expected to number fifteen thousand by the start, the largest derby crowd ever. Across the waving bluegrass to the left, under the brown-topped shed, stood a surging mass of men in black coats and straw hats, cigar smoke rising above them. They were the South's foremost men of politics, the sons and grandsons of historymakers. There, too, stood bankers, farmers, physicians, and laborers, all with one mind—to bet on the winner. They were looking at Kentucky hotshot Manuel, mostly, but wondering if a California horse called Corsine would show out, having come all the way from San Francisco. The others predicted to start were Mazo, His Lordship, and Fontainebleu. Caretakers had groomed and watered the track with industrial sprinklers the evening before.

Stepping off those same steam-powered locomotives that carried the well-suited gamblers from Nashville and other points south were the farmers from Simpson and Logan Counties, on their way to face a jury. They had earlier made a motion for a change of venue to Owensboro, a federal court much closer, but that had been denied. So they had to come to Louisville, the big city. They must have marveled at the grand Union Station, with its tall ceilings, ceramic-tile floors, and Georgia-marble walls, the sunlight filtering in through rose-colored windows. From there they would have either walked or caught a ride in a buggy or on the streetcar to the federal courtroom of Judge Walter Evans, where twelve empaneled white men took their seats in the jury box and prepared to listen to the case of George Dinning v. Doc Moore, et al.

Twelve white men.

Dinning had been here before, but he faced his assailants without the slightest fear or shame.

The past three months had been a nightmare for him. He'd recovered from the assault and found work as a livestock driver. But in March, a young child living in Dinning's home fell ill. Friends and family took care of the child, but the child wasn't getting better. Word got back to the board of health and it was learned the child had smallpox. Dinning pleaded ignorance, saying he couldn't afford to pay a physician and hadn't known the child had the contagious and deadly virus, which was ravaging the country. When the entire family was tested in late March, ten of them had smallpox. The local newspaper reported that a yellow quarantine flag was raised in front of Dinning's "pest infested residence." The board of health seemed more interested in quarantining the afflicted Black residents and protecting the white population from them than it did in eradicating the disease.

Dinning was feeling fine, but he worried about his family.

The judge presiding over the case, Walter Evans, was a man of unimpeachable integrity. As a boy, he had worked on a farm while attending school near Harrodsburg, and in 1861 he joined the Union Army and led a company in the Battle of Fort Donelson. He studied law after the war, was admitted to the bar in 1864, and spent the next decade in private practice at Hopkinsville. He served as a Republican in the Kentucky House and Senate and was then elected twice to a seat in the U.S. House of Representatives. Immediately after his second term, Evans was appointed to a seat on the U.S. District Court for Kentucky by President William McKinley. He was confirmed just two months before the case of Dinning v. Doc Moore, which was scheduled to be heard on May 4, 1899. This unique case, its like never before seen in Kentucky or anywhere, would be among the first for Evans as a federal judge.

The newspapers noted that the rare lawsuit—for bodily injuries to Dinning and his wife and children, and for trespass upon his premises—had attracted widespread attention and was being watched from Boston to Bakersfield. "His suit takes into the United States Courts contentions that, it is claimed by many of his race, are wrongfully ignored in the State Court," the *Courier-Journal* reported.

Bennett Young was raring to go, and he hoped to wrap up the case in a few days, for he had a train to catch to the Confederate reunion in Charleston. Dressed in his finest suit and wearing his usual long salt-and-pepper moustache, he eloquently laid out his case, stating facts that were by then well known.

When he was finished, G. T. Finn gave an altogether different account of the affray. He said the men went to Dinning's house to warn Dinning to stop stealing, and that they went as friends with no intention of harming him or his family. And in the course of events they demanded he leave within ten days' time. Finn said George Dinning's audacious response baffled the men. "You had better make me leave now," Finn quoted Dinning to the jurors. The whites replied that they were men enough to do it, Finn said, and with that they began to walk away.

If we scrutinize this narrative, as the jurors surely did, the spot at which the defense's chronology meets the most skepticism is right there, with two dozen white men hearing that audible manifestation of rebellion from a Black man and simply walking away. If we give Finn and the defendants the benefit of the doubt to that point—they came as friends with no intention of doing harm—and pause the story in that exact moment, before a single shot is fired on that cold and moonlit night, what do we see? What do we choose to see? Self-appointed neighborhood regulators? Gun-hung vigilantes intent on stopping crime in their neighborhood? Farmers trying to carve out a living in an increasingly competitive environment?

These men matured in an age when it was culturally acceptable to own another human. They grew up surrounded by Black servants. For most of his boyhood, George Dinning was the property of a white man. And when it came time for the country as a whole to reckon with a history that was intrinsically unfair to a host of Colored people, when the question of enslavement demanded an answer, these men picked up guns and signed on with the Confederates and marched into battle with their minds made up. They fought, and they lost, and they returned home to a country completely restructured.

To believe that they turned on their heels that night to walk away from a man like George Dinning, who was born a slave and was then set free and had found a way to toil and prosper, who had married and created even more free Black people in Simpson County, who had on that night refused their demands to open the door and come outside, who had been defiant, disobedient, and insubordinate...to believe that is to believe that they were ready to lay down their arms, accept their new lot, and betray the underpinnings of their supremacy.

George Dinning was the first to testify. He was neatly dressed in his three-piece suit. His face was pockmarked and he had only one eye. But he put his hand on the Holy Bible and swore he would tell the truth. He spoke about his peaceful life in Simpson County, how he owned his house, two horses, hogs, and chickens, and had a crop of wheat sown. He told of how he made a living harvesting his own tobacco and hiring himself out to work for other farmers. He told the story of that night unflinchingly. He was followed on the stand by Eva Dinning, his daughter, who testified to the same story as her father and added that the next morning armed men took charge of the premises and took away her brother, Hermann. She named Pluitt and Copeland and King and Randolph. All were armed, she said. She told of the flight of her mother and her siblings.

Hermann testified, too, followed by George's mother, Mary. They each confirmed that the family had been attacked.

The defense took over and called a dozen witnesses, and again tried to make the case that the white men went there peaceably.

Interestingly, Doc Moore testified that he met the group of men near New Hope mill and was asked by Jodie Conn to accompany them to Dinning's house. He said he consented to go to the Dinning house, but did so only in a friendly spirit.

"I went there as his friend," Moore told the court.

"Do you mean to say that you went there as the head of a band of armed men to drive Dinning away from home, and that you went there as his friend?" Young asked incredulously. "Is that your idea of friendship?"

"I don't see any harm in it," Moore said.

Moore said that he marched the crowd out in front of the house to show Dinning that his platoon was large enough to make him leave, whether he wanted to or not.

"I told him to look and see if there were enough of us to make him go," Moore said. When Dinning refused to go, Doc Moore said—shocking the court—he commanded his men to squat and fire.

"Squat and fire?" exclaimed Young indignantly. "That is a military order, isn't it, Mr. Moore?"

The courtroom chuckled in disbelief. Moore countered that he didn't think his men shot to kill. On the stand in a big city, Doc Moore had come unraveled.

The others tried to argue that they either weren't there the night of the shooting or weren't there the next day, when the house was burned down. It was clear to observers that the defense was at a total loss in justifying the trespassing.

The strongest contention the defense could put forward was that Dinning was the first to fire, and that they didn't shoot until he had killed Jodie Conn. But believing that meant believing that Dinning and his family were lying, and that Doc Moore and the peaceful band of regulators were just trying to leave.

Across town, at Churchill Downs, the cheers ascended into the heavens and the hooves pounded the turf and the whiskey was swallowed and the ladies in the rose-covered hats screamed for the horses, and the sloppy men toddled to the rail, and a horse called Manuel won the Kentucky Derby. Some got rich.

Some lost everything. Some broke even.

Chapter 19

"THERE WAS A GREAT REJOICING IN HELL THIS MORNING"

He was one of the best orators in an age of oration. He was astounding in thought and language and in constructing an argument. He was a showman, and this—making his closing argument in federal court—was his carnival. He must have felt a glimmer of the same enthusiasm he had when he climbed out of the Cumberland River under enemy fire and led a naked charge on the Federals. He must have tapped the same source of courage he found after his capture, at Camp Douglas, when the Union guards fired indiscriminately at Confederates in their cells, and he was elected to carry their complaint of injustice to the commandant and unleashed a full-throated prophecy that the day would come when a just God rained punishment upon those who would commit such outrages. He must have felt the same spirit that had swelled in his chest thirty-five years before, when he led a ragtag band of young Confederate soldiers on a raid into Vermont from Canada.

This was a war, too, but the cause was decidedly different.

George Dinning watched his friend Bennett Henderson Young stand and face the jury.

"There was a great rejoicing in hell this morning," Young

began in his closing statement. The gallery was full. Reporters hung on his every word. "When men of the intelligence, the high standing and brilliant talents of the two lawyers who have spoken for the defendants in this case, stand in a court of justice and condone assassination and argue that practically a man may be murdered or driven from his home and his family by a self-constituted mob that may elect to take his life and destroy his property, all the demons smiled and applauded," he said. "Well may we, in view of the brutality towards this man and his wife and children, as detailed from the witnesses, cry out, 'Is God dead?'"

Young, ever the historian, reached back into the past to show that the counties from which the mob came were named in honor of noble Kentuckians who had achieved fame for their courage. Benjamin Logan defended himself time after time from Indian attacks. Captain John Simpson saw military action in both the Northwest Indian War and the War of 1812. Young knew their life stories, and used them to great effect.

"From these two counties, named for these distinguished and heroic Kentuckians, came the men who are guilty of the cowardly and brutal conduct which was exhibited toward this poor, helpless Black man and his innocent family," Young said. "If they be fair representations of the present type of man Kentucky is producing, we must confess that we are degenerate sons of noble sires.

"Far down in Simpson County, on the edge of Logan and close to the Tennessee line, lived the humble, untutored Black man who appears as the plaintiff in this case," Young said, working the room. "By dint of industry and hard, unceasing toil he had secured for himself 125 acres of land. It was poor, unproductive"—Young was not being totally honest here—"but it met all his wants, and there in a rude, uncomfortable log cabin he had lived with his wife and fought the hard battle of toil and twelve children had come to cheer and bless their home.

"There is not in this case a single statement from any witness who has ever said that George Dinning, this Black man, had wronged a living being. Two horses, a few plows, some farming implements, seven hogs, two dozen chickens and four turkeys were all that the pressing demands for food and clothing for his large family had allowed this Black man to accumulate, excepting his farm. There had been no suspicion of crime, he had not interfered with his white neighbors, he had not disturbed their slumbers. But on the twenty-[first] of January, 1897, as he slept in his humble home with his children about him—the youngest four months old and the eldest 15 years of age—unsuspicious of any wrong or any injury from any man, with one child sick and partially delirious from typhoid fever, at half past 12 o'clock at night, he hears a rude, hard knock at his door.

"He calls to know who is there. The cowardly hypocrite responds: 'It is a friend.' This friend was a white man, backed by a gang of whitecaps and kuklux, armed with pistols and guns, who had come to serve notice upon this humble man...." He had to "desert his fireside, filled with so many happy and pleasant associations to him and to those he loved, and depart at once from the neighborhood and put a distance of not less than thirty miles between him and those marauders who in the darkness of the night had come and served this warning upon their black neighbor."

Young recounted the case once more, start to finish, and he made a final impassioned appeal to the jury to uphold the law and the Constitution with their verdict, and then he rested. The courtroom was quiet. George Dinning, with one good eye, watched his friend return to his seat.

The closing statement from the defense, delivered by a former district attorney named W. M. Smith, was unremarkable but for the fact that he admitted his clients had done wrong before the law by trespassing on the Dinning property. But they had not gone to Dinning's house as midnight assassins, he said. His clients were not men who would fire into any man's house needlessly, and Doc Moore's order to squat and fire indicated the battle had already been commenced by Dinning, that death was belching from the upper window, and his clients only shot back in self-defense. One reporter wrote that his argument was of "the depreciating order."

The day was nearly over, and the judge wanted to give the jury instructions and allow them plenty of time to deliberate, so he ordered the twelve to return in the morning and adjourned court for the day.

The following morning, Judge Evans called the court to order and issued stern instructions. He told the jury that, based on the evidence heard, all the defendants except Doc Moore, John Felts, James Flowers, Joseph Flowers, Albert Freeman, and the administrator of Jodie Conn's estate should receive a favorable verdict. In his review of the case, he explained, he had considered the facts most favorable to Dinning, and considering those, responsibility fell on these six men, not the rest. The jury's responsibility, he said, was to determine the amount of damages. He told them the case was such that even punitive damages could rightfully be imposed.

The jury retired to deliberate. The foreman was James E. Breed, an assistant secretary for the Louisville Bridge and Iron Company and son of one of the city's most prosperous merchants before the War Between the States. M. J. Winn owned a tailoring establishment on Fourth Avenue and Green Street. John Stier was a butcher. H. W. Barclay was a real estate man. H. H. Beach was an enterpriser. Irwin Dugan was a steamboat scrutineer respected from New Orleans to Pittsburgh.

The white men on the jury met for just an hour. When they filed back in, the courtroom fell silent. The foreman read the verdict.

Chapter 20

"THE OUTCOME IS REGARDED AS SENSATIONAL"

We of the jury..."

What could George Dinning do with $50,000 in 1899? He could buy 20,000 gallons of twelve-year-old Jay-Eye-See Sour Mash Whisky. Or 270 upright pianos. Or 25,252 mahogany rocking chairs. Or 3,333 suits. Or 833 Rambler Tandem bicycles from Harbison & Gathright on Fourth Avenue. He could afford seven handsome three-story brick mansions in Louisville, a city that hit its stride in the Gilded Age, or take 100,000 round trips on a steamboat to Cincinnati, 150 miles away. With the right investments, he could live the rest of his life without working another day.

"...find against the defendants..."

Maybe he heard the words echo in his ears. Or maybe none of this was about the money. Maybe in his heart it was about the principle of it. He had been wronged. He had been shot. His home had been destroyed, ashes carried on the Kentucky wind. He could never return. A path to reparations had been made available to him. A good lawyer had agreed to help. And here he stood on the brink of justice.

The judge had dismissed all but six of the defendants, and

those were Doc Moore, John Felts, James Flowers, Joseph Flowers, Albert Freeman, and Charles Conn, Jodie Conn's father. All but Conn were Dinning's old neighbors, men he once thought were friends.

"...and assess against them fifty thousand dollars."

It's fair to wonder if their hearts sank that day, if in that moment they pictured lives without their land or livestock, without their homes, without any money. It's fair to wonder whether they felt any shame, or whether they believed their story about going to Dinning's as friends. It's fair to wonder if buried inside their silence in court that day was a violent explosion of anger, for they, white men, were now heavily indebted to a Black man.

Dinning had been born below them, but now they each owed him $8,333.33.

A reporter there in the courtroom that day noted that George Dinning didn't seem to respond at all when the jury read the verdict. He sat motionless, a blank expression on his face.

The verdict was the first of its kind. A Black man in the South had sued his would-be lynchers and won. Many found it remarkable.

"Down on the 'dark and bloody ground' of Kentucky, where the typical southerner lives, and sips mint juleps, and attends horse races, and fights his feuds, and strings up niggers who assault white women, either personally or in print, a case has just been decided which shows what sort of justice a colored man can get when he knows his place, and is in the right," wrote the editor of the *Daily Herald* in Salt Lake City, Utah. "*The Herald* believes the verdict was just. A few cases of this kind will do more to make mobbing unpopular than all the harangues of negro preachers and exhorters that can be crowded into the next century."

Newspaper editors and court observers across the country heaped praise on the judge and jury.

"The outcome is regarded as sensational, indicating an entirely new method of dealing with and punishing mobs," reported the *Fort Wayne News* in Indiana on its front page.

"This was in Kentucky, be it remembered," wrote the editor of the *Mount Carmel Register* in Illinois.

"This is one of the most notable triumphs of law and order ever credited to the record of Kentucky," wrote the editor of the *Buffalo Express* in New York.

"Judge Evans' instructions and the verdict of the jury ought to be a warning to would-be assassins and midnight raiders that Uncle Sam will find a way to punish them when state law fails," wrote the editor of the *Daily Leader* in Lexington.

"One of the best things which has happened lately," wrote the editor of the *Appeal* in St. Paul, Minnesota. "It really is wonderful that Dinning is alive, much less that he could win such a verdict from a jury composed entirely of white men, and in Kentucky."

"All honor to Judge Walter Evans, and praise for a Kentucky jury that followed his instructions and gave George Dinning a verdict of $50,000," wrote the editor of the *Boonville Standard* in Indiana. "An act of glorious justice has been consummated. The wretches should be pursued to their last dollar."

"Whatever may be done with the judgement of $50,000, this verdict by a white jury serves notice that mob law is declining in popular favor in Kentucky, and that the State's standards of procedure are rising," wrote the *Washington Star*. "The leaven is in the lump, and it is working."

A legal journal called *Law Notes* pointed out that many lawyers across the country had been paying attention to the case to see if it was worth bringing action against mobs in other jurisdictions, "indicating a growing determination to put down mob violence."

George Dinning made no purchases that day, or the day after, and the sad fact of the matter was that five of the six farmers he sued were poor. Their lawyer told reporters that they had no money to pay George Dinning, and that they would instead each opt to spend ten days in jail.

"The judgement he secured is not worth the paper the verdict was written on," reported the Jeffersonville *Evening News*, "because none of the defendants have anything."

The announcement was outrageous, but Bennett Young planned to object. He planned to send executions to Logan and Simpson Counties, and if the return was made "no property found," he would demand they take the insolvent debtor's oath, swearing they had not transferred their money or property to a friend or family member or to a trust. There wasn't much he could do besides that. Alas, he still had a suit against the men from Tennessee.

He would pursue the men to his death if necessary. In fact, he was already preparing in his mind a lawsuit against seven of the men who had been dismissed from the case. He knew they were in the crowd who had returned the day after the attack and burned down the Dinning home. He would again call them onto the carpet, and this time ask for $75,000.

And he was hopeful that this shot across the bow would suppress further lawlessness in Kentucky.

The first case of its kind paved the way for others.

A month later, a Black Kentucky farmer named E. A. Woolbright would bring a suit against Ex Wilson, Henry Hollan, Bloomer Dial, John Dial, Pat Sullivan, Getty Ezell, Quince and Finn Grubbs, William Wilson, Sr. and Jr., and James Pool. He would claim that he was working in his field not far from Bowling Green when the white men took him from his plow, tied him to a tree, and gave him fifty lashes. He would claim the same Whitecappers had earlier ordered him to leave the community, and he had refused. After the lashing, he would put his shotgun on his shoulder and walk directly into Bowling Green to hire a lawyer.

And a few months after that, a Black woman named Belle Pritton, of Newark, Indiana, would bring a suit in circuit court against Jacob Young, George Marshall, Benjamin Gooden, Uriah Resler, James Fuller, John Nash, William Sample, S. M. McIntosh, H. Risler, M. D. Wright, W. A. Booker, Era Arthur, George Nash, and Ira Wright, all prominent men in the small community. She would allege that the regulators came to her home at one o'clock in the morning, armed with clubs, sticks, and switches, and that they dragged her and her husband from bed to the front lawn, where they choked her and kicked her and said they would kill her if she would not keep still. She would claim that others beat her husband with clubs and sticks, and that since the night of the beating she had been ill and terribly traumatized, and that she had lost her eyesight. She would seek $10,000 from her attackers.

All that was to come. Meanwhile, a poor Black farmer from Simpson County and an old Confederate soldier quietly celebrated their precedent-setting victory against a mob of white men.

Dinning went home to his wife and children and his new life in Jeffersonville, Indiana, and Young left by train for Charleston, South Carolina, where he was scheduled to deliver a tender eulogy to honor the late Winnie Davis, the Daughter of the Confederacy.

In June 1899, the newspapers reported that Bennett Young had filed another lawsuit on behalf of George Dinning. This time he went after men he knew had land and money: Monroe White, William Ragsdale, Pluitt Copeland, Joseph Copeland, James King, and Sam Randolph. They had been dismissed from the previous suit because the plaintiff couldn't prove they were there the night the shots were fired, the night Dinning was assaulted. But these men, Young could prove, trespassed at the house the next morning, drove Dinning's wife away, and burned the house.

Young had actually filed the suit in late April, but it was not made public until June to give the United States marshal enough time to serve the defendants before they could transfer their property to someone else. The new suit asked for $75,000, alleging the men should be held liable for trespassing on Dinning's property, trespassing in his home, and driving him and his family away from their land.

"In his last trial Dinning was the recipient of a great deal of sympathy from those who held that, no matter what crimes he may have committed, the mob had no right to attempt to drive him from his home," reported the Jeffersonville *Evening News*.

By October, the farmers charged in the Tennessee lawsuit had reached a compromise with Dinning, out of court. They agreed to pay him $3,500 if he dropped his case. They gave him half up front.

Dinning left his mark, an X, witnessed by Bennett H. Young and sworn to by a notary public. The full sum was equal in purchasing power to $108,000 today.

Chapter 21

SQUAT AND FIRE

In December 1899, Governor Bill O. Bradley was working in his office when a delegation of Black men filed into his chambers and surprised him. He was anxious at first, worried that they had come to talk about Maysville.

The week before, a nineteen-year-old Black man named Richard Coleman, who stood accused of killing the wife of the farmer for whom he worked, was carried by train from Covington back to Maysville to be tried. Word of his return had spread, and when the train pulled into the station it was surrounded by thousands of people, armed men on every platform. The sheriff and his new deputies marched a frightened Coleman to the courthouse in Maysville as the crowd launched stones and bricks at him. Two thousand more men were waiting at the courthouse with the farmer, the dead woman's husband. Weapons were drawn and demands made, and the mob bound Coleman and marched him to a cricket pitch outside town. So many took turns thrashing the young man with fists and sticks that by the time he arrived he was barely recognizable. The mob tied him to a sapling, and the crowd fetched brush and built a pyre at his feet. No one wore masks. It was broad daylight. They were above the law.

The husband of the dead woman struck the first match. One of her brothers lit the second. Someone with a knife carved into Coleman's chest. Before long the ropes holding the young man to the tree burned through, and the crowd used poles to push him back onto the pyre.

When word reached Governor Bradley, he immediately offered a $500 reward for the apprehension of the ringleaders.

"This is a terrible disgrace to Kentucky," Bradley said. "This, together with the rest, will keep a decent man from ever coming into Kentucky." Maybe he was truly concerned with racial justice and equality, or maybe, as his statement seems to indicate, his outrage had something to do with economic enterprise.

Coleman was one of eleven people to die in the state that day. Josie Baird was killed by railroad torpedo at Fulton; James Harlan, saloonkeeper, was killed by William Farmer at Louisville; Mrs. Leslie Jump was burned to death in Williamstown; William Carmichael burned to death at Middlesboro; O. D. Saunders, while teaching in church at Akersville, was called out by enemies and killed by William Harlin; Dick Morgan was ambushed on Poor Fork in Harlan County by Will Peach; Stewart Jones was shot by Jack Robbins at Jock's Branch in Bell County; Thomas Jackson was killed by a mad dog at Hopkinsville; Aaron Hughes was killed by John Calise during a craps game at Louisville; and attorney A. M. Tudors's throat was cut by John Hall at Richmond.

One newspaper made note that Kentucky was "the state in which probably occurs more death by violence than any other."

But the men weren't there to chastise Bradley for not doing more to stop Coleman's murder. They presented to the governor a pocket watch, made of solid gold. The charm was set with three diamonds. The chain was heavy gold with twisted links. The face of the watch had old-fashioned figures as indicators instead of Roman numerals. On the outside was the monogram W.O.B., and inside the case appeared the engraving, TO GOVERNOR WILLIAM O. BRADLEY, FROM THE NEGROES OF KENTUCKY, DECEMBER 9, 1899. On the cap of the movement appeared a sentence from one of Bradley's recent campaign speeches: I PLEAD FOR MORE KINDNESS AND MORE JUSTICE FOR THE NEGRO OF KENTUCKY. Above that was a sentence pulled from his endorsement on the application for the pardon of George Dinning: TOO LONG HAVE MOBS DISGRACED THE FAIR NAME OF KENTUCKY.

Bradley thanked the men for their remembrance, and he accepted the gift graciously. He told them he would have been even happier if they had given the money to one of the Black schools.

"I am proud of the fact that I have been the Negro's friend," he said, "and have done all that I could to advance his standing as a citizen and to elevate his race."

By early winter, when the leaves on the beech trees had all turned brown, it was plain to see that Doc Moore was quickly coming unwound. The people of Simpson County noticed that his mind was rapidly deteriorating. He seemed agitated, in constant torment. He told those he trusted that he thought he was being pursued by demons, or devils of some kind. No one could see what he was talking about, but he saw them, plain as day, hounding him from the shadows.

Just before Christmas 1899, Doc Moore, fifty-two years old and alone but for his haunting hallucinations, raised a pistol to his right temple.

If scenes from the life he had lived flitted through his mind in those last moments, he might have recalled signing up to fight for the Eighth Kentucky Cavalry before he turned eighteen, under General John Hunt Morgan, the same as Bennett Young.

He might have recalled returning to live with his parents after the war, just three houses down from where George Dinning lived with his own folks. He might have recollected serving as a deputy sheriff and constable, keeping the peace in that small corner of southwestern Simpson County. He might have recalled meeting Jodie Conn and the rest of the men out near New Hope mill and agreeing to serve as captain of the band of regulators. Maybe George Dinning's defiance echoed in his ears: "You'd better take me out tonight." He might have recalled the gunshot, or shouting, "Squat and fire, boys!" when all hell broke loose. He might have remembered the way the moonlight fell on the yard as the white men fired. He might have remembered lying through his teeth to win a conviction, then lying again when the tables had turned. He might have remembered the satisfied look on one-eyed George Dinning's face when the jury announced that Doc would forever be indebted to a Colored man.

The bullet entered Moore's right temple on December 22. Doc Moore was dead.

A short time after, his mother visited Williams & West clothing store in town and picked out a burial suit, a shirt, a pair of socks, a collar, a tie, and a pair of slippers, totaling $11.40, more money than George Dinning received from Doc Moore.

They buried the degenerate son in the cold earth of Simpson County, Kentucky.

Chapter 22

"I WANT TO DIE IN THE OLD BLUE GRASS"

George Dinning was George Denning now, most likely in order to facilitate being forgotten, but perhaps to distinguish his old self from his new. Dinning was a slave's name.

Over the better part of the next decade, he maintained his legal antagonism against the farmers of Simpson and Logan Counties, which kept his story fresh in the minds of the readers of the country's newspapers. There was a price to pay for terrorizing innocent people.

With the help of Bennett Young, Denning sued Jodie Conn's father time and again for various amounts over the next seven years. And he gained, little by little, over time. In 1902, he was paid $500 as part of a compromise with three of the original defendants. A month later, he claimed $31.13 from Charles T. Conn, who said he had no more to give. Denning sued Conn again in 1903, and this time roped in the creditors whom Conn had paid off with proceeds from his son's estate. The case was argued to the state Supreme Court, and a judge ruled against Denning on a technicality. The court record trail runs cold there.

Denning lived the rest of his life peacefully in Jeffersonville, Indiana, working as a teamster and laborer. He raised his family there, and by 1900, five of his children were in school, and four of them knew how to read and write, a gift never afforded George and Mollie. His children were soon having children of their own, and grandchildren, and some of them would remain in the area for a very long time.

Shortly after the turn of the century, Bennett Young, still president of the orphanage for Black children, drew up articles of incorporation for the Booker T. Washington Community Center, a place devoted to the social welfare and recreation of young Black citizens of Louisville. He raised an endowment for the center and would stay on as its chief for the rest of his life. He continued to represent African Americans in the criminal and civil courts, and rarely took payment. And even though he moved to the outskirts of town, to a mansion he called Youngland, he still served as superintendent of the afternoon Sunday school at the Stuart Robinson Memorial Church.

In 1903, he published another book, *The Battle of the Thames*, recounting the battle that turned the tide of the land war with Britain in 1813. In 1912, Chapel Company of Boston published Young's magnum opus, *Confederate Wizards of the Saddle*. In the book Young details, and mostly glorifies, the chivalry, skill, and accomplishments of his Civil War heroes, John Hunt Morgan among them. His unabashed respect and admiration for those who fought so hard to preserve enslavement leaves behind a fraught legacy.

He recounts one story in the book that's worth noting, not about a general, but about a poor mountaineer. In telling the story, Young wrote that he witnessed "one of the bravest things I have ever observed."

On a brutally hot July 5, 1863, on the front end of Morgan's raid, his handpicked cavalrymen rode upon a brick railroad depot filled with several hundred Union troops unwilling to surrender.

The Eighth Kentucky was ordered to charge the front of the depot. Young was among those in the onslaught. They were advancing through a field covered in waist-high weeds, which made marching difficult. Within a few hundred feet of the large front door of the depot, the Confederates were ordered to "lie down," and they did, and the Federals fired into the weeds. A number were hit, including the man beside Bennett Young. Young knew him well. He was a cattle drover from around Somerset, in eastern Kentucky, on the edge of the Appalachian Mountains. Uneducated, but brave. Young never could fathom why the young man had joined the war. He had no property, no enslaved people, no relatives in the Confederacy. He had made a few acquaintances as a drover, but those limited relationships couldn't explain why he had risked his life for the Southland. And he certainly hadn't joined the effort for adventure.

He was quiet, too. Uncommunicative. But one night, on a dark and lonely scout through the mountains, he had opened up to Young and told him why he went to war. He was thirty-two years old and had fallen in love with a white girl who lived along the Wilderness Road, during an overnight stay at her father's house. His desire got the better of him, but he couldn't bring himself to tell her of his love. Instead, he bought her presents. Small mirrors. Plain rings. Garnet breastpins. He imagined a day when he would build her a log cabin and propose.

Upon returning from a long cattle drive, he learned that she had married another man.

He had nothing else to live for. So one day when John Hunt Morgan came riding through Somerset, he mounted his black steed and rode away to war, not caring about the outcome.

He always took the front, Young wrote. When they were lying in the field that day, the Enfield ball passed clean through his body. His groans were agonizing. He begged to be taken off the field, but no one could move. Any man who rose would surely be shot by the Federals.

This is when the astonishing happened. Young watched as the Second Kentucky Regiment charged the south side of the depot with their pistols, hustled up to the open window, and fired into the mass of Union troops inside.

The distraction gave Young a chance to lift his friend onto his back and storm off the field, bullets whizzing by. He barely had time to commend his friend to the surgeons and bid him good-bye. The man put Young's fingers to his lips, and his black eyes filled with tears.

In 1868, after Young returned to Louisville from exile, he visited Cave Hill Cemetery and found the grave of Vincent Eastham of Somerset, Company B, Eighth Kentucky Cavalry. From then on, every Decoration Day he brought armloads of flowers to make beautiful the grave. He ordered his children and his children's children to forever keep green the spot where his friend slept.

This sort of pledge, to honor the war dead, to remember his friends from the Lost Cause, drove Bennett Young for the rest of his life. He wanted, he said, to "hold up again the wreaths that crown the brows of the men who, on the sanguinary battlefields of the West did and dared all that men could do to win from the inexorable decrees of fate, the liberty and independence of the South." This sentiment, of course, only referred to the liberty and independence of the white South.

As commander of the Kentucky division, and later commander in chief of the United Confederate Veterans, Young was a key player in a movement to build monuments to the Confederate dead across the South. He oversaw the erection of an obelisk in memory of General Felix Zollicoffer and his troops near the battleground of Mill Springs in Pulaski County, Tennessee.

When Young learned that the federal government had taken over the birthplace of President Lincoln in LaRue County, Kentucky, and planned to erect a monument there, Young started an effort to buy and preserve Jefferson Davis's birthplace at Fairview in Todd County. He advanced the money out of his own pocket. "The North has honored Lincoln's birthplace," he said. "The South will do as much for Mr. Davis." He soon began planning and raising money for an obelisk 351 feet tall that would be "majestic and imposing, not only to this generation, but to all other generations for a thousand years to come." The arc of history would rightfully bend against that ambition in just one hundred years, and communities of color would splash paint and harsh words onto those same memorials and make plain to white America the pain they caused.

In February 1911, Young gave the verbose oration at the unveiling of a statue of Davis on Canal Street in New Orleans. Little children wearing red, white, and blue sang "Dixie" and stood in the shape of the Confederate flag. "Jefferson Davis, misjudged in life and disfranchised until death, is finding his true place in history," Young said that day. "These words were not spoken to awaken a single question of prejudice or ill-will; they are only given utterance to emphasize the duties of the South to the memory of Mr. Davis." Young called for monuments to Davis in every major city in the South. "As he stood for the South, the South will stand for him and all that his life and suffering implied," Young said, "and the South will see that he shall be understood and appreciated, and that no shadow shall darken his fame and that no misrepresentation shall dim the splendor of his character."

The statue would stand until 2017, when the New Orleans city council, prodded by a grassroots effort to take down such Confederate statuary and symbols of white supremacy, ordered the monument removed. For a century, Black and Brown children played at the feet of the figurehead of a movement that kept them impoverished, void of political power, suffering. By 2017, the statue had been defaced a number of times, and the words SLAVE OWNER had been spray-painted upon its granite base. The removal was protested by Rebel sons bearing Confederate flags and carrying guns, who surrounded the statue for weeks. But on May 11, 2017, workers came and quickly loaded the bronze Jefferson Davis onto a truck and took it to storage in an undisclosed location. The workers who removed the statue wore masks over their faces to protect their identities, a sign of the lingering power of the threat of white supremacy.

In his final year, as his health began to fail, Young started composing a collection of stories for the children at the Kentucky School for the Blind, which he visited often. The stories wouldn't be published until after his death, but one stands as a parable.

A large and powerful goose named Dr. Gander lived on the barnyard at Youngland and minded the affairs on the farm in Young's absence. One day Dr. Gander saw a hungry sow get loose from her pen and gobble up a barnyard hen, to the surprise of all the animals. The sow enjoyed the meal so much that she then set her sights on Dr. Gander. The goose was horribly frightened. He weighed just twenty-four pounds and the pig weighed three hundred. But he put up a fight. "Now is the time to get in your work," he told himself. And the gander attacked, flapping about the sow's head, staging counterattacks, pecking her eyes. She was massive, though, and he was growing tired. Then a little dog jumped through the fence and went after the sow's hind legs. Soon both goose and dog were doing their best against the huge and aggressive animal, to no real avail. A Jersey cow noticed the commotion and sidled over, bending her head down as if she was about to charge. The pig stopped cold and reconsidered. Order was restored to the barnyard.

Young retired in the fall of 1918 to Jacksonville, Florida, to see if the mild climate might improve his health, but he seemed to sense death approaching. "I want to die in the old Blue Grass State," he told his physician. "I want to cross the river and bivouac there with my gallant comrades who have gone before." He and his wife took a taxicab to the train depot and rode in a private suite home to Louisville. An ambulance met them at Union Station, and Young made it to his home on West Ormsby, where he was surrounded by family. He died the afternoon of February 23, 1919, at age seventy-six. The *Courier-Journal* announced his death on its front page, above the fold. "One of the last survivors of a memorable and heroic generation, Gen. Young was long a conspicuous figure in the business life of Louisville and the courts of the State and Jefferson County," the paper reported. "He was an eloquent pleader before the bar, and, twenty years ago, the announcement that Gen Young was to argue could fill a courtroom always."

Among the first to pay respects at the Young home was the Reverend H. C. Weeden, a Black Methodist minister, who was reared and educated by Young.

"Gen. Young's death is a great loss to the colored people of Louisville," the Reverend Weeden said. "He was foremost in work of charity among our race."

"Courageous as a lion, he had the gentle spirit of a child," wrote the editor of the *Owensboro Inquirer*. "He loved the good and the beautiful. He was always the champion of the cause that needed the assistance of a square deal."

Of note was the fact that many African American associations in Louisville adopted resolutions bemoaning Young's death, leaving for posterity an odd juxtaposition of causes.

"He endeared himself particularly to his comrades of the Confederacy, at the head of whose organization of surviving veterans he served for a time," the editor of the *Courier-Journal* noted. "He was zealous in his labors in the cause of Louisville's public library, while the breadth of his sympathies is indicated by the fact that perhaps among none is his death more regretted than among the negroes, who had ample reasons for regarding him as a friend."

They buried him at Cave Hill Cemetery under an unadorned slab upon which was inscribed:

I HAVE KEPT THE FAITH

Bennett Henderson Young's grave marker in Cave Hill Cemetery, Louisville, Ky. (*Courtesy of the author*)

Chapter 23

"SOME OF THIS FALLS DOWN TO US"

On December 9, 2019, a rainy Monday afternoon, Anthony Denning pulled to a stop on the narrow road near the southern edge of Eastern Cemetery in Jeffersonville, Indiana, where he grew up. The cemetery is ringed by single-family houses, and beyond those to the south, past the Maple Elementary School and Bethel AME Church and the Howard Steamboat Museum, is the Ohio River, and beyond that is downtown Louisville. Anthony's father, George, used to bring Anthony and his siblings out here to visit the graves of their people.

"I can see it from here," he said, stepping out of the car.

He walked past rows of eroded headstones that stretched to the northwest and stopped in front of a modest cement marker that read MOLLIE DENNING, GONE BUT NOT FORGOTTEN. His great-grandmother, who died in 1944, somewhere close to age eighty-nine, is buried here, a half mile north of the Mason-Dixon Line. He pulled a white kerchief from his pocket and rubbed it back and forth across the face of the headstone. It made little difference; the engraving was still difficult to decipher. "I've got to come back out here and clean this up better," he said, plucking some weeds around the base of the marker.

Anthony is fifty-seven now and has a bum knee and a back that makes him think twice about international flights. His hair and beard are turning white. He speaks with a slight Kentucky drawl, even though he was born and raised in Indiana. He moved north himself, after high school, and a stint in the Navy, and he has owned a barbershop in Indianapolis since the early 1990s. It's called Teek's because Anthony picked up the nickname Antique when he was younger, and that was eventually shortened to Tique, but Teek looks better on a sign. As it turns out, he is a bit of a collector. He owns a vintage barber's chair and two beautiful cars built in the 1970s, including a beige Cadillac with 69,000 original miles. He keeps them both in storage and only drives them once a month. His latest restoration project has been a 1930 Philco Art Deco radio and wet bar combination, which he claimed after his grandmother died. It was chipped and scratched when he first laid eyes on it, but he saw its potential. He lugged it to a professional, who took on the tedious task of restoring the bar and the original radio electronics. It is now a thing of beauty. He says he'll never sell it because it belongs in the family, but he has seen the same restored radio bar for sale online for $30,000.

When Anthony was a boy, he heard curt whispered stories about George and Mollie Dinning, how his great-grandfather killed a man in Simpson County and how his great-grandmother had to flee with her children, including his grandfather, also named George. But it wasn't something that was openly discussed. Anthony heard only the rough corners of the story, and none of the details.

"It seemed like one of those family secrets that nobody really wanted to talk about," he said.

A few years ago, he noticed a blog post from a St. Louis newspaper editor and historian who sketched out his great-

Anthony Denning uses a handkerchief to clean the headstone of Mollie Denning, his great-grandmother, at Eastern Cemetery in Jeffersonville, Indiana, on December 9, 2019. (*Courtesy of the author*)

grandfather's story in more detail. Anthony learned for the first time about Bennett Henderson Young and the civil lawsuit. He never met his great-grandfather George, who died of apoplexy on March 13, 1930, or his great-grandmother, who died in 1944, but knowing more of the details helped bring them to life.

"Reading that stuff about them," he said, "it brought a tear to my eye."

Since then, he has been on a mission to fill in the gaps, to learn more about the man who defended his family from the regulators. That night exists as a signpost in his lineage, a historic marker he can point to as a moment that helped create him three generations before. If things had gone differently that night, if George Dinning had failed to grab his rifle, or hadn't taken a bullet in the head, or hadn't mustered the courage to squeeze the trigger, Anthony Denning might not have been born.

"I would not be here," he said. "If it would've went any other way, I would not exist."

How do you thank a man you never knew, who died decades before you were born?

Anthony's quest to learn more has taken him to the Family History Library, the world's largest genealogical collection, in Salt Lake City. He went for the first time to a family reunion in Simpson County, where he met distant relatives but was mostly confused by how they were related. He has collected dozens of historical records, legal documents, and newspaper clippings about his great-grandfather. When he reads about George Dinning, he sees himself between the lines.

"Some of this falls down to us," he said. "We've been fighters. I feel like we were raised off of the things that he went through, to stand up and have courage to face the things that come your way."

Not long ago, Anthony's brother was working at a nursing home when one of the elderly patients saw his name tag. "You're too young to be a Denning," the woman said. She was Anthony's oldest living cousin, in her eighties. Her grandfather was George Dinning's son, Ben Dinning. Since then, Anthony visits the woman every chance he gets, kissing her forehead before he leaves. She, too, is reluctant to talk about what happened in the 1890s, she said, because she is uncertain about the line between truth and folklore.

One interesting piece of the story has survived in the family's oral history. It was never mentioned in the newspapers or any public records. Anthony's mother, Imogene Denning, recalls hearing that Mollie Denning and her children were hiding in barrels when they crossed the Ohio River and arrived in Jeffersonville. Whether that means barrels on a barge or barrels floating on the river has been lost to time. Alas, it seems plausible that they were in fear for their lives and could have been frightened enough to hide in order to be spirited away to Indiana.

Those Dennings who remain know very little about George Denning, including why he changed the spelling of the family's last name from Dinning. Perhaps he lived in fear of being pursued to Indiana, or maybe he tired of the attention.

The remaining Dennings say the Georges who came after him, the ones they did know, were disciplined, resolute, headstrong, and stubborn. Maybe even a little mean. There's a family story that George Denning's grandson George, Anthony's father, was walking mules across the bridge from Louisville one day when some men who were painting the bridge began throwing rocks at him out of pure meanness. He walked the mules home and returned with an ax handle, and when he was finished not a single bridge painter was standing. The story doesn't seem far-fetched. George Denning's son George built an attractive house on Spring Street in Jeffersonville in 1926, four years before his father died, and moved his family in soon after. They were among the first Black families to live on Spring Street, a point of pride for George's descendants. He lived there until his death after a car accident in 1961, at seventy-four years old. Anthony's mother lives in the house now, a direct recipient of the modest generational wealth that sprang from George Denning's courageous lawsuit.

The George Denning who left Simpson County for good is buried somewhere in Eastern Cemetery, but no one in the family has been able to locate his headstone. A great flood in 1937 ruined the burial records at the funeral home that handled his remains, and the family has been unable to find his plot. They know he's here somewhere, though, buried on free soil in a town that welcomed him and his family.

They know that his passing mustered none of the pomp and ceremony of Bennett H. Young's death, just the sterile and bureaucratic filing of a certificate with the Indiana State Board of Health. His last public record was spare, much like his first, in the 1860 slave roster. The Indiana record states: Male, 74, Colored, Married. Lived at 313 East 14th Street, Jeffersonville, Clark County, Indiana. Death was "sudden."

The family has been unable to locate even an obituary or a news article noting his death.

Anthony has walked all over the cemetery, searching for his great-grandfather's grave. He hopes to find him someday, to rub his fingers across the stone marking the final resting place of a stubborn man who would not quit fighting.

"I've always thought of it," he said. "I've tried to put myself in his shoes, a man with children in the house, and a wife, trying to protect what's rightfully his."

How do you honor a man who came before you? Is it enough to be a good man yourself?

"For that time, that was unheard of."

How do you thank a man who did something like that when you cannot find his grave?

Anthony won't stop searching. Courage like his great-grandfather's inspired the men and women who fought for the right to vote, who fought for equal treatment, who fought against Black Codes and Jim Crow, who fought the Second Klan, who fought for this country in foreign wars, who fought against government persecution and police prosecution, who fought for liberty, who are still fighting, chanting "Black Lives Matter."

Anthony dreams of buying one of the historic houses on Riverside Drive in Jeffersonville, not far from where his people are buried. The houses sit along the Ohio River. He would work hard to restore it to its former glory. Maybe it would take months or years to bring it back. No matter. When he was finished, he'd park his antique cars in the driveway and open his Philco radio bar and pour a glass of bourbon. He'd sit on the front porch, firmly in Indiana but facing the South, looking out over the river to Louisville, and Simpson County beyond, so far, far away.

ACKNOWLEDGMENTS

I'd like to offer my deepest thanks to the following people for their help, friendship, inspiration, guidance, and grace in the past few years, as this story traveled from curiosity to book: Michael Kruse; Thomas Lake; Mike Wilson; Kelley and Tom French; Bill Duryea; Lane DeGregory; Leonora LaPeter; Brendan Meyers; Corey Johnson; DeMorris Lee; Erin Scheffels; Demian Miller; Scott Lambert; John Capouya; Tony Rehagen; Justin Heckert; Joshua Sharpe; the Lake family of Ludowici, Georgia, and beyond; Wright Thompson; Chris Jones; Kim Cross; Mosi Secret; Charles McNair; Brooke Jarvis; Bronwen Dickey; Michael Hall; Michael Graff; Michael Mooney; Tommy and Alix Tomlinson; Justin George; Erin Sullivan; Andrew Pantazi; Amy Wallace; Denise Wills; Hafizah Geter; Christopher Goffard; Caitlin Flanagan; Max Marshall; Leah Sottile; Matt LaWell; Roy Peter Clark; Paige Williams; Matthew Glowicki; Hampton Sides; Stacy Brick; Jeff Klinkenberg; Kathy Floyd; George Getschow; James Scott; Jason Ryan; Ashley Porter; Eric Nishimoto; Julia Flynn Siler; and the whole Archer City crew. I'd like to thank the journalism faculty at the University of Montana in Missoula, where this story started to take shape, especially Carol Van Valkenburg, Dennis Swibold, Joe Eaton, Keith Graham, Kevin Tompkins, Nadia White, and Jeff Gailus.

I'm grateful to Allen G. Breed and Roland Klose, who both reported on George Denning's story before me, and their work helped point the way. Thanks to the good people at the African American Heritage Center and the Simpson County Historical Society, both in Franklin, Kentucky; the Filson Historical Society in Louisville; Diane Stepro at the Jeffersonville Township Public Library and Jeanne Burke at the Clark County Museum, both in Indiana; Desiree Wallen at the National Archives in Atlanta; and Thomas Owen in special collections at the University of Louisville.

For their invaluable help with research and genealogy, my intense thanks go to Jennifer P. Brown, Caryn Bush-Baird, Melanie Osborn, and Gary Osborn.

Special gratitude for Ian Straus, my editor, who made this book much better, and for Tracy Behar, Jessica Chun, and the crew at Little, Brown Spark. Thanks to my literary agent, Jane Dystel, who is the very best.

When I met Anthony Denning, I felt like I had made a new friend. Thanks to Anthony and his family for their warmth, and for their help in telling their ancestor's important story.

Thanks also to my family—to my mother, Donna; my stepdad, John; and my brothers, Matt, Paul, and Blake. Lorraine Monteagut provided support in many ways, and this book would not exist without her help. I so appreciate it.

Finally, for their patience and criticism, my warmest gratitude goes to my children, Asher and Morissey, and to Bey, whom we miss very much.

BIBLIOGRAPHY

Baker, John F. *The Washingtons of Wessyngton Plantation: Stories of My Family's Journey to Freedom*. New York: Atria Books, 2009.

Beach, Mrs. James, and James Henry Snider. *Franklin and Simpson County: A Picture of Progress, 1819–1975*. Tompkinsville: Simpson County Bicentennial Commission, 1976.

Brooks, Lucille. *African American Heritage of Simpson County, Kentucky*. Utica: African American Heritage Committee, 2001.

Brooks, Roy L. *Atonement and Forgiveness: A New Model for Black Reparations*. Berkeley: University of California Press, 2004.

Durrett, Reuben T., editor. *Bryant's Station and the Memorial Proceedings*. Louisville: John P. Morton and Co., 1897.

Egerton, Douglas R. *The Wars of Reconstruction: the Brief, Violent History of America's Most Progressive Era*. New York: Bloomsbury Press, 2014.

Falk, Gary. *Louisville Remembered*. Charleston: History Press, 2009.

Federal Works Agency. *Kentucky: A Guide to the Bluegrass State*. New York: Hastings House, 1954.

Foner, Eric. *Reconstruction: America's Unfinished Revolution, 1863–1877: Updated Edition*. New York: Harper Perennial Classics, 2014.

Glazier, Jack. *Been Coming Through Some Hard Times: Race, History, and Memory in Western Kentucky*. Knoxville: University of Tennessee Press, 2012.

Harrison, Lowell H. *Kentucky's Governors*. Lexington: University Press of Kentucky, 2004.

Harrison, Lowell H., and James C. Klotter. *A New History of Kentucky*. Lexington: University Press of Kentucky, 1997.

Jaspin, Elliot. *Buried in the Bitter Waters: The Hidden History of Racial Cleansing in America*. New York: Basic Books, 2007.

Kinchen, Oscar A. *Daredevils of the Confederate Army: The Story of the St. Albans Raiders*. Boston: Christopher Publishing House, 1959.

Kinchen, Oscar Arvle. *General Bennett H. Young, Confederate Raider and a Man of Many Adventures*. Boston: Christopher Publishing House, 1981.

Kleber, John E. *The Encyclopedia of Louisville*. Lexington: University Press of Kentucky, 2001.

Locke, John, and Crawford Brough Macpherson. *Second Treatise of Government*. Indianapolis: Hackett Publishing Co., 1980.

Lucas, Marion B. *A History of Blacks in Kentucky: From Slavery to Segregation, 1760–1891*. Lexington: University Press of Kentucky, 2003.

McQueen, Keven. *Louisville Murder & Mayhem: Historic Crimes of the Derby City*. Charleston: History Press, 2012.

Milewski, Melissa. *Litigating Across the Color Line: Civil Cases Between Black and White Southerners from the End of Slavery to Civil Rights*. New York: Oxford University Press, 2018.

Raper, Arthur F. *The Tragedy of Lynching*. New York: New American Library, 1969.

Simpson County, Kentucky: *Families Past and Present*. Paducah: Turner Pub. Co., 1974.

Simpson, John A. *Edith D. Pope and Her Nashville Friends: Guardians of the Lost Cause in the Confederate Veteran*. Knoxville: University of Tennessee Press, 2003.

Smith, Gerald L., Karen Cotton McDaniel, and John A. Hardin. *The Kentucky African American Encyclopedia*. Lexington: University Press of Kentucky, 2015.

Snider, James Henry, and Mrs. James Beach. *Franklin and Simpson County: Reflections of 1976 and a Supplement to A Picture of Progress, 1819–1975*. Tompkinsville: Monroe County Press, 1977.

Welch, Kimberly M. *Black Litigants in the Antebellum American South*. Chapel Hill: University of North Carolina Press, 2018.

Wells-Barnett, Ida B. *Southern Horrors: Lynch Law in All Its Phases*. OUTLOOK Verlag, 2018.

Wright, George C. *A History of Blacks in Kentucky in Pursuit of Equality, 1890–1980*. Lexington: University Press of Kentucky, 1992.

Wright, George C. *Life Behind a Veil: Blacks in Louisville, Kentucky, 1865–1930*. Baton Rouge: Louisiana State University Press, 1985.

Wright, George C. *Racial Violence in Kentucky, 1865–1940: Lynchings, Mob Rule, and "Legal Lynchings."* Baton Rouge: Louisiana State University Press, 1990.

Young, Bennett H. *Confederate Wizards of the Saddle: Being Reminiscences and Observations of One Who Rode with Morgan*. Nashville: J. S. Sanders & Co., 1999.

Young, Bennett H. *History and Texts of the Three Constitutions of Kentucky: With Illustrative State History Prefacing Them and Marginal Notes Showing All Alterations in the Fundamental Law* . . . Louisville: Courier-Journal Job Printing Co., 1890.

Young, Bennett H. *The Battle of the Thames: In Which Kentuckians Defeated the British, French, and Indians, October 5, 1813*. Louisville: John P. Morton & Co, 1903.

Young, Bennett H. *The Prehistoric Men of Kentucky: a History of What Is Known of Their Lives and Habits, Together with a Description of Their Implements and Other Relics and of the Tumuli Which Have Earned for Them the Designation of Mound Builders: a Paper Prepared to Commemorate the Silver Anniversary of the Filson Club*. Louisville: John P. Morton & Co., Printers, 1910.

Young, Bennett H., and S. M. Duncan. *A History of Jessamine County, Kentucky: From Its Earliest Settlement to 1898*. Delhi: Pranava Books, 2019.

Young, Bennett H., editor. *Kentucky Eloquence, Past and Present: Library of Orations, after-Dinner Speeches, Popular and…Classic Lectures, Addresses and Poetry*. Louisville: Ben La Bree, 1907.

Young, Bennett H. *Dr. S. M. Neel, the Self-Appointed Moses of the Southern Church: Being a Response to Dr. Neel's Article Entitled "Col. Young's So-Called Reply"*. Delhi: Pranava Books, 2019.

INDEX

Note: Italic page numbers refer to illustrations.

abolitionism, 11
Afro-American League of Jefferson County, 173
Alpha Baptist Church in Franklin, 173
American Lawyer, 204
American Revolution, 116, 118
Angel, Robert, 153
Anti-Mob and Lynch Law Association, 29
Arthur, Chester A., 211
Arthur, Era, 245
Atkinson, William Yates, 221–22
Atlanta Journal, 222
Atlantic Monthly, 13

Babb, W. P. "Lum," 131, 134, 146–47, 153, 185, 220
Baird, Henry, 29
Baird, J. C., 38
Baird, Josie, 248
Ballard, Bland, 27
Ballard, William, 101, 220
Barclay, H. W., 239
Bates, C. P., 172
Beach, H. H., 239–40
Beall, John Yates, 120
Ben Holton v. the Duncans (1882), 204
Bennett, Eliza Sharp, 213
Berry, L. G., 154–56, 157, 185
Bingham, Henry, 222
Bittner, Gustave, 191

Black Codes, 265
Black Lives Matter, 265
Black people. *See also* enslavement; lynchings
  ability to testify in federal courts, 205
  arming against white violence, 27–29
  attacks on Ku Klux Klan, 18–19
  damage suits for lynchings, 204, 244–45
  inability to testify against whites in state court, 26–27, 93–94
  Ku Klux Klan's intimidation of, 14–15, 17–19
  lack of justice for white crimes against, 26–29, 41, 93–94, 169
  law suits against whites, 204–6
  Union Army service of, 13
  voting rights of, 94
  Bennett Young as advocate for, 126–27
Blackstone, William, 169
Bloodworth, J. H., 84, 107, 220
Bloodworth, W. T., 84, 220
Booker, W. A., 245
Booker T. Washington Community Center, 252
Boone, Daniel, 183
Boonville Standard, 243
Boston Globe, 193
Bowling Green Times, 29
Boyle, St. John, 210

Bradley, W. O. "Bill"
 on Civil War, 229
 and Richard Coleman's lynching, 248
 Colorado Springs trip of, 50, 170
 correspondence on George Dinning
  case, 170–81, 182
 and delegation of Black men, 247–49
 and George Dinning's safety before
  trial, 24–25, 30, 31, 32, 35–38, 50–
  51, 53
 and George Dinning's safety during
  trial, 105
 George Dinning's sworn statement to,
  42–43
 Molly Dinning's correspondence with,
  40–41
 hanging in effigy on courthouse lawn,
  51
 on Louisville attack on George Dinning, 206
 on lynchings, 25, 29, 30
 on mob violence, 31
 opposition to Ku Klux Klan, 27
 pardon for George Dinning, 183–89,
  192–94, 208, 249
 and race-based killings in Kentucky, 26
 as Republican, 25, 29–30
 signing of antilynching bill, 44
 speaking engagements of, 208–9
 Tol Stone protected by, 127, 128
 support for pardon of George Dinning,
  164, 165–79, 181
 and transcript of trial of George Dinning, 181–82, 184–85
Breckinridge, John, 104
Breckinridge, John C., 104, 125
Breckinridge, William Campbell Preston,
 104–5, 165–67, 176, 180–81
Breed, James E., 239
Brooklyn Times, 194
Bryant, Tom, 51
Buchanan, James, 104
Buffalo Express, 243
Butler, Benjamin, 123

Calise, John, 248
Campbell, Arch, 100, 112
Carmichael, William, 248
Caron, Charles K., 191
Carver, John, 29
castle doctrine, 169
Christian, Matt, 23, 93
Christianity, 125

Cincinnati Enquirer, 47
Civil Rights Act of 1866, 95
civil rights movement, xiv
Civil War
 attack on Fort Sumter, 12, 119
 continuation of, xii, xv
 and judgment of history, xiii–xiv
 Kentucky's neutrality in, 12, 26, 119
 monuments of, 128, 228–29, 254–55
 and rights of Black people, 169
Clark, Bud
 as Democrat, 24
 George Dinning's testimony on, 147
 and George Dinning in jail, 22, 23, 24
 and George Dinning's protection before
  trial, 24–25, 33, 37, 38, 200
 George Dinning turning himself in to,
  6, 9, 29, 30, 135, 188, 189, 200,
  217
 ushering of jury for deliberations, 160
Clark, George Rogers, 190
Clark, William, 183
Cody, Bill, 227
Coin, Charles, 47
Coke, Edward, 168
Coleman, Richard, 247–48
Colored Orphans' Home Society, 126, 195,
 252
Confederacy
 former Confederates, 37
 legacy of, xvi
 monuments of, 128, 254–56
 veterans groups, xi–xii, xvi–xvii, 254,
  258
 Bennett Young as Confederate, 116,
  119–27, 128, 232, 236, 249, 252–
  55, 258
Confederate battle flag, xi–xii, xvi–xvii
Conn, Alexander, 96
Conn, Ben, 65, 69, 95–98, 152–53, 185
Conn, Caroline J. Baird, 87
Conn, Charles T., 7, 38, 86–87, 154, 220,
 239, 242, 251
Conn, Jodie L.
 attack on George Dinning's home, 7,
  32, 215, 218, 234, 250
 Tom Bloodworth's testimony on, 84
 clothing worn in attack on George Dinning's home, 60, 87
 Ben Conn's testimony on, 96
 Eva Dinning's testimony on, 106
 George Dinning's relationship with,
  102

George Dinning's shooting of, 5, 6, 38, 40, 42, 136, 154, 178, 194, 215, 217, 219, 220, 234

George Dinning's testimony on, 135–36, 138–39

family background of, 86–87, 96

Albert Green Freeman's testimony on, 56–62, 64, 67, 68, 69–70, 71

friends avenging death of, 7, 8, 22–23, 30, 32–33, 53, 92, 160–61

Isen Hollis's testimony on, 92

image from Louisville *Times,* 88

William S. Moore's testimony on, 72, 73, 75, 78, 79, 81, 82

obituary of, 87–88

J. M. Phelps's testimony on, 90

press characterizations of, 7, 9, 86

press reports of shooting of, 6–8, 9, 22–23, 31

Nick Williams's testimony on, 91

Conn, Matilda Hardin, 96

Conn, Natley, 96

Conn, Notley Thomas, 86, 96

Conn family, 105, 130, 197

Cook, George, 220

Cook, Jesse, 220

Cooper, Ahmed, xi–xii, xvii

Cooper, Simon, 24

Copeland, Joseph, 71, 220, 233, 246

Copeland, Pluitt, 220, 233, 246

Cotton, Bud, 222

Cox, E. H., 171

Craik, Charles E., 173–74

Cranford, Alfred, 221, 223, 225–26

Crockett, Joseph, 118

Cuscaden, George W., 191

Cutbirth, Benjamin, 183

damage suits of George Dinning

    damages sought in, 216, 246, 251

    defense's strategies in, 217–19, 230, 232–34, 239

    Eva Dinning's testimony in, 233

    George Dinning's ability to collect damages, 244, 246, 264

    George Dinning's response to verdict, 242, 245

    George Dinning's testimony in, 233

    Hermann Dinning's testimony in, 233

    Mary Dinning's testimony in, 233

    filing of lawsuit, 214

    hearing of, 221

    judge's dismissal of some defendants, 239, 241, 244, 246

    jury deliberations in, 239–40

    jury's verdict in, 241, 242, 243

    plans for, 195, 200, 202–4, 207

    press reports on, 216–17, 231–32, 237, 239, 242–43, 246

    summons issued on defendants, 216

    and witnesses in trial of George Dinning, 33

    Bennett Young as attorney in, 195, 204, 206, 210–14, 217, 218, 219–20, 232, 234, 236–38, 241, 244, 245–46, 251, 261

    Bennett Young on facts of case, 214–16, 232

Davis, Jefferson, xii, 122, 229, 255–56

Davis, Winnie, 245

Deaux, Joe, 83, 220

Denning, Anthony, 259–65, *261*

Denning, George, 259, 263

Denning, Imogene, 263–64

Dial, Bloomer, 244

Dial, John, 244

Dilliard, E. H., 153

Dinning, Benjamin (son), 102, 139, 262

Dinning, David (Irish immigrant), 10

Dinning, David M. (slave owner), 10, 13, 19

Dinning, Emma (daughter), 4, 137

Dinning, Eva (daughter), 4, 20, 105–14, 136, 137, 214, 233

Dinning, George. *See also* damage suits of George Dinning; trial of George Dinning

    ancestry of, 10–11, 13

    assigned lawyers of, 34–38, 50, 55

    burial of, 264

    childhood of, 11–12

    Jodie Conn shot by, 5, 6, 38, 40, 42, 136, 154, 178, 194, 215, 217, 219, 220, 234

    death of, 261, 264

    depiction in Louisville *Times,* 52

    and family oral history, 263

    farming of, 19–20, 28, 39–40

    G. T. Finn's questioning of, 140–47

    as former slave, 10–11, 166, 232, 233, 264

    John Grider's questioning of, 130–40, 147–49, 154

    gunshot wounds of, 4, 5, 23, 93, 134, 139–40, 145, 146, 149–50, 187–88

    house and land bought by, 39–40, 200, 214, 218–19, 233

Dinning, George. (cont.)
indictment for willful murder, 38, 160
in jail, 22–23, 31, 38, 41, 46, 47, 49–
53, 158–60, 162–63, 188, 190, 200
in Jeffersonville, Indiana, 197–98, 199,
200, 202, 213–14, 245, 251–52,
263–64
Louisville attack on, 201–3, 203, 206–
8, 210, 213, 230
marriage of, 19–20, 39–40, 102
name change to Denning, 251, 263
pardon of, 183–89, 192–94, 208, 249
press characterizations of, 7, 8, 22, 31–
32, 47
press reports of making profiting from
trial, 197–98
press reports of self-defense of, 33,
166, 167–69
press reports of shooting of Jodie Conn,
6–8, 9, 22–23, 31
press reports on pardon of, 192–94
protection before trial, 24–25, 30–31,
32, 33, 34–38, 42, 45–46, 47, 50–
51, 53, 188, 200
protection during trial, 53–55, 85, 105,
158–60, 168, 177–79
and quarantine of home for smallpox,
230–31
reputation for truth and honesty, 20,
151, 152, 153, 166, 185, 194, 200
self-defense of, 33, 36, 42–43, 166,
170–71, 172, 173, 175–76, 189,
194
speaking tour of, 196–97, 199
state penitentiary release, 183–84,
189–90
state penitentiary sentencing, 163, 165,
168, 169, 171, 183
sworn statement sent to Bill Bradley,
42–43
turning himself in to Bud Clark, 6, 9,
29, 30, 135, 188, 189, 200, 217
white men attacking home of, 3–5, 32–
33, 40, 41–42, 188–89, 200, 215,
232–34
white men burning home of, 20–21,
33, 40–41, 92, 186, 188, 200, 216,
217, 218, 234, 246
white men's accusations of stealing, 5,
8, 9, 42, 57
white neighbors of, 36, 40, 41, 73, 132,
151, 153, 185, 200, 238, 242
Bennett Young as advocate for, 128

Dinning, George, Jr. (son), 4, 137, 260, 263
Dinning, George (father), 11, 19
Dinning, Hermann (son), 9, 20, 102–4,
151, 214, 233
Dinning, Isaac, 13
Dinning, John, 39
Dinning, Mary (mother), 9, 19, 162, 199,
233
Dinning, Mertrude, (daughter), 4, 137
Dinning, Mollie (wife)
correspondence with Bill Bradley, 40–
41
death of, 261
George Dinning's concerns for safety
of, 192–93
George Dinning's testimony on, 131,
133, 136, 137
Claud Hackney's visit following attack,
100
Daniel Gilbert Hackney's visit following attack, 98–99
headstone of, 259, 261
in Jeffersonville, Indiana, 199, 263
John King's testimony on, 151
marriage of, 19–20, 39–40, 102
sworn affidavit of, 41–42
at trial of George Dinning, 85, 130
John Webb's testimony on, 152
white men attacking home of, 3, 4–5
white men ordering to leave county, 9–
10, 20, 39, 41, 215–16, 218, 246
white men returning to home after
attack, 84, 215
Dinning, Nannie (daughter), 4, 137
Dinning, Viola (daughter), 4, 106, 136
Dixon, Moses, 216
Doss, Pete, 92, 153
Du Bois, W. E. B., 13
Dugan, Irwin, 240
Duncan family, 204

Earle, Ben P., 171
Early, John H., 174
Eastham, Vincent, 253–54
Edison, Thomas, 211
Edmund Pettus Bridge, Alabama, xiv
Emancipation Proclamation, 13, 26
English common law, 169
enslavement
abolition of, 229
and lack of property rights, 169
legal forms of, xii, 93
reparations for, xii

Stuart Robinson on, 125
Bennett Young on, 126–27
Evans, Robert, 101
Evans, Walter, 230, 231, 239, 243
extrajudicial killings. See lynchings
Ezell, Getty, 244

Family History Library, Salt Lake City, 262
Farmer, William, 248
Felts, John, 220, 239, 242
Ferguson, Benjamin, 153
Ferguson, Patrick, 118
Fifteenth Amendment, 94
Fifth Street Baptist Church, Louisville
  George Dinning speaking at, 194–96
  donation of clothes for George Din-
    ning's trial, 36, 51, 130, 195
  offering collected for George Dinning,
    195–96
Finn, G. T.
  as attorney for defendants in damage
    suit of George Dinning, 217–18,
    232
  closing arguments of, 158
  family background of, 151
  objections in George Dinning's trial,
    90, 107, 108, 133, 139, 152
  questioning of W. P. Babb, 153
  questioning of L. G. Berry, 155–56
  questioning of Ben Conn, 97–98
  questioning of Eva Dinning, 108–14
  questioning of George Dinning, 140–47
  questioning of Hermann Dinning, 103–
    4
  questioning of Albert Green Freeman,
    56–64, 70
  questioning of Claud Hackney, 100–
    101
  questioning of Bill King, 152
  questioning of John King, 151–52
  questioning of William S. Moore, 72–
    75, 80
  questioning of Zack Murray, 150–51
  questioning of John Webb, 152
  theory that George Dinning blamed
    Jodie Conn for arrest of son, 102
Finn, L. B., 151
Flowers, James Wesley, 71, 91, 220, 239,
  242
Flowers, Joseph Laranzy, 91, 220, 239, 242
Floyd, George, xii
Forsyth, Charles, 24
Fort Wayne News, 7, 243

Fourth Amendment, 169
Francis, W. R., 23, 115, 146
Frank, John H., 36, 51, 194–95
Franklin, Benjamin, 46
Franklin, Kentucky. See also trial of George
  Dinning
  Black porter killed in, 51
  illustration of downtown, 46
  postcard depicting typical court day, 35
  Simpson County Courthouse, 71, 95,
    161
Franklin Favorite, 179–81, 217
Freedmen's Bureau, 26, 27, 94
Freedom's Watchman, 16
Freeman, Albert Green, 56–71, 220, 239,
  242
Frémont, John, 11
Fuller, James, 245

Gaines, Noel, 82, 158, 159, 160
Gaither, E. H., 52–54, 130, 157, 160, 177–
  79
Garfield, James, 208
George Dinning v. Doc Moore, et al., 230–
  31. See also damage suits of George Din-
  ning
Gibson, J. H., 55
Gibson, Joe, 55
Gibson, John, 55
Gilded Age, 228
Gilliam, Perry, 49
Gooden, Benjamin, 245
Gordon, F. L., 51, 158–60
Gould, George M., 202
Grainger, John Henry, 49
Grant, U. S., 122–23, 208
Grider, John B.
  absent-mindedness of, 90–91
  closing arguments of, 158
  George Dinning's testimony on, 147
  educational background of, 91
  introduction of George Dinning's
    undershirt as evidence, 154
  motion for continuance denied, 157–58
  motion for new trial denied, 163
  and pardon request, 184–86
  questioning of L. G. Berry, 154–56
  questioning of Matt Christian, 93
  questioning of Ben Conn, 95, 96–97
  questioning of Joe Deaux, 83
  questioning of Eva Dinning, 105–8
  questioning of George Dinning, 130–
    40, 147–49, 154

Grider, John B. (cont.)
  questioning of Hermann Dinning, 102–3
  questioning of Robert Evans, 101
  questioning of James Wesley Flowers, 9
  questioning of Joseph Laranzy Flowers, 91
  questioning of Albert Green Freeman, 64–70
  questioning of Claud Hackney, 99–100
  questioning of Daniel Gilbert Hackney, 98–99
  questioning of Bill King, 152–53
  questioning of William S. Moore, 75–82, 92
  questioning of Zack Murray, 149–50
  questioning of J. M. Phelps, 88–90
  questioning of William Townsend, 84
  questioning of Nick Williams, 91–92
Grider & Moss, 35, 91
Grierson, Benjamin, 123
Grigsly, B. P., 171
Grubbs, Finn, 244
Grubbs, Quince, 244

Hackney, Claud, 99–101, 103, 112, 152, 185
Hackney, Daniel Gilbert "Gib," 4, 98–99, 107, 112, 133, 185
Hagerman, C. J., 30
Hagerman, Virgil, 35–37, 186
Hagood, L. M., 172
Hall, John, 248
Hall, Tom, 173
Hannah-Jones, Nikole, xii
Happy (warden), 183, 184, 192
Harlan, James, 248
Harlan, John Marshall, 175
Harlin, William, 248
Hartford Courant, 193
Henry, Dick, 6, 138
Henson, William, 55
Hickman *Courier*, 16
Hodges, Frannie, 130
Hollan, Henry, 244
Hollis, Isen, 92, 138
Holton, Ben, 204
Howell, John, 29
Hudson, Tip, 222
Hughes, Aaron, 248
Hunter, David, 123

inflation calculations, xvi

Jackson, Thomas, 248
Jefferson, Thomas, 11, 118
Jeffersonville, Indiana, George Dinning settling in, 196–98, 199, 200, 202, 213–14, 245, 251–52, 263–64
Jeffersonville *Evening News*, 244, 246
Jeffersonville *National Democrat*, 199–200
Jenkins, Henry, 220
Johnson, Andrew, 125
Johnson, John, 24
Johnson, S. F., 26
Joiner, Arch, 24
Jones, E., 55
Jones, Sam, 181
Jones, Stewart, 248
Jump, Mrs. Leslie, 248

Kelley, R. P., 153
Kentucky
  antilynching bill of, 43–44
  Black men joining Union Army, 13
  Black people granted right to testify against whites, 95
  Black settlers of, 10
  Confederate invasion of, 12–13
  fears of slave insurrection in, 11–12
  as frontier, 183
  inability of Black people to testify against whites in court, 93–94, 95
  lynchings without trial in, 47–48, 247–48
  neutrality in Civil War, 12, 26, 119
  progressive politics in, 179, 186
  race-based killings in, 26, 27, 28
  as slave state, 10, 190
Kentucky Conference of the African Methodist Episcopal Church, 208–9
Kentucky School for the Blind, 116, 256
Kentucky state penitentiary
  Black people as majority of inmates, 102
  George Dinning released from, 183–84, 189–90
  George Dinning sentenced to, 163, 165, 168, 169, 171, 183
King, Bill, 103, 107, 111–12, 152
King, James, 220, 233, 246
King, J. M., 91
King, John, 103, 107, 111–12, 151–52, 219
King, Martin Luther, Jr., xiv
Kirby, J. M., 55
Knoxville Sentinel, 54

Ku Klux Klan. *See also* Whitecappers
  Black people attacking, 18–19
  costumes of, 14–15, 16, 17–18
  intimidation of Black people, 14–15,
    17–19, 28
  intimidation of juries in courtrooms, 27
  and Mount Rushmore, xiii
  as night riders, xv, 27, 185
  origin of name, 14–15
  raids of, 17–18
  Second Klan, 265
  spread of, 16–17
  support for, 18, 27
  violence of, 16, 27, 31

Lafayette, Marquis de, 118
Lapaille, Melville, 130
Law Notes, 243
legal system
  Black people's law suits against whites,
    204–6
  lack for justice for white crimes against
    Black people, 26–29, 41, 93–94,
    169
  and mobs raiding jails, 24, 30
Lewis, Meriwether, 183
Lexington *Daily Leader,* 216, 243
Lexington Morning Herald, 54–55, 104,
  165–67
Lexington *Observer and Reporter,* 104
Lincoln, Abraham, 13, 119, 151, 208, 229,
  255
Little Rock Central High School, xiv
Locke, John, 168–69
Logan, Benjamin, 237
Lost Cause, xvi, 127, 254
Louisville, Kentucky
  Derby Day in, 227–30, 235
  George Dinning attacked in, 201–3,
    203, 206–8, 210
  George Dinning released to, 183–84,
    189–90, 192
  history of, 190–91
Louisville Board of Aldermen, 174
Louisville City Hospital, 202
Louisville Commercial, 170, 172
Louisville *Courier-Journal*
  on attack on George Dinning, 207
  on damage suit of George Dinning, 231
  on George Dinning's fame, 197
  interview with George Dinning, 192–
    93
  on pardon of George Dinning, 192

  on petitions for pardon of George Din-
    ning, 177
  on shooting of Jodie Conn, 7
  on trial of George Dinning, 32, 115,
    127, 191–92
  on trial of Tol Stone, 127–28
  on verdict in trial of George Dinning,
    164, 168, 174, 180, 181
  on Bennett Young, 126, 257, 258
Louisville *Dispatch,* 180
Louisville *Evening Post,* 8, 173, 207–8
Louisville *Times*
  on trial of George Dinning, 32, 34, 51,
    53, 115
  on verdict in trial of George Dinning,
    169–70, 180, 181
Lovell, John, 146–47
Lucas, Bob, 5–6, 73, 96, 131–32, 134, 136
Lynching Memorial, Montgomery, Alabama,
  xv
lynchings
  antilynching bill introduced and passed
    in Kentucky Senate, 43–44
  Bill Bradley's promises to end, 25, 29,
    30
  Bill Bradley's proposed legislation on,
    37
  damage suits for, 204, 244–45
  deaths of victims, xv, 26, 28, 29
  and extrajudicial killings, xv, 49
  and fears of slave insurrection, 12
  and mob violence, 24, 28, 34, 43–44,
    48–49, 204, 221–26
  motivations for, 47–48, 49
  without trial, 47–48, 247–48

McAfee, Andrew, 213
MacArthur, Arthur, 228
McCain, T. H. B., 16
McDaniel, Arch, 220
McDonald, Elbert, 220
McDonald, S. A., 91, 220
McDonald, T., 153
McFerrin, John P., 171
McIntosh, S. M., 245
McKinley, William, 37, 231
Madison, James, 11
Marion, Thomas, 172
Marshall, George, 245
Mayes, Burle, 55
Menne, Frank J., 191
Milewski, Melissa, 204–5, 206
Milroy, Robert H., 123

mob violence. *See also* damage suits of
  George Dinning
  Bill Bradley on, 31
  and Richard Coleman, 247–48
  and Ku Klux Klan, 27
  and legal system, 24, 30
  and Louisville attack on George Din-
    ning, 201–3
  and lynchings, 24, 28, 34, 43–44, 48–
    49, 204, 221–26
  and white men attacking home of
    George Dinning, 3–5, 32–33, 40, 41
    –42, 188–89, 200, 215, 232–34
Moore, William S. "Doc"
  and damage suit of George Dinning,
    218–19, 220, 234, 239, 242
  Joe Deaux's testimony on, 83
  G. T. Finn's questioning of, 72–75, 80
  James Wesley Flowers's testimony on,
    91
  Albert Green Freeman's testimony on,
    57, 66, 68–69
  John Grider's questioning of, 75–82, 92
  J. M. Phelps's testimony on, 88–89
  suicide of, 249–50
  William Townsend's testimony on, 84
Morgan, Dick, 248
Morgan, John Hunt, 13, 104, 119–20, 182,
  249, 252–53
Moses, Adolph, 171
Mount Carmel Register, 243
Mount Rushmore, xiii
Murray, Zack, 4–5, 133–34, 145–47, 149–51
Myall, William, 171

Nash, George, 245
Nash, John, 245
Nashville *Banner,* 18–19
Nashville *Tennessean,* 8–9, 22, 23, 33, 47
Nashville *Union and Dispatch,* 15
National Memorial for Peace and Justice,
  Montgomery, Alabama, xv
Neal, Allie Mae, xv
Neal, Claude, xv
New York Freeman, 28
New York Sun, 203–4
New York Times, xiii–xiv, 11, 31, 33, 46,
  160, 205
night riders/raiders, xv, 27, 32, 33, 168, 185,
  243

Oakley, Annie, 227
Odd Fellows' Hall, Louisville, 196

Ohio County News, 194
Ohio River, 190, 196–97
Overstreet, J. W., 173
Owensboro Inquirer, 6–7, 162, 167–68, 257
Owensboro Messenger, 22–23
Owsley, Dave, 130

Paducah Sun, 170
Parks, Rosa, xiv
Peach, Will, 248
Perry, Will C., 162
Phelps, J. M., 88–90
Pierce, Joe, 29
Pistole, J. M., 55
Plummer, Joseph, 40
police brutality, xii, xiii, xvi
Pool, James, 244
Porter, John, 29
Powell, Gibbs, 220
Powell, Jasper, 220
Powell, Mayberry, 220
Pritton, Belle, 245
progressivism, 179, 186, 228
Proud Boys, xii
Pulaski Citizen, 14, 15
Pyle, Walter L., 202

racial violence, xii, 179. *See also* lynchings
Ragsdale, William, 220, 246
Rainwater, William, 220
Randolph, Samuel, 220, 233, 246
Ray, J. S., 153
Reconstruction, 93
Redfern, John, 34
Reeves, W. L. (judge)
  asking jury for verdict, 162–63
  on L. G. Berry hearsay testimony, 156
  William C. P. Breckinridge on, 105
  conference with attorneys in trial of
    George Dinning, 90
  image from Louisville *Times,* 54
  instructions to jury, 160
  as judge in trial of George Dinning, 55,
    71, 105, 154
  overruling John Grider's motion for
    continuance, 157–58
  overruling John Grider's motion for new
    trial, 163
  overruling motion for change of venue
    in trial of George Dinning, 50
  overruling request for banning of guns
    at trial in trial of George Dinning,
    53, 54, 105

Resler, Uriah, 245
Richmond Climax, 53
Risler, H., 245
Roark, G. W., 217
Robbins, Jack, 248
Robinson, Stuart, 125
Rodes (sheriff), 31
Roosevelt, Theodore, 228
Ross, A. J., 171
Ruby, Tennie (or Tina Ruley), 34
Russellville Ledger, 50–51, 162, 197–98

St. Louis Daily Globe-Democrat, 47, 160–61
St. Paul *Appeal,* 243
Salt Lake City *Daily Herald,* 242
Sample, William, 245
Samuels, W. H., 153
Sarver, Bob, 34
Saunders, O. D., 248
Scott, Suydam, 171
Scroggins, Thomas, 27
Second Klan, 265
Seddon, James A., 120–21
Sellers, William, 27
Shepherd, John, 17
Sheridan, Philip, 122–23
Sherman, William T., 122–23
Simpson, John, 237
Simpson, Ophelia, 190
Simpson County Courthouse, Franklin,
    Kentucky, 71, 95, 161, *See also* trial of
    George Dinning
Simpson County Jail, cell in, 48
Smith, John Gregory, 121
Smith, W. M., 217, 239
Snider, John, 55, 163
Snider, Tom, 55
Sons of Confederate Veterans, xi–xii, xvi–
    xvii
Spanish-American War, 210, 228
Stanford *Interior Journal,* 32, 168
State Board of Equalization, 173
Stevenson, John, 94
Stier, John, 239
Stone, Tol, 127–28
Strickland, Elijah "Lige," 223–26
Stuart Robinson Memorial Church,
    Louisville, 252
Sullivan, Pat, 244
sundown towns, xii

Taylor, Breonna, xiii
Temple, Nute, 55

Thirteenth Amendment, 13–14, 26, 40
Thomas, Major, 224–25
Todd, George, 172, 207
Toronto Globe, 123
Townsend, William, 83–84
trial of George Dinning
    J. H. Bloodworth's testimony in, 84
    Tom Bloodworth's testimony in, 84
    William C. P. Breckinridge's column
        on, 104–5
    Ben Conn's testimony to G. T. Finn in,
        97–98
    Ben Conn's testimony to John Grider
        in, 95, 96–97
    crowd in courtroom, 55, 158
    Joe Deaux's testimony to John Grider
        in, 83
    Eva Dinning's testimony to G. T. Finn
        in, 108–14
    Eva Dinning's testimony to John Grider
        in, 105–8
    George Dinning as witness in own
        behalf, 127
    George Dinning's testimony to G. T.
        Finn in, 140–47
    George Dinning's testimony to John
        Grider in, 130–40, 147–49
    Hermann Dinning's testimony to G. T.
        Finn in, 103–4
    Hermann Dinning's testimony to John
        Grider in, 102–3
    Mollie Dinning attending in gallery, 85,
        130
    drawing of east end of George Din-
        ning's cabin used in, 59, 77, 80, 99
    Robert Evans's testimony to John
        Grider in, 101
    Fifth Street Baptist Church's donation
        of suit for, 36, 51, 130, 195
    James Wesley Flowers's testimony to
        John Grider in, 91
    Joseph Lazansky Flowers's testimony to
        John Grider in, 91
    Albert Green Freeman's testimony to
        G. T. Finn in, 56–64
    Albert Green Freeman's testimony to
        John Grider in, 64–71
    Claud Hackney's testimony to G. T.
        Finn in, 100–101
    Claud Hackney's testimony to John
        Grider in, 99–100
    Daniel Gilbert Hackney's testimony to
        John Grider in, 98–99

trial of George Dinning (cont.)
    heat wave during, 55, 63–64, 82, 129–
        30, 135, 157, 162
    jury deliberations in, 160–62, 195
    jury for, 55
    jury's verdict of manslaughter, 163, 165
    William S. Moore's testimony to G. T.
        Finn in, 72–75, 80
    William S. Moore's testimony to John
        Grider in, 75–82, 92
    Zack Murray's testimony to G. T. Finn
        in, 150–51
    Zack Murray's testimony to John Grider
        in, 149–50
    J. M. Phelps's testimony to John
        Grider, 88–89
    press reports of, 33, 46–47, 50–51, 53,
        54–55, 71, 86, 115, 127, 130, 160–
        62, 164, 165–70, 172, 173, 177,
        179–81
    protection of George Dinning during,
        53–55, 85, 105, 158–60, 168, 177–
        79
    scheduling of, 43
    transcript of, 181–82, 184–85, 191–92
    Nick Williams's testimony to John
        Grider, 91–92
    witnesses testifying in, 32–33, 55
    Bennett Young on, 115, 127–28
Trump, Donald, xiii
truth and reconciliation, xii
Tudors, A. M., 248

Uhls, J. D., 55
Underground Railroad, 196–97
Union Army, Black men serving in, 13
United Confederate Veterans, 254, 258
United Nations, xii–xiii
U.S. House of Representatives, Committee
    on Freedmen's Affairs, 16

Waddle (sheriff), 31
Walker, Stephen, 220
Warren, Newt, 8
Washington, George, 11, 118, 208
Washington Star, 243
Weaver, Sylvester, 191
Webb, John, 92, 107, 111–12, 152, 220
Weeden, H. C., 257
Wells, Ida B., 28–29
Wells, Prince, 191
White, Monroe, 220, 246
White, Thomas, 71

White, Willis, 24
Whitecappers
    antilynching bill's penalties for, 43
    and damage suit of George Dinning,
        238
    and George Dinning's indictment, 37,
        200
    power of, 27, 256
    press reports of, 7, 29
    and trial of George Dinning, 92, 157,
        174
    and E. A. Woolbright, 245
white supremacy
    Confederate statuary as symbols of,
        255–56
    legal rights denied Black people, 93
    reckoning with, xv, 232–33
    terror tactics of, 26
    and Bennett Young, 126, 127
Wilkes, Sam, 221, 223–26
Williams, Gus, 24
Williams, Nick, 73, 82, 91–92, 154–56,
    157, 220
Willson, Augustus E., 174–77
Willson, Forceythe, 174–75
Wilson, Ex, 244
Wilson, J. Rice, 129
Wilson, William, Jr., 244
Wilson, William, Sr., 244
Winn, M. J., 239
Witt, Bell, 49
Woolbright, E. A., 244–45
Woolworth's, Greensboro, North Carolina,
    xiv
Worthington, William Jackson, 50–51, 165,
    167, 170, 177
Wright, Ira, 245
Wright, M. D., 245
Wynn, Ed, 222

Young, Bennett H.
    as advocate for George Dinning, 128
    as attorney, 115–16, 126, 128, 252
    as attorney in damage suits of George
        Dinning, 195, 204, 206, 210–14,
        217, 218, 219–20, 232, 234, 236–
        38, 241, 244, 245–46, 251, 261
    as author, 116, 252–54, 256–57
    and Booker T. Washington Community
        Center, 252
    as Confederate in Civil War, 116, 119–
        27, 128, 232, 236, 249, 252–55,
        258

and Confederate monuments, 128,
254–55
death of, 257–58, 264
education of, 119, 125
family background of, 118–19
grave marker of, 258
as historian, 116–18, 252–55
lectures and speeches of, 116–18
on pardon for George Dinning, 182
portrait of, *117*
as president of second Southern Exposition in Louisville, 211
promotion of Kentucky and Indiana

Bridge over Ohio River, 212
railroad interests of, 117, 210–11, 212
and state constitution, 212–13
on trial of George Dinning, 115, 127–
28
Young, Eliza Sharp, 213
Young, Jacob, 245
Young, John, 118
Young, Martha Robinson, 125
Young, Robert, 118–19

Zollicoffer, Felix, 254

ABOUT THE AUTHOR

Ben Montgomery is a former enterprise reporter for the *Tampa Bay Times,* founder of the narrative journalism website Gangrey.com, and author of *Grandma Gatewood's Walk, The Leper Spy,* and *The Man Who Walked Backward.* In 2010, he was a finalist for the Pulitzer Prize in local reporting and won the Dart Award and the Casey Medal for a series called "For Their Own Good," about abuse at Florida's oldest reform school. He lives in Tampa with his children.